AF757539

THE DEFETISHIZED SOCIETY

THE DEFETISHIZED SOCIETY

NEW ECONOMIC DEMOCRACY AS A LIBERTARIAN ALTERNATIVE TO CAPITALISM

CHRIS WYATT

continuum

2011
Continuum International Publishing Group
80 Maiden Lane, New York, NY 10038
The Tower Building, 11 York Road, London SE1 7NX

www.continuumbooks.com

© 2011 by Chris Wyatt

All rights reserved. No part of this book may be reproduced, stored in a retrieval system, or transmitted, in any form or by any means, electronic, mechanical, photocopying, recording, or otherwise, without the written permission of the publishers.

Library of Congress Cataloging-in-Publication Data
A catalog record for this book is available from the Library of Congress.

ISBN: 978-1-4411-5933-5 (Hardcover)

Typeset by Newgen Imaging Systems Pvt Ltd, Chennai, India
Printed and bound in the United States of America

For my mother;
in loving memory,
my father

Contents

Acknowledgements

I would first like to acknowledge Neil Stammers, Mark Erickson and Neil Curry for reading through early drafts of the introductory chapter, their comments on the outline of the book proved to be invaluable, and were gratefully received. My many conversations with Darrow Schecter served a similar purpose; Darrow's work and teachings continue to be a great source of inspiration to me and all who know him. I am indebted to all four. Further thanks goes to Marie-Claire and all at Continuum for their ongoing support and encouragement during the process of writing the book. On a personal note, I would like to extend my gratitude to Andy Winter, Jewls Wingfield and Sarah Miles for the laudable work they do; their teachings have helped make the stress of writing the book (almost) manageable. Finally, my thanks go to all my colleagues and students at the School of Applied Social Science for making the University of Brighton such a stimulating, and humorous, place to work.

Introduction

There is every indication that due to the spiralling lack of faith and increasing disinterest in the existing economic and political structures, modern industrial society is at a crossroads. In light of the contemporary global economic crisis, attempts to continue the theoretical task of sketching the institutional contours of a feasible rival to liberal capitalism could hardly be more urgent. The two basic options are still reform from within or a radical restructure. Given that social democracy increasingly appears a spent force, it is the latter option that is taken up in this book. In what follows, the left libertarian scheme (inspired initially by the English theorist of libertarian socialism G. D. H. Cole) referred to as New Economic Democracy (NED) is presented as a genuine alternative that successfully combines non-statist socialism with a participatory democratic ethic. In my recent work on John Rawls (justice) and Cole (libertarian socialism),[1] I analysed NED's political constitution and its mechanisms for distributing goods and resources. Now, adopting a new framework of analysis, I wish to continue with this goal. In *Beyond Rawls* (Continuum 2008), I coupled two distinct traditions, the analytical political theory of Rawls and left libertarianism. I argued that Rawls' difference principle (that inequalities are only permitted if they benefit the least well-off) will be more easily realized in NED. The argument in the present book may be seen as a complement to the one developed in *Beyond Rawls*.

The new framework of analysis is inspired by the Marxian critique of the fetishism of commodities. Chapter 1 provides a full exposition of Marx's critique of commodity fetishism, but in order to establish the rationale of the book, this introductory chapter will now offer a briefer preliminary summary. In Marx's day the verb to fetishize referred to the tendency to worship an inanimate object due to its supposedly mystical and magical powers. Marx applies this to his argument that classical

1. *The Difference Principle Beyond Rawls*, referred to hereafter as *Beyond Rawls*.

political economy creates pervasive illusions. He uses the term fetishism to explain how the social relations of producers are displaced and relocated in the illusionary 'natural' qualities of commodities. His claim is that, in capitalist society, commodities have certain qualities bestowed upon them, qualities that are then regarded as existing in them naturally. Commodities masquerade as exhibitors of non-social properties, one step removed from any human aspects. These qualities and properties can of course only be possessed by people. By attributing autonomy to commodities, though, people transpose to them magical powers for conducting their lives. Objects are treated as subjects – the personification of the inanimate. It is this personification of things which is captured in the notion of commodity fetishism. This is the root of the mystification of fetishism. Mystification confuses social facts as natural. This is because social relations appear to, and are interpreted by producers as, comparative relations between commodities. Commodities are products of private labours; it is only through market exchange that interactions are established. So with commodity production, only exchange-value brings together otherwise isolated producers. Key to the commodity fetishism thesis is that producers, rather than being united, are initially divided and become linked indirectly through their market transactions. Social relations between people secured through the act of exchange are hence *indirect*, and are channelled through *direct* relations to commodities (1977: 436–7). The market integrates the labour of producers in a duplicate illusory form. So the enigma of why commodities are fetishes occurs because the social character of production is presented not in the actual sphere of production, but through exchange relations.

The commodity fetishism thesis, then, apprehends how the products of labour are misconceived as soon as they are exchanged on the market. Under the spell of fetishism, individuals bestow onto commodities their personal relations. The appearance of this relationship between the objects of labour is, Marx adds, not false; it actually exists, but it does obscure the primary relationship between producers. *Commodity fetishism conceals the underlying social relations*; it engenders a divide between outward appearance and hidden reality. The effect:

> Marx's notion of commodity fetishism…echoes the contradictory experience of a society where, for example, car ownership and the apparent freedom purchased by the buying of a car is an everyday aspiration and yet the conditions of the car worker are the most mind-enslaving drudgery. (Wainwright, H. 1994: 168)

In demystified consciousness it is evident that the exchange-value of a commodity is perceived through its relation to labour and people's needs. But in mystified consciousness, goods seem to exchange at the rate they do due to their inherent properties. In Marx's theory, the displacement of interpersonal relations to the relations producers have to things is a key contradiction of commodity-producing society; a contradiction he seeks to expose in the term commodity fetishism.

The phenomenon of the fetishism of commodities is still one of the most serious problems in contemporary capitalist society. Even the most cursory glance at advertising strategies will reveal that commodities are, in general, portrayed as holding magical properties: this razor attracts a beautiful woman, this perfume allures the man of your dreams, this slick car confirms the composure of the driver; the list is endless. It is not only that capitalism permits the fetishism of commodities; it is, rather, that fetishism is actually indispensable to it. Capitalism is not just an economic system that is profit based; it commands the maximization of profit. If enterprises do not expand, they run the risk of being subsumed by larger corporations (for this reason Marx himself was not unduly critical towards individual capitalists (1977: 417) – it is capitalism in its entirety, as a series of social relations, that he lambasted). In the relentless quest to expand output, the more consumers fetishize, the more sales will increase. A key aspect of commodity fetishism is that it deliberately focuses attention on idealized surface appearances, while the material social relations through which the commodities are produced tend to fall from view. This helps contribute towards problems like political apathy and environmental ruin. Along with the often shameful history of imperialism and colonialism, we may add developing world sweatshops, in which indigenous labour is frequently paid near-on starvation wages. Sadly, these places exist in great numbers. It is probable that sweatshops are located in most countries throughout the world, but it seems as if they are especially concentrated in Bangladesh, China, Mexico, Costa Rica, Dominican Republic, El Salvador, Haiti, Honduras, Indonesia, Nicaragua and Vietnam (Powell, B. & Karbek, D. B. 2004: 5).

The literature abounds with vivid accounts of just how brutal life in a sweatshop actually is. For example at the Alejandro Apparel sweatshop in Honduras, which is typical of sweatshops throughout the developing world, workers are driven relentlessly. One worker reported that it was demanded 1,200 sleeves be sown onto shirts during a 10-hour shift; her pay is $35 a month! Other workers earn 86 cents per hour for similar tasks. Workers are given only 10 minutes for food breaks, and toilet use is monitored by management. Talking between employees is forbidden and supervisors frequently berate workers. The situation is similar at Southeast Textiles, here workers are required to ask the supervisor to stamp a toilet pass. Further, quotas for work shifts were set at a deliberately impossible high level so that workers were forced to work unpaid overtime to meet the goal. At both plants, repetitive strain injuries are common. Management cite the constant pressures from the giant corporations for increasingly cheaper clothing as the reason for this excessively strident treatment. At Niagra Textiles, a plant in Bangladesh, workers receive 11–20 cents per hour for sewing garments. Work shifts are 14 hours a day, every day of the week; and once a week employees are forced to endure a 19-hour shift. If workers are caught talking during working hours, they are fined a day's pay. At Western Dresses in Dhaka, workers toil from 7.45 to 10–11.00 PM. Outrageously, mistakes are punished by physical beatings. At a sweatshop in Thailand, the drink containers were spiked with amphetamines, which ensured employees could work for 2 whole days without rest. Elich (2010) reports that this practice was so frequent that some workers became addicted and brought the drugs illegally. Such is the domination of the labour-force that workers seen yawning are subject to an $11 fine. At Daxu Cosmetics in Anshan, workers receive $24 per month; from this they are required to pay $13 for cramp and meagre accommodation. Employees are only permitted one shower each week, and they are locked within the compound for the vast majority of the time. Any worker wishing to leave is required to pay a penalty of $58 to the owner; not many are in a position to save such a sum (Elich, G. 2010: 1–4).

The current global economic climate does not bode well for the large armies of indigenous labour. Breman (2009) reports that with regards to income distribution, the global recession has affected more severely those who are already the most downtrodden and vulnerable: the massed ranks of low-paid, asset-less workers who constitute the subordinated sections of the global economy. She is referring to the hundreds of millions who are incorporated into the productive process as *informal* labour. Due to the plethora of market-driven policies and the dismantling of organized labour and job security, these workers are at the mercy of fluctuating employment; they also lack any contractual or labour rights. It is this kind of labour, she confirms, that now predominates within the global labour force. 'The International Labour Organization estimates that informal workers comprise over half the workforce in Latin America, over 70 per cent in Sub-Saharan Africa and over 80 per cent in India; an Indian government report suggests a figure of more than 90 per cent' (2009: 1). The increasing imbalance between capital and labour is, she concludes, intensified by the trend towards informalization (Breman, J. 2009: 1, 3–4). Others, too, have been keen to draw attention to the dismal plight of informal labour. For instance Davis (2004) points out that 'the informal working class – everywhere subject to micro- and macro-exploitation – is almost universally deprived of protection by labour laws and standards' (2004: 9). With this in mind, it can be inferred that capitalism may be an efficient system of generating wealth – a point fully acknowledged by Marx (1977: 223–6), albeit at the expense of the exploitation of labour – but it is even more efficient at concentrating it. 'Over half of the world's population subsists on less than $2 a day, while the 200 richest individuals own more wealth than 41 percent of the world's population, or in other words, more than 2.6 billion people' (Elich, G. 2010: 1). These conditions are ripe for the unmerciful exploitation of sweatshop labour.

It is extremely doubtful whether the existing financial world system can alleviate commodity fetishism and the exploitation and misery it conceals. On the contrary, the global economic structures that are now thoroughly solidified seem well suited only to intensifying the problem. At the risk of over-generalizing, in the 1980/90s neo-liberalism replaced Keynesianism as the dominant economic orthodoxy. The Thatcher and Reagan administrations together pioneered free-market policies, thus reconstructing their economies along neo-liberal lines. Williamson (1990) sought to capture the emerging neo-liberal agenda by coining the term 'Washington Consensus', which refers to the development strategies advocated by the key global decision-makers. Williamson's items can be organized into two main groups. First, economic stability through fiscal discipline and the 'free-market', and, secondly, a sweeping decrease in state intervention in the economy. High on the list was tax reform, the liberation of finance and trade, foreign investment, deregulation and privatization. So, the Washington Consensus is closely associated with a 'market fundamentalism': the idea that unfettered markets are the solution to economic problems.[2] This set the trend for the decisive and far-reaching economic policies that were to follow. In 1993 Congress approved the North American Free Trade Agreement (NAFTA), and in 1999 the World Trade Organisation (WTO) promoted the liberalization of trade in services, which were, as intended, compatible with the interests of the Multinational Corporations (MNCs) and investment banks. This empowered bodies like

2. Serra et al. point out that Williamson has put distance between himself and this view (2008: 3).

the International Monetary Fund (IMF), the World Bank and the US treasury to pressurize Third World governments into accepting neo-liberal programmes of 'structural adjustment'. Simultaneously, the traditional left redress of state-centred public ownership was progressively undermined by the enormous power of global capital: witness, for example, the recent capitulation of social democratic policies to market imperatives under Blair's regime in the UK. As a consequence of which, all the chief economic and political players came to accept liberal capitalism. Although it has always been contested – as the protests in Washington, Milan, Melbourne, Prague, Seoul and Nice testify – the Washington consensus served as the frame of reference for the major policy formations which reverberated throughout most of the world (Stiglitz, J. E. 2008: 41; Serra, N. et al. 2008: 3–4; Callinicos, A. 2003: 1–6).

The policies of the Washington Consensus have, however, been subject to intense criticism. The Washington Consensus strategies were upheld zealously by Wall Street and the US Treasury who, together with international financial institutions, restructured foreign economies to ensure they were suitable for overseas investment. A predominant expectation placed upon economies experiencing structural adjustment was that they did not restrict the flow of capital through their borders. This left them susceptible to market contingencies, and in such times when market fluctuations are not favourable to further investment, the tendency is for capital to flee. With regards to indigenous workers, unemployment and poverty commonly follow. Although rescue packages by bodies like the IMF and the G7 may be assembled, this routinely comes with conditions which put developing countries in an impossible situation:

> if governments failed to comply, they lost credibility, as they were accused of not doing what was right for their country. If governments acceded to the demands, they also lost credibility, as they appeared to be simply following the orders of the new colonial masters. When the reforms failed to deliver on the promises, which happened in county after country, the governments again lost credibility. (Stiglitz, J. E. 2008: 51)

Stiglitz (2008) stresses that other market failures are also clearly noticeable, especially in developing countries where poor information, weak competition and fragmentary markets are common. He states that for markets to engender efficient outcomes there can be no externalities and no public goods. Further, there can be no 'imperfections of information, changes in the information structure, or asymmetries of information' (2008: 42). These conditions require, he infers, capital markets to be 'impossibly perfect'. He argues that these failures in market fundamentalism were actually present before the term Washington Consensus passed into popular usage. In the economies that implemented the Washington Consensus recommendations, growth was not only slow, it benefited mostly those who were already at the top; and even here, there were no significant decreases in poverty. Development strategies that engender an increase in GDP, while simultaneously failing to create the opportunity for most citizens to enjoy the potential benefits it could bring, cannot, Stiglitz contends, be considered a success. Disillusion throughout the developing world should, then, come as no surprise. In light of this, he reaches a distressing conclusion. 'If there were fruits of the Washington Consensus, they are yet to be enjoyed, at least by the average citizen of many developing countries' (2008: 44, 42–4, 47, 54; 2002: 86; Serra, N. et al. 2008: 4; Callinicos, A. 2003: 32–3).

In recent years, as the deficiencies of the Washington Consensus strategies became increasingly difficult to deny, its meaning has changed. Since it first appeared in 1990, Stiglitz and Serra et al. (2008) stress that it is now seen in both narrower and broader terms than were intended in its initial inception. It is narrower in the sense that it concentrates mostly on privatization, liberalization and price stability, and it is broader as it includes capital market liberalization. These stages of amendment have been captured in the terms 'Washington Consensus Plus', and, almost comically, the 'Washington Consensus Plus Plus'. At each stage of revision, its advocates have attempted to modify the prescription. The latter set of reforms now includes public institutions. The Washington Consensus had always seen governments as the problem, it assumed they could not be reformed, and regarded unshackled markets as the solution. But as it became clear that the countries within which development was stagnating often suffered from too little government, it reluctantly acknowledged that governments can and should be reformed. For Stiglitz, though, such reforms remained unbalanced and too narrow, as privatization was still regarded as the central policy. A more radical change in mindset is, he insists, needed. In sum, he concludes that there is a broadly shared view that the market fundamentalism of the Washington Consensus is seriously flawed. 'There is also a broad consensus that the international economic institutions have created unfair rules of the game... and have foisted failed policies on developing countries that are dependent on these institutions and on donors for assistance' (2008: 53). In terms of the strategies needed to help poor countries develop, then, the Washington Consensus provides no answer (Stiglitz, J. E. 2008: 41, 48–51, 53; Serra, N. et al. 2008: 3–4).

This short narrative may be rather simplified, but today, in spite of the above critiques, there can be no doubt as to the global hegemony neo-liberalism continues to assert. Neo-liberalism has created a global monoculture, ensuring the operations of the giant corporations can advance without obstruction. The global culture is subject to an unremitting commercial exploitation. Indispensable to neo-liberal international free trade are the kind of aggressive advertising campaigns that offer glorified representation of the product, often in the hope of stimulating imaginary appetites. In the process, they deliberately depict commodities as endowers of miraculous attributes they simply do not have. It is as if there is an imagined halo of mysticism attached to the desired commodity; imagined in the sense that the commodity actually possesses supernatural properties, the illusion itself is, ontologically speaking, real enough. It is an illusion that the marketing departments of capitalist corporations are only too happy to keep alive. Meanwhile, the appalling conditions of sweatshop labour continue to go, relatively speaking, unnoticed. Is it any wonder that the World Bank, the IMF and the WTO have been dubbed the 'iron triangle of the global sweatshop economy' (James 2000; Morrison, R. 1997: 225). It would seem that global liberal capitalism, however modified, offers little hope for a solution to the fetishism of commodities and associated problems. A far more radical resolution is called for. It is for these reasons that the normative quest to theorize the institutional bases of the defetishized society is vital.

Although it is as yet too early to tell how neo-liberalism will respond to the contemporary global economic meltdown, alternative policies are already being suggested. Stiglitz outlines what he terms a 'Post-Washington Consensus Consensus': the developing world must participate meaningfully in development strategies, there is no standard policy that will succeed for all countries everywhere, countries should have the opportunity to exercise their own judgement and experiment as they wish; GDP should not be the only measure of success – it must also include distribution and social/environmental sustainability. Policy objectives should also seek to improve standards of living, and they should advance democratic and equitable development. Finally, and crucially, the roles of the state and the market must be balanced. A common critique of the Washington Consensus is that along with its failure to understand economics, it not only neglected to consider political processes, but also the interaction between the two. By way of contrast, the Post-Washington Consensus Consensus establishes a role for both markets and governments. It recognizes there are both government and market failures, but it stresses there are systematic ways of enhancing the performances of both. Governments and markets are, from this perspective, complementary (Stiglitz, J. E. 2008: 41, 47, 51–4; 2002: 87–8). It is here that NED offers something original to the debate. NED provides a left-libertarian solution to the glaring inadequacies of the Washington Consensus strategies and the appalling conditions of developing world sweatshops. This introductory chapter will go on to explain exactly how NED articulates political processes and economic relations; it will also clarify how they are democratically integrated through deliberative and participatory means. Before this, it will be incumbent to establish some antecedent points that will help clear the path for the discussions that follow.

The solution to the riddle of the fetish commodity form and the mystified thinking of individuals does not lie with professional experts like the psychiatrist or the career politician. In the manner in which these formal offices are ascribed an elevated status, they can even add to the tendency to fetishize – the former a culture of dependency, the latter a hero saviour. Neither is it an issue merely internal to Marxian scholarship. It is a collective problem in contemporary social life, and as such the solution must also be social. Only a radical restructuring of the economic and political institutions that regulate human interactions can provide the social climate in which the phenomena of fetishism may be transcended. This was Marx's position, yet for all of their undoubted excellence, his writings leave many organizational questions unanswered. The dictatorial turn of the Soviet Revolution and the collapse of social democracy that we are presently witnessing indicate that this is by no means only an academic problem or an issue of merely historical interest. Given that both the Soviet and Fabien inspired attempts to remodel society have only resulted in authoritarian forms of control, the guiding principles to the real solution have to be libertarian and democratic. The libertarian socialism articulated in NED holds that to have a substantive content, democracy must apply to the economic domain as well as the political. It claims further that full democracy can only be achieved within a system of workers' control; it cannot be attained if the means of production are either privately or state owned. Following Cole, I contend there is no question about the ideological dimension to the liberal separation of politics and economics. Thus, there is an agreement with the argument of the young Marx that if capitalists and workers enjoy equality as they are both citizens, there is a serious problem with existing forms of citizenship.

Further, the libertarian critique of the social democratic and command socialist states has fuelled neo-liberalism enthusiasm for free markets. By articulating a left-libertarianism that is as equally opposed to a market forces economy as it is to state socialisms, this book redresses the balance. Libertarianism is not the exclusive domain of the 'free market' right. Marx indicates that a non-authoritarian, indeed, a libertarian socialist alternative to social democracy and state socialism, is possible (bearing in mind that he never actually witnessed the Soviet fiasco but was prescient enough to disclaim certain social democratic interpretations of his work to the point of declaring 'I, in that case, am not a Marxist'), but he fails to sketch its institutional profile in any great detail. The present work offers an interpretative completion of his work. Marx's analyses of commodity production and a mode of production still contain important arguments. However, they need to be complemented by an equally important analysis of a 'mode of consumption'. And in both the productive and consumptive spheres, a discussion of the 'mode of organization' is the key imperative. I sketch what all three mean further on in this chapter, and it will become clear as the book unfolds that the latter is absolutely crucial to the task of theorizing the defetishization process.

The rationale to the argument that NED represents the defetishized society can be briefly summarized as follows. The first point to note is that the theory of commodity fetishism provides an account of the socio-economic situation which ensures alienation. 'The social power...which arises through the co-operation of different individuals...appears to these individuals...not as their own united power, but as an alien force existing outside them' (Marx, K. *GI*: 46 *quoted in* Brus, W. 1973: 47). Commodity fetishism is the result of market-driven activity; as is alienated labour. At their place of work, workers, typically, have little (if any) input into the organization of production. Major decisions are commonly made privately by a distant board of directors. Autocracy in the workplace is the predominant feature in the capitalist enterprise. A key accusation against capitalism by Marxist-inspired theorists like Horvat (1982) is that it fails to engender individual self-determination. The problem is therefore threefold: commodity fetishism, alienated labour and a lack of any real opportunity to experience genuine freedom. The solution must, correspondingly, be the diametrical opposite: defetishization, non-alienating (i.e. creative) labour and self-governing organization in which associates share control.[3] A real

3. There is more to the defetishized society than an appropriately organized political economy. Other domains of social life also seem to be guilty of fetishism, especially when

democracy, in contrast to the kind of liberal democracy typically offered for export by neo-liberal regimes, embraces popular participation in the organization and maintenance of society. Wainwright captures this position deftly, 'the extent to which political institutions are constructed to make possible popular participation in their administration should be one criterion by which their democracy should be judged' (1994: xii). She adds, plausibly, that for this to be realistic an egalitarian and cooperative economy is as essential prerequisite. It is in the same spirit that this book is written. The following two sections of this introductory chapter, 'The Problem' and 'The Solution', outline the problem and proposed solution in more detail. The subsequent section, 'The Solution in Organizational Terms', sketches the constitution of NED in fairly condensed terms. Finally, the existing social tendencies that point in a NED direction and the structure of the book are laid out.

The Problem

In this section I will, in the briefest of terms, summarize Marx's account of value in capitalism and its close association with commodity fetishism. It then shows how the young Marx's critique of alienated labour interrelates with his mature critique of commodity fetishism. Finally, it will be explained that although Marx did propose a solution to commodity fetishism – the abolition of the private ownership of the means of production – he was inconsistent on what this would amount to in organizational terms.

Marx distinguishes the elements of capital in regards to the process of production, the means of production (constant capital) and labour power (variable capital). Capitalism therefore has a double nature, variable capital first reproduces its own value, and, secondly, it produces fresh value, a surplus value. Drawing from his distinction between labour and labour

---

encouraged by the mass media. In terms of gossip for example, the over-documentation of the frequent sex scandals of renowned professional footballers in the UK is a case in point. But for all people, finance is the primary concern. In the first place, if any society cannot provide for the material needs of its people, it will obviously have grave difficulties surviving. Secondly, work, understood as socially necessary labour, is the central activity of most people's lives. The organization of economic life impacts directly on the capability of people to form more meaningful and satisfying relationships, not just in the workplace, but also in an extra-productive sense. How society organizes its economy, then, has an immediate effect on everyone. So the way production and consumption are organized must take precedence over other domains of social experience.

power, Marx then provides an account of the value-extending process. As non-owners of the means of production, the workers cannot make use of the value of labour power; only by selling their labour power can they gain access to productive assets. So although capital is investment used to secure greater profit margins, the forces which expand capital stem from propertied relations in which only a minority own the accumulated wealth embodied in productive resources. It is here, in the sphere of production, that capital exploits labour through the extraction of surplus value. In sum, capital is value in motion, a social relation attached to things like money and commodities. Marx's theory of value and his doctrine on fetishism are closely linked. The social character of labour is reproduced in the product as value. Although value expresses the relations of people, it does not convey them as such, but as relations between the items produced. That is, labour is a universal category, yet it is only with commodity production that it is expressed objectively as the value of products. In capitalism, producers work independently within a complex division of labour, interactions between people occur impersonally through market transactions. Note, however, that such social relations are effected only in the exchange of products, and not chiefly in the social character of labour, which appears indirectly in the value of commodities. This is the illusion of fetishism – *value appears as a natural attribute of commodities.* To put another way, the labour time that goes into the production of a commodity equals its exchange-value; the form of capital production is people operating the means of production. But although the forms may be visible, their basis in labour is not. Exchange-value appears to emanate from the commodity itself, rather than from the labour through which it was produced. In this sense, it seems as though exchange-value transcends its material premise. So, labour assumes the form of the exchange-value of commodities, and even though commodities do not have exchange-value autonomously, they nevertheless appear to. To summarize, while value is a relation between people, it is expressed as a relation between things; and it is through exchange-value that relations between people in their place of work remain hidden (Geras, N. 1991: 191; Cohen, G. A. 1978: 115–16).

Marx's analysis of commodity fetishism clearly recalls his earlier discussion on alienation. Chapter 3 provides a full exposition of his critique of alienated labour; here I will provide a summary in fairly succinct terms. He uses the term to describe how people in capitalist society become separated from their essence. The essence of a human being is captured in his term 'species being' – what it means to be human, to produce through creative labour in cooperation with one's associates. According to Marx, expression of human subjectivity understood in these terms is denied to workers in commodity production and, therefore, forms one of the central aspects of his alienation thesis. As non-owners of productive assets, workers have no choice but to exchange their labour power for wages. In the process, they become separated from their own producing activities. It follows that workers are equally alienated from the items produced through their labour. When labour power is treated as a commodity, there can be no self-determination. As such, the society of alienated labour has no autonomy, individuals' lives are ruled indeterminately by impersonal exchange relations; the labour process is beyond their control. A deleterious effect is that, with commodity production, the items produced engender independent and anti-human powers. So for Marx, both alienation and fetishism emerge when commodities are exchanged through an impersonal market. In either case, individuals experience a separation from each other and, equally, from the general interest. It is clear that domination is a reoccurring theme in the critiques of alienation and commodity fetishism; the properties conferred upon commodities are not under the direct control of people. Objects rule people, rather than being ruled by them. Labour is expressed as an objective property of the commodities it produces. Commodities, as alien entities, appear to have a life of their own. People are rendered subject to the process of commodity production and to the attributes bestowed, falsely as being natural, onto the commodities themselves.

That Marx's mature critique of commodity fetishism has distinct parallels with his earlier critique of alienated labour can, then, be clearly demonstrated. So how exactly does this inform the theoretical challenge of articulating the organizational bases of the defetishized society? The argument of this book is that we must visualize the material conditions capable of upholding creative labour and, of equal importance, genuinely democratic organizations. This, I contend, is best realized through a radical political economy of a left libertarianism.[4] Here, though, care needs to be taken to clarify that this is not necessarily Marx's position. It is by no means clear that Marx would agree with my proposed solution. On the one hand, the young Marx who brilliantly demonstrated the limits of

4. At the most general level, political economy asks how societies reproduce themselves materially. More specifically, it addresses how the labour of economic agents is regulated. It takes into account people's working activity, not in technical terms but in relation to its social form. It can, then, be understood as the science of productive and social relations (Perlman, F. 1972: x; Rubin, I. I. 1972: 3).

political emancipation, and Marx the advocate of the Paris Commune, is hostile to the authoritarian state. Yet on the other hand, in texts like the *Manifesto* of 1848 he is an advocate of a centralized common plan. So although the Bolshevik appropriation of Marxism was, in Schecter's words, 'often accomplished only with great distortion to the letter and spirit of Marx's work, especially the socialist humanism of Marx's early writings' (1994: 2), there is an ambiguity in Marx's thought. This ambiguity enabled Lenin to present Marx as a centralist. The Leninist version of Marxism installs hierarchy; discipline is enforced through the leadership of the Vanguard Party (Schecter, D. 1994: 4, 8–9; Morrison, R. 1997: 157). As I will now show, this book presents a very different solution.

The Solution

Following Marx, the solution will consist of transcending the state-civil society dualism, and cooperative labour will be central to this process. But in contrast to certain sections of Marx's comments, a genuine communal ownership of productive assets cannot, I will argue, give rise to a centralized state. So although Marx identifies the problem of commodity fetishism in masterly fashion, the solution presented here goes beyond his work. There are two indispensable features to the defetishized society – transparency in the social relations of production and demystified commodities. These can only be realized through the systemic implementation of creative labour and genuinely democratic organizations. These two facets are not reducible to each other, they interrelate strongly – *self-determination is the negation of alienation, and self-determination can only be realized when workers' cooperatives are managed along inclusive, participatory lines* – and without the institutionalization of both, the process towards defetishization cannot be sustained. This claim will now be explained in slightly more detail. In the process, the work of Roberto Michels will be introduced.

Through their practical activity, labour of various kinds, people transform the external world – society and nature – which in turn become the outcome of human endeavours. Therefore, people remodel both the conditions of their existence and also themselves as a species. The work process is simultaneously the process of self-creation. For Marx these are the terms on which freedom, an essential human characteristic, must be understood. Self-realization is indispensable to a non-alienated existence. As such, a share in the control over the economic conditions for one's life demands creative labour and democratic structures in the workplace. In this sense there are direct links between creative labour and democratic organizations; and, as a corollary, between both and commodity fetishism. This implies that a genuine cooperative control over the working environment is a prerequisite for superseding the phenomena of commodity fetishism, alienation and reification.[5] NED has no role for capital. But if the unaccountable power of capital is merely replaced by the equality unaccountable power of political elites, the opportunity for workers to coordinate their own activities through mechanisms of self-management is not advanced in the slightest. Defetishization, therefore, cannot possibly materialize in a system of oligarchic organizations. It follows that the most important imperative to the defetished society is a federation of genuine democratic organizations; otherwise there is no guarantee that the processes of production will not remain hidden. This point cannot be over-emphasized. The external form of democracy will only correspond to its intrinsic content if organizations are non-oligarchic. This implies that only the transparency of authentic democratic structures can reveal the actual social relations through which products and commodities are produced.

So, it is essential to a defetishized society that the most immediate organizations are able to withstand the formidable oligarchic impetus. There is no better way of articulating what this entails than through a debate with the paradigm writer on oligarchy, Roberto Michels. Michels is arguably the most feared critic of democracy. His main text *Political Parties* (1911) represents a landmark in the study of organizational dynamics. Since its publication, the descent of organizational democracy into oligarchic control has been widely accepted as largely unavoidable. It is now clear that organizational democracy is an elusive goal. The tendency for power to concentrate at the summit of an organization is an (almost) omnipresent phenomenon. Oligarchic structures are easily identified almost everywhere one cares to look. His seemingly accurate predictions about the future behaviour of democratic organizations have ensured that *Political Parties* is a pivotal text in the canon of political sociology. A critical response to Michels is, therefore, the best means by which to show why NED's organizational structures are non-oligarchic.

Michels' key claim is that power in organizations will, inexorably, concentrate in the higher echelons of their bureaucratic hierarchies. Organizations are subject and will succumb to the unyielding and deterministic tendencies that constitute what he termed 'the iron law of oligarchy' (1999: 342). The iron law has, as its name suggests, universal application. The

5. The term reification is explained fully in Chapter 1.

argument is that due to certain structural features inherent in their internal edifices, mass parties, trade unions and large-scale pressure groups will inevitably degenerate into self-perpetuating oligarchies. The complex of tendencies which prevent the fulfilment of democracy may be classified as being dependent upon organizational necessities and irreducible psychological imperatives. First, organizations are characterized by an extensive differentiation of function, and the expert leadership required to fulfil technical imperatives of efficiency ensures that the power of determination quickly concentrates, disproportionately, in their hands. Therefore, leaders become independent of the control of the collective will. This, the technical indispensability of leadership, is the principal cause of oligarchy. Secondly, leaders become accustomed to oligarchic privilege and develop an urge to dominate others while the masses have a need to be guided and require leaders they can venerate; feelings of gratitude help guarantee the leaders' continual re-election. These are the two main premises upon which Michels develops his thesis that democracy contains an 'oligarchical nucleus' (1999: 6, 364–6). The interests of elites and those of the masses will, he insists, polarize. From here a leadership clique evolves into a remote institution, forms a kind of cartel and builds up what he calls a 'metaphysical wall'. Democratic control, Michels concludes, is reduced to a minimum. Expressed laconically, the underlying sociological law of all modern democratic parties is 'who says organisation, says oligarchy' (1999: 365).

Perhaps the most encouraging response to what may be termed Michelian oligarchies has come from the literature on producer cooperatives. Michels is characteristically sceptical of the survival of workplace democracy. Significantly, this has not always been confirmed by empirical evidence. On the contrary, the empirical inquiries into participatory workplaces have shown that oligarchic tendencies can, although not easily, be resisted. At the very least, the prediction that politico-economic organizations are destined to be dominated by the dictates of oligarchs is, as this book will show, open to question. My argument is that through the adoption of certain procedures, the organizations central to the basic structure of NED will be able to maintain their internal democracies.

The Solution in Organizational Terms

Chapter 2 provides a full exposition of the political economy of NED; this section encapsulates it concisely. It is this scheme that harbours the conditions in which defetishization will occur. This is a double-edged process. First, there must be transparency in the social relations of production so that material relations between producers are no longer subordinated to the social relations between things. Secondly, the material conditions through which commodities are produced must be made evident in order to invoke their demystification. As both processes relate directly to the market, the first step is to ask whether there is still a role for markets in NED. If so, how may they be arranged so that they no longer engender fetishized social relations and fetishized commodities? In order to answer this question, it is instructive to summarize here in a few lines the constitution that markets will be embedded within. NED's two sectors, 'needs' and 'wants', are then briefly detailed. The section concludes by stating how products and commodities are ascribed value in NED.

In stark contrast to both the state socialisms of Marxist-Leninism and social democracy, NED incorporates a system of social governance embedded within a pluralist democracy. In the political sense, in place of the modern state is a commune system.[6] With regards to the economy, on the supply side production is divided into economic and technological homogeneous industries that form the guilds – which are decentralized into semi-autonomous cooperatives, and on the demand side consumer interests are aggregated through consumer councils. The general idea is that in addition to workplace democracies, consumer interests must be represented as a right of citizenship, rather than determined through prerogatives of private wealth as they are in market economies. The guilds and consumer councils are self-governing bodies in which government functions are devolved and carried out. The private sphere becomes one of cooperation and collective governance. Although the community own productive property, the guild cooperatives possess it collectively. This scheme establishes both a self-governing civil society and a state with pluralized component functions. It thereby transforms the prevailing divide between state and civil society. The guilds and consumer councils are constructed into the commune system through mechanisms of representation and consultation. Administrative machinery is simultaneously distributed to these functionally demarcated spheres of democratic authority. It will be clear that NED conceives of democracy in a radically different way to Western liberal democracies. The latter, typically, asserts that democracy involves universal franchise, frequent elections and mass political parties. This sits within a particular type of society, one that upholds a possessive individualism, markets, competition and supposedly consumer sovereignty. As this

6. This book does not analyse the commune system to any great extent. See *Beyond Rawls* chapter four, part two, for a discussion on the communes and sovereignty.

book will show, NED seeks to provide higher standards of accountability and increased levels of participation.

NED has two sectors. The principle sphere is a needs sector in which products are produced to satisfy democratically chosen needs. High-pressure capitalist intensive advertising contributes to grotesquely inflated needs. But in NED use-values pass from producer to consumer without the medium of the market. Democratic planning through the guilds and consumer councils determines the production and distribution of these *primary* goods. The second sector is a wants sector in which *specialized* products are determined, in consultation with the consumer councils and through the dictates of demarcated markets. Here the guilds are responsible for regulating competition within their own domains; as with NED's participatory approach to planning; these demarcated markets have been inserted with the consumer councils to aid their socialization. So with the production of need goods, the activities of the guild cooperatives are incorporated into the democratic plan, and in the wants sector they enjoy a higher degree of autonomy. Although exchange-value is expanded in the wants sector, it is subordinated to the use-value of the needs sector. Exchange-value is no longer the centrepiece of economic life. In both spheres of the economy, continuous producer-consumer dialogue is the chief determining factor. Unlike capitalist modes of appearance which are subject to a transformation that renders them mystified, in NED it is politics that links value and exchange; social relations are not reduced to commodity exchange. It is within this politico-economic setting that social relations are first disclosed and rendered transparent, and secondly they are beyond the distortion of mystifying ideologies.

Use-values in NED are, in the needs sector, ascribed to products; in the wants sector they take the form of commodities, and as such they are also exchange-values. A use-value is a commodity as soon as it is exchanged for other use-values. The distinction between products and commodities is therefore significant. If a person produces something just for herself, it is not a commodity. Equally, when use-values are produced not through market imperatives but in order to satisfy predetermined needs, with a knowledge of who is going to consume them – as they are in NED's needs sector – they are not commodities. In the sense that products are determined through democratic planning, they have a sociality before they are produced. In contrast, commodity status may be ascribed to a use-value only when it is in the sphere of exchange. So in NED's wants sector, commodities will be produced. For many Marxists socialist commodity production is a contradiction in terms. We can either build socialism, or we can stay with commodity production. But we cannot have both, as the latter denotes the market relationships which engender alienation and commodity fetishism. Other Marxists, however, dispute this reasoning. Their argument is that a market in which labour power no longer exists as a commodity is consistent with socialism. It is the latter position that is consistent with NED. That said, as there is still a subordinated role for markets in certain consumer goods, an immediate problem is encountered. Financial incentives and competitive material relations bolster acquisitive interests, rather than cooperation. Horvat is confident that with high levels of living, the danger is minimized. 'The more fully lower level needs are satisfied, the less important pecuniary incentives become, and the greater the emphasis on things that "money cannot buy"' (1982: 503). This is another good reason why, in NED, the democratically planned needs sector takes precedent over the market-orientated wants sector. But the issue of financial incentives engendering acquisitive interests is still pertinent. The position defended in this book is that it is only by demarcating markets so that they are compatible to the guild system, where competition can be regulated internally within each guild, will market laws lose their influence. NED socializes the market so that the antagonistic nature of self-interested competition is negated to the greatest possible extent. The general idea is to initiate activities in which cooperation is the key to success.

In NED's needs sector, goods will not simply exhibit the value of the labour they embody. They will meet the basic needs determined through the two consumer councils, by the people themselves. As prices will not always mirror purely the cost of labour consumed in the production of the goods, Marx's labour theory of value is not fully invoked.[7] The price of goods will be political prices, the price system being a key aspect of NED's mode of consumption. In addition, as there is no wage-labour and no private ownership of the means of production in NED, the Marxian categories of paid and unpaid – or necessary and surplus-labour are not relevant.[8] Neither does the concept of abstract labour have the same usage. Abstract labour is labour that can be measured and quantified; it is also removed from the workers performing it, that is commodity-labour. In NED as products have value partly in that they are the outcome of creative labour, the abstraction does not involve reification. Briefly

---

7. This should come as no surprise, for Marx believed that the labour theory of value would have no application in post-capitalist society.

8. There is still of course the issue of the appropriation of surplus value, but as Chapter 2 Part Three explains, this is subject to democratic adjudication.

put, *products and commodities are ascribed value through the institutionalization of creative cooperative labour, and through the requests of consumers – aggregated democratically via the consumer councils.* This offers a new angle for analysing the circulation of commodities, one that expands upon the Marxian treatment of commodities which concentrates on productive factors in value analysis. It stresses the trajectory of products in their entirety, from democratically deciding what gets produced, to production itself, to their distribution and exchange, and then to their consumption. If the overemphasis on the primacy of production is counterbalanced by attending to consumption factors on equal terms, and if both domains are thoroughly democratized, products can assume value by virtue of the political process. The idea that products are ascribed value partly through extra-productive means is not new to NED – Marx's labour theory of value has received heavy criticism for its insufficient treatment of demand – but what is new is the role consumer councils will play in the determination of products.

One final point, in Marx's analysis there is a triad of commodity fetishism, alienated labour and the labour theory of value. As the latter is of a limited applicability in NED, do the other two notions lose some of their strength in a strict Marxist sense? I do not believe they do. For instance Elster believes Marx is right in terms of the exchange-value of commodities, but he adds that Marx strayed when ascribing the relations involved as stemming from the productive process. A rare object may have an exchange value yet not be the outcome of organized production. So for Elster although the cost of production is a determinant of value, it is not universal. He does not dispute that Marx's theory of fetishism is useful, but it is, he argues, weakened through its reliance upon the labour theory of value (1985: 97–9). Yet as Cohen explains, the reliance is not exclusive:

> Some of Marx's doctrine of fetishism is expressed in terms presupposing the labour theory of value. That is not the only theory which grounds value in material conditions of production, and most of the fetishism doctrine may be stated within a competing material theory…in which value ratios are technically determined, but not by labour alone. (Cohen, G. A. 1978: 116)

Whether value in market economies is determined solely by a) labour, or more likely by b) labour and other technical factors of production or, even likelier still, by c) the latter combined with consumer demand, the ascendancy of exchange relations remains. As such, the fetishism doctrine can still 'be stated'. It is, therefore, permissible to analyse Marx's doctrine of fetishism and his theory of alienated labour largely in the absence of the labour theory of value.

Sociological Tendencies that Prefigure New Economic Democracy

The approach in this book is for the most part a radicalized analytical political theory. But I also wish to show that NED is more than an analytically rigorous response to the problems of social inequality and political alienation. The articulation of theoretical claims without any reference to empirical documentation runs the risk of 'fetishizing the text', so to speak. So although the present analysis of NED keeps a theoretical focus, it does move beyond the boundaries of academic analytical political theory and into an engagement with sociological literature. In this way, the existing demands for a greater control over the working environment (the evidence is overwhelming that most people would like their work to be more interesting and fulfilling, i.e. non-alienating) and the painful disillusions with prevailing capitalist consumption patterns (where many items produced are cheap and tasteless, providing no lasting pleasure to consumers and no real satisfaction to the workers who produced them) will not be treated as distant echoes. There are existing sociological tendencies which point in an NED direction.

An understanding of praxis is vital to radical political discourse. 'The philosophers have only interpreted the world, in various ways; the point, however, is to change it' (Marx: The 11th Thesis on Feuerbach). So the difficult question of where the agents of change are located must be addressed. In my opinion the agency question is best addressed by invoking the *functional* principle – that only inherent interest in all individuals, and not the individuals themselves, is suitable for representation. The correct starting point is, therefore, to devise appropriate political structures that seek to represent people in only one demarcated capacity, that part of themselves they put into associated effort, rather than an indiscriminate medley of interests in one large body, as, for example, the sovereign state attempts to do. This approach asserts that there is not an agency of complete individuals that can be approximated by a class, a nation, a gender, a race and certainly not an undifferentiated mass political party. The claim that there is not a generic humanity at the level of material interests informs NED's treatment of agency. It is incorrect to assume the interests of the people can be aggregated. What can be aggregated, however, are the most prominent interests that people share. The functional democratic ethic that informs the theoretical articulation of NED stresses in particular the interests people have as producers/providers of a service and as consumers. As such, there is what may be termed a twin agency.

Let us first take consumer behaviour. The Fair Trade Labelling Organisation (FLO) provides a channel for ethical considerations. As an alternative market, FLO products consist of more than just food, clothes and other products. They are packaged with knowledge of where production occurred, and their connection to wider political and social trends forms a key part of consumer choice. FLO is celebrated for restructuring producer–consumer interactions through a more humanized market; and the continued success of FLO indicates that people are, in their role as consumers, perhaps thinking progressively and in terms that go beyond purely personal desire satisfaction.[9] Another case in point is the attitude contemporary consumers are adopting towards domestic waste. It is now commonplace for households to separate their rubbish into recyclable sections, glass, paper, tin cans, plastics, etc. Until fairly recently this was largely the reserve of 'greens', and in some quarters may have even been considered eccentric. Today recyclable bins are provided free of charge to most houses. There is no direct financial incentive for consumers to act in this way, and yet an increasing number appear to be taking the time to dispose of their waste thoughtfully. This may initially seem a trivial matter, but it does suggest that even within the existing market economy – in which individuals are encouraged to be self-interested in how they satisfy their (often inflated) needs, and with little financial incentive for altruistic behaviour – positive change in consumer attitudes is occurring on a large scale. This is by no means the full picture; there are other examples of collective consumer action. The popular boycotting of dubious goods produced through adverse economic conditions, or in politically repressive regimes, has a rich history. During the 1970–80s consumer campaigns were used as instruments of political pressure and sought to organize boycotts of, for example, South African fruit (this was during the racially segregated era of Apartheid). Environmentalists took the initiative to expose the bioaccumulative consequences of CFCs. Animal welfare activists publicized the appalling conditions of factory farms and the inhumane treatment of laboratory animals. Feminists campaigned against the stereotyping of women in overly sexual terms. Many of these protest activities continue today, and have come to be theorized under the umbrella term 'new social

---

9. The degree to which FLO negates commodity fetishism is, though, another matter. See Lyon (2006) for a discussion of this question.

movements' (NSMs). When the cases of FLO, the disposal of domestic waste and the NSMs are taken together, they illustrate that a new collective consumer consciousness is emerging.[10]

Wainwright stresses that crucially, and in contrast to a central precept of neo-liberalism, these movements indicate that, in their capacities as consumers, people do far more than calculate the price of goods against marginal utility. While this remains an important concern for consumers, people also regard themselves as citizens with distinct interests in the effects commodity production have on the social and natural environments (1994: 166–8). These sociological tendencies certainly anticipate and prefigure NED's mode of consumption. NED captures these concerns; it also offers an advance on the existing market mechanisms for guiding consumer choices – which are at present distorted terribly by the huge inequalities in income and wealth – through the decentralized system of consumer councils. The general idea is that in a defetishized society in which the social conditions of production are revealed, consumption will be political and ethical. Rather than purchasing solely on the basis of fashion trends or designer labels, consumers will be more concerned about issues such as the effect of productive technologies on the environment and what conditions are like for the workers who produce the items they consume. Further, in order that no one should experience shortage through the excessive accumulation of things, citizens in NED will not be wholly dependent upon objects for their happiness; there will be no retail ceremonies or the ritualization of town-centre shopping complexes as a substitute for the worship of religious deities.[11]

As the idea of consumer councils will be new to most contemporary readers, it is worth briefly clarifying their rationale. Cole is perhaps at his most innovative when he is articulating how people's interests as consumers can be represented democratically. His suggestion that consumer interest may be aggregated at individual, local and regional levels by consumer councils remains one of the most original ideas in the history of radical political economy. The result is that debates in this field are steered beyond the plan-market impasse. This ingenious idea can no longer be marginalized in contemporary literature. Self-management in the workplace and hierarchy beyond it are contradictory. This calls for an equality of access to consumption goods. Following Cole, in NED this is realized through

10. I do not mean to imply that the NSMs are *only* concerned with identity and consumption, but it is apparent that they have interests in both.

11. The terminology in this last line is adapted from Morrison (1997: 108).

continuous dialogues between organized production, the guild cooperatives and organized consumption, the consumer councils. Articulating consumer interests in a formally inclusive setting establishes structural mechanisms through which political action can be channelled. This represents a vast improvement upon anything that is available at present. Consumers do have room for political manoeuvre in market economies, but, one might add, why wait until products have been produced and thrown out onto the market before boycotts are organized and enforced? I do not mean to be dismissive of consumer-led boycotts. My point is simply that in NED, if the same level of protest is channelled through and expressed in the consumer councils, the opposed commodity would never get produced in the first place.[12] This is a crucial point. Although I have stated that creative labour and democratic organizations are fundamental to the defetishized society, it is conceivable that controversial products such as instruments of warfare/torture/vivisection can be produced in this way; unlikely, but conceivable. With the mandate of consumer support, the consumer councils will be legally empowered to prevent these disputable products going to market. Consumer councils, therefore, are an indispensable aspect of NED's mode of consumption. The 'invisible hand' of the market is replaced by the 'visible hand' of the two consumer councils.

Corresponding to consumer democracy, the productive side of NED is no less democratic. In responding to Michels, the empirical studies on workers' cooperatives are consulted. This body of literature has drawn some promising conclusions. In terms of sustaining their internal democratic structures, engendering a pleasant workplace environment and securing high productivity, producers' cooperatives have enjoyed notable successes. While this on its own falls short of an extensive treatment of the agency issue, it does nevertheless make an important link between the domains of empirical and theoretical inquiry: adopting a theoretical approach that does not abstract from social processes gives political expression to existing social currents. In particular, the literature on the Mondragon system of cooperatives in the Basque region of Spain is engaged with. The internal structure of the cooperatives and the organization of the complex's superstructure are explained fully in Chapter 2. By way of a very brief summary, there are over 160 cooperatives with a combined total of approximately 22,000 workers. The products range from household appliances to

12. This does of course depend on the lack of any counter protest. In the unlikely event of an impasse between two well-supported and conflicting campaigns, the case goes before the local Commune.

engineering goods. The cooperatives form part of inter-cooperative federations, and they are also united externally through branches of a cooperative bank. There are important lessons to be learnt from the Mondragon experience; there is also much to be admired in its remarkable achievements. Significantly, the Mondragon cooperatives have an impressive proven track record of resisting oligarchic tendencies while simultaneously remaining highly efficient. For these reasons, their organization directly informs the theoretical formulation of NED's guild cooperatives.

Structure of the Book

The book is divided into two sections. Section I 'Commodity Fetishism, Anti-Fetishism and New Economic Democracy', has two chapters. Chapter 1, 'The Fetish Character of the Commodity Form and Defetishization', provides a full exposition of Marx's theory of the fetishism of commodities, as briefly summarized above. It then discusses John Holloway's work on 'anti-fetishism'. His *Change the World Without Taking Power* (2002) discusses fetishism at some length, and in doing so he distinguishes 'power-over' from 'power-to'. The former occurs when one class is in a position to appropriate the 'done' of a subordinate class. The latter implies no separation between the 'doers' and their done; there is no disconnection in what he calls the 'social flow of doing'. This is a useful distinction, and it can be used to shed light on NED's anti-fetishism. Holloway provides a sophisticated critique of capitalism. But although he stresses the solution is to re-appropriate the means of doing and to reconnect the social flow of doing, he does not get drawn into mapping out the contours of an alternative society, contending there is no choice but to follow the 'utopian star'. This strikes me as being partly off the mark. In my opinion, the anti-capitalist movement needs to have some idea of where it is going. Given that defetishizing the commodity form presupposes the reversal of the concealment of the social relations through which commodities are produced, and inversing the tendency to bestow upon commodities magical characteristics falsely presumed to be intrinsic to them, it is crucial to explain extensively the organizational set-up through which these processes can be realized. It is true that attempts to design a libertarian blueprint which is both theoretically sophisticated and practical enough to replace contemporary corporate capitalism can only be tentative and provisional. The finer micro details cannot be exhaustively anticipated in advance. But there is now a plethora of collective knowledge of the experience of command socialisms and social democracies to permit an informed projection of the principles that will need to be embedded in the political economy of a future society. As Breitenback et al. point out, how can anyone proposing alternatives to capitalism be persuasive if their stipulations do not go beyond the level of the 'pithy epithet' (1990: 5)? It is, I agree, vital to chart as systematically as possible the defining features of post-capitalist society.

The second chapter in Section I, 'Radical Political Economy and the Constitution of New Economic Democracy', details the organizational bases to NED's radical political economy. Before this though, the real-life example of the Mondragon complex is introduced. I have stressed that a system of semi-autonomous workers' cooperatives, united into federations by suitable external political structures, and in constant dialogue with the consumer councils, is the key premise upon which to engender defetishized social relations of production. As the Mondragon system has successfully organized production along these general lines, it will serve as an empirical reference point throughout. The design of NED's guild cooperatives has been substantially informed by the Mondragon cooperatives. However, although Mondragon provides an empirical lens by which to construct and analyse the guilds' internal design, caution must be shown when questioning the degree to which this system itself transcends fetishism. Despite its proud growth record, Mondragon is still a relatively small federation of worker-controlled enterprises operating within a wider mixed economy. To be successful the defetishization process requires a radical retransformation of the entire economy. Only when the organization of Mondragon is placed within a sympathetic wider context, like NED, is it legitimate to ask whether anti-fetishism will have a lasting value. But what Mondragon does illustrate well is that production in actually existing cooperatives – the workplace organizations required to maintain a non-fetishized economy – can be highly efficient. The significance of this empirically verified fact can hardly be exaggerated; it reinforces the proposition defended in this book that the defetishized society is not utopian in the unrealistic sense of corresponding in any way to existing reality. Holloway's work is fascinating, but his analysis needs to be completed by an extended critical discussion of what anti-fetishism demands in organizational terms. To serve this purpose, Chapter 2 begins by providing an exposition of the Mondragon system.

This task continues by outlining the institutional contours of NED thoroughly. The constitution of NED – the functional principle, the guild idea, the guild cooperatives, the consumer and civil councils, democratic investment planning and the commune system – are laid out in detail. This section of Chapter 2 is largely intended for the reader unfamiliar with *Beyond*

Rawls. The organizational contours of NED's political economy have not changed significantly from that outlined and analysed in *Beyond Rawls*. The only exception is the guild cooperatives, which have now been theorized with tighter precision. The reader already familiar with the argument in *Beyond Rawls* may wish to skip this section. The third and final section of Chapter 2 clarifies NED's plan-market synthesis. Through an analysis of the most immediate contestable issues discussed in the literature on socialist political economy, I illustrate that although both democratic planning and functionally demarcated markets will constitute NED's defetishized economy, it will not be within the frameworks of socialist centralized planning or the mixed economy typical of social democracies. In NED, planning proceeds via the institutions of a re-politicized civil society, through continuous dialogue between organized producers and organized consumers. This ensures that producers are directly accountable to consumers, and not state planners. Likewise, the task of regulating the market is also realized through these interacting bodies, organizations that citizens are more intimately involved with. The outcome is that producer–consumer relations are as transparent as economic realities allow. By the end of this chapter it will be clear why the combination of the unconventional approaches to planning and market is original, and hence unique to NED.

Section II 'Defetishization in the Economy of New Economic Democracy', argues that NED contains the politico-economic structures capable of neutralizing the tendency to fetishize. It has four chapters – Chapters 3 to 6. Chapter 3 'Superseding Alienation', introduces Marx's critique of alienated labour in full. Then, responding to commentators who argue it is inevitable in all modern advanced economies, it is shown that once the quantity and quality of products has been determined through NED's participatory and inclusive democratic planning, they are produced through conditions favourable to creative labour. The division of labour is analysed at both the macro and micro levels. I begin by highlighting how NED's use of the functional principle offers an original approach to dealienation. It is illustrated how placing organized consumption on an equal par with organized production diminishes Marx's elevation of the latter. NED stands in the Marxist-humanist tradition, but it makes a very important revision: that a mode of consumption is no longer regarded as subordinate to the mode of production. As I will show, this leads the debate on the possibility of transcending alienated labour into a new direction. I then contend that through the assimilation of a procedure for democratically planning investment, an ingenious scheme devised by David Schweickart (1993, 1998), creative labour can be enshrined in the constitution of NED. Finally, I explain how the guild cooperatives themselves can institutionalize certain structures that will also be conducive to upholding creative labour. In sum, workers in NED are not subjected to stupefying work, and they will only have to work towards goals that have been subject to public debate. In the guild cooperatives, labour is not carried out impersonally, independent of workers' personalities; guilds have networks of interconnected flows, coordinated through self-organized collectives. As the chapter makes clear, these conditions are ripe for the sustainability of creative labour. The chapter concludes by addressing what Horvat terms 'alienated consumption'. Here it is argued that the organizations that largely constitute NED's mode of consumption, the consumer councils, will be indispensable to the transparency and demystification dealienation requires. As such, they will play a significant role in the negation of alienation and commodity fetishism.

Chapter 4 'Towards a New Economic Democracy Critique of Oligarchy', introduces the work of Michels. A debate is then constructed between Michels and the democratic socialist theorist whose writings initially inspired the theorization of NED, G. D. H. Cole. Comparing the work of Michels and Cole ignites a dynamic that informs the analytical defence of NED, and in so doing steers a path towards the defetishized society. Reference to Cole is also important for a number of other reasons. Cole held, for good reason, that only when the representative ethic is functional and specific, and not general and undifferentiated, can democracy be real. This position is fully endorsed in NED. He also sketches the institutional contours of a guild in considerable detail. In the process, he provides an account of how they will retain their internal democracies. Some of his suggestions are still useful, but his position now needs to be augmented. Since the period in which he designed the guild system on paper (1914–20), the literature on workplace democracy has expanded considerably. There is now a more theoretically sophisticated, and as the commentaries on Mondragon illustrate, a more empirically validated response on how to negate oligarchic tendencies in workplace democracies. So in order to complete the analysis, there is recourse to move beyond Cole's libertarian socialist texts. Nevertheless, his ideas can still provide a useful reference point, and despite the innovation in NED of semi-autonomous guild cooperatives in which a profit criterion for efficient production is sanctioned, the overall structure of his ideal-typical guild is retained.

Michels provides three different yet interrelated theories about the origins and development of oligarchy, even though the relationship between them is not always clear. He has what Herbert Kitschelt (1990) calls two weak and one strong conception of oligarchy. They are a theory of transaction costs, a theory of membership lethargy (weak, or preliminary, theories), and a theory of elite control (strong theory). Chapters 5 and 6 are, respectively, named after these weak and strong theories. The weak notion is critical of direct democracy, in particular of the idea that all members of an organization are able to participate equally in collective decision-making. Due to the actual numbers involved, this is mechanically and technically impossible. The strong notion stresses that the interests of elites and those of the masses will polarize. Initially a leadership clique may be responsive to its constituency, but as the organization matures, professional leaders become stable and evolve into a distant mini-community. Michels undoubtedly defines what are clearly formidable tendencies; it is indisputable that they exist, and that they are strong. Chapters 5 and 6 argue, however, that through the introduction of certain democratic procedures, the organizational structures in NED are sufficiently robust to resist the onslaught of Michelian oligarchies. They will, in other words, be capable of sustaining non-oligarchic structures of accountability between the leadership and the rank and file.

The concluding chapter summarizes and reiterates the central argument of the book. As NED has the economic and political structures capable of penetrating beneath superficial appearances, and as it can sustain both transparency in the social relations of production and demystified commodities, it can instigate and sustain non-fetishized social relations. The task is to articulate an alternative cooperative mode of production and, of equal importance, a corresponding mode of consumption. This is achieved by redefining the lines of demarcation between a cooperative economy and a pluralized state, or to be more precise through a re-politicized civil society in which both the productive and the consumptive spheres are fully democratized. Democratizing the social relations of production in the unique way NED does, adhering to the functional principle of representation, institutionalizing continuous dialogue between organized producers and organized consumers (the correct mode of coordination), abolishing any significant role for capital by democratizing investment planning and establishing a fair criterion for surplus appropriation provides the most desirable socialization of productive assets. It is within this radical political economy that the defetishization process can unfold. The implementation of creative labour on a macro scale, a conceivable critique of oligarchy, the subordination of exchange-value to use-value and the illuminating role of the consumer councils support the conclusion that NED can plausibly be thought of as the defetishized society. In light of this, my contention is that in terms of alternatives to liberal capitalism, although NED cannot be touted as a panacea, it is the best option available. Obviously, an alternative to capitalism cannot possibly have a substantial role for capital – market socialism is often guilty of this. It is equally obvious that a real democracy must not, logically, be constituted through oligarchic organizations – Marxist-Leninism and social democracy both make this error. As NED fulfils both objectives, it can help fill the vacuum left by the more commonly known socialisms.

SECTION I

COMMODITY FETISHISM, ANTI-FETISHISM AND NEW ECONOMIC DEMOCRACY

1

The Fetish Character of the Commodity Form and Defetishization

Marx holds that a necessary condition of scientific inquiry is that it must seek to reveal the true reality which stands behind concealing appearances. In formulating this requirement he often uses terminology like form/content, illusion/reality and appearance/essence. In capitalism for example he identifies a severance between existing social relations and how they are experienced. As 'all science would be superfluous if the outward appearance and the essence of things directly coincided' (1974: 817), his analytical method is to penetrate beneath immediate appearances and uncover the underlying reality (Geras, N. 1971: 1–2). It is in this respect that the theory of the fetishism of commodities must be understood. This chapter begins by explaining Marx's theory; Part One, 'Marx and Commodity Fetishism', undertakes this task. Having established the bases to commodity fetishism, Part Two, 'Anti-Fetishism', explores what exactly is involved in the antidote to fetishism. Here the requirements of the defetishized society are clarified. The task is to articulate the economic relations of what may be termed a defetishized political economy.

Part One: Marx and Commodity Fetishism

Marx begins his discussion on the fetishism of commodities by inferring that although a commodity initially appears a trivial thing, further analysis reveals it is 'a very queer thing, abounding in metaphysical subtleties and theological niceties' (1977: 435). The enigmatical character of a commodity arises:

> simply because in it the social character of men's [sic] labour appears to them as an objective character stamped upon the product of that

> labour; because the relation of the producers to the sum total of their own labour is presented to them as a social relation, existing not between themselves, but between the products of their labour. (Marx, K. 1977: 436)

This chapter will clarify precisely what Marx means by this. Commodity fetishism is a penetrating critique of capitalist social relations. In order to explain it thoroughly, this exposition is divided into four sections, a), 'The Illusion of the 'Natural' Properties of Commodities', b), 'Reification of the Productive Relations between People and the Personification of Things', c), 'The Mystified Appearance of Capitalist Society' and d), 'The Objectivity of Commodity Fetishism'. The contents of these sections interrelate and overlap, and they are not intended for analytical purposes. They are solely to aid the explanation of what is, as Rubin puts it, among the most 'daring and ingenious' of Marx's generalizations (1972: 5).

The Illusion of the 'Natural' Properties of Commodities

The theory of commodity fetishism tries to specify how the market affects workers in their capacities as producers and consumers. Marx infers that in capitalist society commodities have certain qualities bestowed upon them, qualities that are then regarded as 'natural'. He uses the term fetishism to explain how the social relations of producers are displaced and relocated in the ostensible qualities of commodities. In portraying capitalist social relations as natural, social objects are naturalized. This is the root of the mystification of fetishism. Mystification confuses social facts as natural, and it is from here that the value form is fetishized. That is, fetishism metamorphoses the social character of things into a natural character. To illustrate his point he invokes the analogy of religion, in which an imagined entity, god, is conferred with supernatural powers. Likewise, commodities, which are plainly the result of labour, also come to appear in an autonomous sense, independent from those who produced them. But unlike the religious fetish, the economic fetish is not the outcome of a thought process; it derives from the way production is organized. Commodities exist in a way god does not (1977: 436). The qualities accorded to commodities are real. These qualities though are not natural but social; they are taken for natural because their essence is not immediately apparent. Commodities are comprehended only in terms of their peculiar attributes; and not, more accurately, as stemming from the actual social relations which produced them. What is mistakenly conferred to the commodity is then interpreted as something inherent in it (see reification below). In this way the fetishized commodity is infused with an independent power which, beyond the world of illusion, it does not have (Marx, K. 1977: 436, 439; Geras, N. 1971: 6; 1991: 190–1; Cohen, G. A. 1978: 115–16; Ollman, B. 1976: 195; Carver, 1982: 68–71).

Reification of the Productive Relations between People and the Personification of Things

Geras (1971) explains that for Marx fetishism inflicts itself upon people as mystification and domination. The latter is addressed in Chapter 3. In respects of the former, Geras draws a secondary distinction: a), appearances/forms of manifestation in which social relations are not false as such, that is, they correspond to an objective reality; they are mystified when understood as products of nature, and b), appearances/forms of manifestations which are plainly false, illusions that do not correspond to objective reality. For Marx, that social relations are mediated by the relations between things is a form of manifestation that actually exists. '[T]he relations connecting the labour of one individual with that of the rest appear, not as direct social relations between individuals at work, *but as what they really are,* material relations between persons and social relations between things' (1977: 437).[1] Relations between people secured through the act of exchange are hence *indirect*, and are channelled through *direct* relations to commodities. This is a key step to understanding fetishism. In commodity production, it is not that social relations between people assume an imaginary appearance as a relation between objects, it is that these social relations genuinely do assume the form of relations between objects. So the fetishism thesis is that social relations come into view and are interpreted by producers as comparative relations between commodities. Material relations between producers are subordinated to the social relations between things. Social form is alienated from productive content. Marx regards it as absurd, but the absurdity is of reality, not an illusion (Marx, K. 1977: 436–7; Geras, N. 1971: 4–5; Elster, J. 1985: 95–6; 1986: 57–8).

It is important to realize that the process through which things become personified must be analysed as the outcome of the process through which the social relations of production become reified – to treat an abstraction as if it has a real material existence. When people go to the market to sell their

1. My italics.

wares it is as owners of things. Possession of a thing is a necessary requirement to form direct social relations of production. As such, it appears as though it is the thing itself that is endowed with the capability to instigate these social productive relations. As it allows the owner to enter into exchange relations, the thing stands as the possessor of the extraordinary quality of exchangeability. The thing not only serves as a use-value, it also has a social function, it connects people; it is here that things come to acquire particular social characteristics. Social relations are established through things because there are no direct relations between the owners of different productive factors. Commodities are products of private labour conducted independently of other private labours. Capitalists, landowners and workers all own commodities, but they are independent from each other, both in inter and intra terms. It is only in the form of purchase and sale that interactions are established. It is the productive relations that are realized through market exchange that are reified social relations. To say productive relations are reifications is to say they are congealed in the properties of things, properties that appear to emulate from the things themselves, detached from the actual productive relations. As things appear as bearers of fixed social characteristics, they are endowed with the power to induce people to enter into concrete social relations of production. It appears to be the social character of the things that engenders the social character of the people who own them (Marx, K. 1977: 436–7, 438–9; Rubin, I. I. 1972: 21–4; Perlman, F. 1972: xxvi).

But, of course, the social characteristics of things do not belong to them naturally; they are expressions of human relations attached to things. That is, the manner in which commodities appear to relate to other commodities and to people is an objective expression of relations between people. The appearance of the relationship between the objects of labour is, as explained above, not false, it actually exists, but it does obscure the underlying material relations between producers. Commodity fetishism conceals the social character of private labour and the social relations of individual producers; it engenders a divide between surface appearance and hidden reality. Producers' relations appear this way because the qualities that commodities are compared with seem to have no connection with the social relations of the people who produced them; they are no longer treated as the products of human endeavours. In demystified consciousness – which is not mesmerized by the enchantment of fetishism – it is evident that a commodity's exchange-value is through its relation to labour and people's needs. But in mystified consciousness (or inverted/bewitched consciousness as Marx sometimes refers to it), goods seem to exchange at the rate they do due to their inherent properties. It is in this sense that the phenomena of the personification of things comes into being. As Rubin explains, the social characteristics of commodities shape *individual* productive links between people only to the extent that the social characteristics themselves are an expression of the *social* productive links (1972: 25). In Marx's theory, the displacement of interpersonal relations to the relations producers have to things is a key contradiction of commodity-producing society; a contradiction he seeks to expose in the usage of the term commodity fetishism. In sum, there are two properties, the personification of things and the conversion of productive relations into relations between things (Marx, K. 1977: 436–7, 438–9; Rubin, I. I. 1972: 24–7; Perlman, F. 1972: xxvi; Elster, J. 1985: 95–6; 1986: 57–8).

Commodity fetishism, then, captures how the products of labour are misconceived as soon as they are exchanged on the market. The story of the metamorphosis of productive relations into relations between objects is concerned to explain what happens in the process of production and the articles produced. Confusing this to be a narrative about the adventures of inanimate objects, commodities are attributed qualities only people can possess. As a consequence, the relationship between people and their products has, Marx argues, two aspects: commodities become people's master, and workers become object-less beings (1977: 438, 442). The laws that regulate economic processes do not exist outside people, and commodities are objectifications of inter-subjective relationships. But the subjective aspect contained in the commodity becomes reified; it is here that human relations are turned into relations between objects. Hence the dual process, as commodities are endowed with human attributes, so are workers debased to the level of objects. Rather than being seen as a web of social relations that are not static but changeable, society is interpreted as being subject to independent items and objective laws. It is in this sense that the society of commodity fetishism has no autonomy. As Marx concludes, 'the process of production has the mastery over man [sic], instead of being controlled by him' (1977: 442; Ollman, B. 1976: 195; Carver, 1982: 68–71; Avineri, S. 1968: 117–19).

The Mystified Appearance of Capitalist Society

By extension, fetishism also applies to other economic categories like money and capital. In capitalist society money mediates between people and their objects, and so comes to have real power. As explained above, people's relations are reified in their products, and these reified products then interact back with them ensuring that the false appearance is taken to be true. With capital fetishism the social relations of production which specify productive assets as capital are also disguised. The real power of capital appears mystifyingly as natural. The appearance that mystifies though is not unreal; it is an objective social form which masks the underlying relations. The reversal of this mystifying metamorphosis, Marx insists, is to treat capital as a finite social relation – demystification through a 'de-naturalization'. Yet this is not a de-objectification, for capital is an objective form. Hence, the false appearances of fetishized forms are not entirely due to any subjective deficiencies in the cognition of social agents. As Geras explains, when capitalism is experienced as something different to what it actually is, this is due to *capitalism displaying itself as something different to what it actually is.* Subjects do not deceive themselves; they are deceived by reality. For Marx then, capitalism presents itself in a camouflaged form, commodity values draw a veil over the social character of labour, in much the same way wages conceal exploitation.[2] So although commodities, money, capital, etc., do not have supernatural properties, the false believe that they do is, ontologically speaking, real (Ollman, B. 1976: 195–6, 200; Geras, N. 1971: 6; 1991: 191).

The Objectivity of Commodity Fetishism

It has been generally accepted that Marx makes certain claims in his fetishism thesis. As illustrated above, he argues that in commodity economies the products of labour, things, are assigned characteristics whose source is in the social relations of production through which they were produced; social relations are expressed in exchange; the exchangeability of a commodity is considered its natural property; and the characteristics that are assigned to the commodity appear in a mysterious way because they were not immediately apparent in the underlying relations of producers. Rubin

2. Geras concludes his discussion on appearance/essence by addressing the forms which are purely illusions, that is, they are nothing more than appearances. In the wage form, the value of labour-power falsely appears as the value of labour. Exploitation is concealed, as no distinction is drawn between paid and un-paid labour. Capitalists appear to pay for labour, but for Marx they actually hire labour-power, although this is not immediately apparent. An equal exchange of equivalents is only an appearance. So in contrast to the metamorphosis of material relations into relations between things, the wage form does not correspond to any objective reality (Geras, N. 1971: 7–8).

agrees that these interpretations are not inaccurate, but they do not, he adds, exhaust the full content of Marx's fetishism thesis. The productive relations are veiled, but they *inevitably* take the form of things; they can *only* be expressed through things. That is, things play this role due to the actual structure of commodity economies. 'Marx', Rubin confirms, 'discovered the objective economic bases which govern commodity fetishism' (1972: 6, 5–6).

Commodities are evaluated and exchanged on the market. It is the market that regulates the products of labour; society only indirectly regulates working activity. Due to variations in consumer purchasing behaviour, the prices of commodities fluctuate, and this influences the various directions in which economic agents channel their working activity. Separate commodity producers constantly enter and exit different productions. Within this atomistic structure, connections between autonomous enterprises are maintained through things. This does not imply that producers are only connected with the consumer they directly sell to. Indirect relations are also established. As commodity producers make goods to be sold impersonally on the market, they are forced to consider the conditions of the market. That is, private enterprises work independently of each other, and direct connections are only established through exchange. 'Since the producers do not come into social contact with each other until they exchange their products, the specific social character of each producer's labour does not show itself except in the act of exchange' (Marx, K. 1977: 436). Exchange then comes to assert an influence upon their productive activity. An enterprise relies on market signals, which implies the orientation of its productive methods will be indirectly influenced by the productive methods of other enterprises. If an innovation in the production of watches lowers the cost of watch production, then all watch producers are forced to adopt similar measures to upgrade their productive technology. It is clear that producers must take into account the working activity of others. So commodity producers, independent from each other with regards to their productive methods, are related through market exchange. The role of exchange ensures that people's working activity influences each other only by virtue of the movement of things. It is in this sense that exchange influences working activity. Production and exchange are inseparably linked components of reproduction. Seen in this light, commodity fetishism conveys to people and to the market an objective reality that is coercive of economic agents. It follows that fetishism is inseparable from commodity-producing society (Marx, K. 1977: 436–7; Rubin, I. I. 1972: 7–10).

Summary

Marx suggests that in capitalist society the content (the interior reality) behind the form (fetishized surface relations) is private labour producing use-values for exchange, rather than immediate consumption. This implies that with commodity production only exchange-value brings together otherwise fragmented producers. Here the interactions between atomic individuals are predominantly through the exchange of products. The market integrates the labour of producers 'behind their backs', so to speak. Central to the commodity fetishism thesis is that producers, rather than being united are initially divided, are linked indirectly in a duplicate illusory form. This, as Cohen explains, may be seen as 'surrogate coherence' (1978: 119–22, 125). So the enigma of why commodities are fetishes occurs because the social character of production is presented not in the actual sphere of production, but through exchange relations. The relations of producers are only *indirectly* social; producers, who only have minimal *direct* social relations, connect through exchange via the market. This engenders the mystification and concealing aspects of commodity fetishism. The root of mystification is that in market forces economies commodities have attributes accorded to them, attributes that are then regarded as obtaining in them naturally. Mystification collapses the socially objective appearances of capitalist relations into a natural objectivity. The first step to understanding fetishism is that this metamorphosis of material relations between producers into the social relations between things actually occurs. The reification of the products of labour ensures that false appearances are interpreted as true; this is an objective reality of capitalist society, and it ensures that attention is focused away from society's real essence, production. To conclude, the processes explained in this chapter – the illusionary natural attributes of commodities, the personification of inanimate objects and the reification of productive relations and the resulting concealment of productive relations – are the key aspects of the theory of commodity fetishism. With the theory of commodity fetishism now fully clarified, the next step is to consider what the essential criteria of the defetishized society will consist of, and from there how it may be expressed in organizational terms.

Part Two: Anti-Fetishism

> *Capitalism is the daily repeated violent separation of the object from the subject, the daily snatching of the object-creation-product from*

> *the subject-creator-producer, the daily seizure from the doer not only of her done but of her act of doing, her creativity, her subjectivity, her humanity.*
>
> *(Holloway, J. 2002: 143)*

This second part of the chapter introduces John Holloway's (2002) intriguing discussion of fetishism. This is done through three sections, 'Power-To and Power-Over', 'Hard Fetishism and Fetishization-As-Process' and 'Reconnecting the Social Flow of Doing'. Holloway's critique has much intrinsic appeal, and he captures deftly what defetishization entails. He does not, though, stipulate the institutional form that may sustain defetishized relations. In contrast, I contend that it is legitimate to sketch the organizational contours of the defetishized society; indeed, I argue it is vital.

Power-To and Power-Over

In order to establish the relevance of Holloway's analysis, it will be instructive to outline his critique of capitalism and his distinction between 'power-to', and its opposite 'power-over'. The former is transformed into the latter when the 'social flow of doing' is ruptured. When power-to exists as power-over, the greater number of 'doers' become the 'done-to'. Power-to unites, it brings people's 'doings' together, whereas power-over separates the done from the doing, it separates each other's doings and it separates the doers from the means of doing. Power-over, therefore, encompasses control over the done. As a consequence, the exercisers of power over deny the subjectivity of those they are able to dominate. In capitalism the means of doing are the means of production. The non-owners of the means of doing, the workers, have to sell their 'capacity-to-do', labour power, to the owners of the means of doing. The done is defined as private property. Capitalists appropriate the done (dead labour, capital), and the relentless drive to accumulate escalates the speed of the doing. The done increasingly stands dominant over both the doing and the doer. The doing becomes concealed and the done, commodities, appear with their own value. The social flow of doing, the doers *and* the wielders of power-over, the capitalists, all stand in subordination to the real subject in capitalism: value (Holloway, J. 2002: 28–34).

Holloway argues that the commodity form fractures the social flow of doing. As a commodity is produced solely to be exchanged impersonality on the market, it unhinges social doing. Only the commodity is recognized socially through the act of exchange. So in capitalist society things rule, labour relations are not immediately apparent; the done is severed from the doing and the sociality of doing is disrupted. Inherent in the commodity form is the appropriation of the done by those who own the previous done, and so the means of doing. Accumulation is the habitual practice of disconnecting done from doing. This form of doing (abstract labour, creation of surplus value) and the done (commodity, capital) engenders the rupturing of the social flow of doing. To clarify this process of fragmentation, Holloway supposes he makes a chair. In terms of the social flow of doing, the chair is briefly objectified. When put to use, it is integrated into the collective flow. But in capitalism, the chair's objectification is more than brief. The chair now exists as the property of someone else, a commodity to be sold. Its existence is disconnected from its constitution – the doing that created it, which falls from view. Although the buyer uses the chair, the social flow is broken; direct relations between the user and the maker do not exist. The disintegration of the social flow of doing engenders an individualization of doers. As commodities are intended to be exchanged through the market, they must be abstracted from the doing. Communities then appear as the aggregation of atomized individuals (Holloway, J. 2002: 47–50, 59–60).

It is clear that Holloway endorses much of the Marxian critique of capitalism. As the previous section indicated, for Marx the mystical character of commodities does not stem from their use-value, it generates from the commodity form, from the social character of the labour through which they are produced. Commodities are produced by private labour, which is only indirectly social. Holloway captures Marx's position deftly, '[t]here is an objectification of the subject and a subjectification of the object: things (money, capital, machines) become the subjects of society, while people (workers) become the objects' (2002: 51). He agrees with Marx that social relations appear as the relations between things, an appearance that incorporates the fracturing of done from doing. The categories of fetishized social relations include money, commodities and capital, all of which appear to emanate from the sphere of circulation. The subjectivity of the producers is hidden, all that is visible is the interaction of commodities and the individuals who own them (Holloway, J. 2002: 50–2).

Hard Fetishism and Fetishization-As-Process

From here Holloway develops his theory of fetishism. He states there are two ways to understand fetishism, a) 'hard fetishism', and b) 'fetishization-as-process'. The former is fetishism as established fact, a stable feature of capitalism, the latter treats fetishism as a constant battle, never settled. These two have very different political implications. Hard fetishism is the more common approach. In capitalism social relations really are the relations between things, people exist as dehumanized objects. Fetishized social relations are seen as stable. Value appears as a permanent social relation, and is regarded as dominant. It follows that the social relations through which value is created are also understood as stable. The 'closed logic' that Holloway is referring to infers that commodities, money, capital, state, etc., actually are reified forms of social relations, but they are interpreted as closed categories. An immediate problem for the 'fetishism as accomplished fact' theory is how fetishized social relations are best transcended. Holloway rejects out of hand any idea that the political party or the state can be the vehicles through which emancipation will occur. Fetishism as established fact implies anti-fetishism can only emerge from somewhere outside the existing system. Fetishism and anti-fetishism are separated; fetishism rules daily life, while anti-fetishism lies on the periphery. The solution, Holloway suggests, is a concept that does not assert this disengagement. He infers that fetishism implies its opposite as 'resistance, refusal and rejection'. Only with a theory of anti-fetishism can fetishism be conceived. Fetishism and anti-fetishism co-exist as antagonistic processes. Fetishism separates subject and object, and done from doing. It is antagonistic to anti-fetishization, the movement to reunify subject and object, and done with doing (Holloway, J. 2002: 7880, 82–9).

Holloway suggests that as people live in an antagonistic society, they fetishize and are in opposition to fetishism. Antagonism exists in the way doing is organized. In capitalism people do not control their creative activity; it is subject to market imperatives. The antagonism is between labour power and those who appropriate it. The domain in which the done is severed from the doing is production; it is here that subject and object are separated. In producing a commodity, workers simultaneously produce their alienation from it. Capitalist production separates subject and object; it then brings them together as alienated subject and object. Value is the relation between them, as it conceptualizes the detachment between labour and the commodities it produces (2002: 147–8). This, then, is the bases to Holloway's argument that fetishism must be understood as fetishization. The next section engages critically with his work.

Reconnecting the Social Flow of Doing

Holloway, following Marx, asserts that the fetishism illusion is real. Fetishism occurs not just in people's minds, but also to the material disconnection of done from doing. It cannot be overcome just in thought; it requires the reunification of doing with done. If material exploitation is separated from the fetishization of thought, then fetishization is merely a 'tool of cultural critique', a 'sophisticated moan'. Rather, the means of doing need to be re-appropriated. He immediately points out that state ownership did not transform doing, and that to use property terms does not move beyond fetishism. Property is an active process of separating. The struggle, he infers, is to dissolve property and the means of production. But then what exactly does this entail? What will a society that has dissolved both property and the means of production look like in organizational terms? Holloway proposes that we should not engage with capital on capital's terms. The struggle must occur on a different dimension, one in which capital cannot exist (2002: 210, 213–14). Certainly a genuine alternative to capitalism can have no significant role for capital, but the different dimension can move beyond fetishism without abandoning all property forms. On the provision that property relations can be arranged so that they are not an active process of separating, organizational design can, to my mind, be justified. Yet for Holloway:

> It is surely wrong to think in terms of a continuous process of organisation-building. Certainly there must be an accumulation of practices of oppositional self-organisation, but this should be thought of not as a linear accumulation, but as a cumulative breaking of linearity. (Holloway, J. 2002: 214)

This is to beg the question how the constitution of the new society will function. A society with a continuous social flow of doing, in which doing and done are not severed, will need to harbour patterned relations, and for this a linear accumulation is required. We can as Holloway suggests think of organization in terms of doing, rather than in terms of being (2002: 214), but this does not rule out a unity of organization.

Holloway's answer to the question of how to change the world without taking power is 'we do not know' (2002: 215). I too believe that it should not be through the state. But then, one wonders, through what? His book deliberately provides no definitive answers, although he does acknowledge that to reject state power does not imply rejecting organization. Rather than trying to control the state, the goal must be social self-determination (2002: 215, 217). He claims, reasonably, that the question of what constitutes self-determination must be posed in terms of the articulation of decision-making, rather than being directed by the party or the state. This implies that the movement towards self-determination intimates a critique of representation, a 'moving against-and-beyond representation' (2002: 228).

For Holloway representation defines, excludes and separates. It establishes who is the representative and who is the represented, and for what duration. In elections the electoral select a representative to act on their behalf. Representation, Holloway contends, imposes hierarchical structures, and is incompatible with self-determination. Self-determination requires responsibility; people must participate in the determination of social doing (2002: 229). To reject representation is, he adds, to reject leadership. Inasmuch, Holloway does not believe there can be an organizational model. 'What is important is not the detail but the thrust of the moving…out into the unknown. What else can we do but follow the utopian star…?' (2002: 231). But why must it be unknown? We can at least give our journey some direction. NED's organizational forms are subject to revision upon further analysis, but in contrast to Holloway, I would suggest theorizing the detail is not only important, it is essential.

Take, for example, what self-determination entails. Holloway contends that '[t]he drive towards self-determination moves against-and-beyond representation, against-and-beyond the state, above all, against-and-beyond labour' (2002: 238). In regards to the latter two, I concur fully. It is on the issue of moving 'against-and-beyond representation' that we part company. Self-determination, understood as the development of power-to-do beyond power-over, can be realized as long as what is being represented is not people, but demarcated interests inherent in all individuals. This is probably the major sticking point between Holloway and NED. Holloway seeks to move against-and-beyond representation; I seek to move against-and-beyond undifferentiated representation. Provided it is people's productive, consumptive and political interests – and not the actual individuals – that are being represented in functionally dichotomized bodies,[3] and provided that the representative bodies are genuinely non-oligarchic, the representative ethic will not exclude or separate. It is along these organizational lines that social self-determination can be realized.

A genuine social self-determination signifies collective participation in the social flow of doing. Producer cooperatives are essential to the solution, yet for Holloway their limitations are evident:

> in so far as they produce for a market, they are forced to produce under the same conditions as any capitalist enterprise. The problem is not the ownership of the enterprise, but the form of articulation

3. Functional organizations are explained fully in the following chapter.

> between different doings. If these doings are articulated through the market, then the doers lose control of their own doing, which becomes transformed into abstract labour. (2002: 240)

His argument is that along with the creation of cooperatives, the interaction between different groups of doers must also be addressed. Self-determination is not just about particular activities; it also involves the relations between them. Rearticulating the social flow of doing involves setting out an appropriate interaction between production and circulation. Cooperatives are inadequate all the time they fail to innovate new intercommunications between consumers and other producers external to the particular cooperative (2002: 240). This is an excellent argument. It is not difficult to appreciate why cooperatives operating in market economies will be under the dictates of market imperatives. Market socialism has been heavily, and deservedly, critiqued for precisely this reason. Self-determination does involve rearticulating interactions between producers and consumers. As Chapter 2 explains, this is central to the rational of NED's construction. The 'form of articulation between different doings', which in NED translates to the form of articulation between different groups of guild cooperatives (doers), is a concern that has been addressed in detail in the theorization of NED's political economy. The guild cooperatives will not, I will argue, suffer from the fragmentation Holloway points too.

Conclusion

In non-commodity production, Marx suggests that 'the social relations between individuals in the performance of their labour, appear at all events as their own mutual personal relations, and are not disguised under the shape of social relations between the products of labour' (1977: 440). In primitive communist, tribal and feudal societies the product has a sociality before it changes hands; there is some agreement in advance about its quality and quantity, and, importantly, who it is intended for. The task taken up in the following chapters is to show how this sociality can remain in a modern complex economy; moreover, how it can remain in undisguized form. In other words, it is indicated how material relations can be sustained without being distorted by passing through the exchange relations of a market forces economy. The solution cannot be found through the introduction of therapeutic interventions at the level of the individual. Marx did identify a reduction of forms to a social subjectivity. But as Geras points out, although this is still a form of mystification, it is not fetishism. The material forms of social relations in capitalist society are not natural, but they are objective. As the previous section explained, objects, whose content is accumulated labour, become independent and dominate social agents. So the source of subjective mystification is not caused by any frailties of human subjectivity, it is due to the way in which capitalism presents itself in disguised form (1971: 7). The solution, therefore, cannot be an advanced consciousness. Rather than through an informed thought, the resolution to fetishism can only be found in a radical material transformation.

Holloway takes up the challenge of theorizing what this involves. He infers that the liberation of power-to from power-over entails the defragmentation of the social flow of doing. A collective participation in the social flow of doing implies an anti-power, not power-over. He seeks to move not just against-and-beyond capital, but also representation. In short, all the fetishized forms that the struggle towards social self-determination seeks to obliterate. He acknowledges the need for 'recognizable forms of organization', but warns the danger is the omnipresent threat that existence will become severed from constitution, that is, 'we do' – the drive towards social self-determination, will be subordinated to 'what is' – institution. As such, the precepts of direct democracy must aim to assure the alternative organizational form is 'anti-institutional'. This argument has real strengths, especially with regards to the need to transcend alienated labour and the necessity of establishing horizontal networks linking producers and consumers independently of the state. Equally, the request to articulate communicative bonds between cooperatives is well founded. I pointed out, however, that although state ownership is an inappropriate way to re-appropriate the means of doing, it does not follow that all property forms should be abandoned. I have contended further that an ethic of differentiated representation is compatible with social self-determination. I shall return to Holloway's work towards the end of the concluding chapter, after the constitution of NED has been fully laid-out and analysed. The purpose of this passage has been to explain his veracious critique of capitalism and to establish the key criteria of what must supersede it, a defetishized political economy in which the social flow of doing is not disrupted by a severance of the done from both the doing and the doers. Holloway's work, I will conclude, prefigures NED.

2

Radical Political Economy and the Constitution of New Economic Democracy

Chapter 1 established the bases to Marx's theory of commodity fetishism and what defetishization entails. The next task is to consider what the required thorough material transformation involves. In NED there is no rigid divide between state and civil society. Democratic participation is extended to the economic and civil realms, yet restricted to the various functional bodies individuals belong to. Self-governance applies both within and between the functional agencies. In the design of NED, care has been taken to reconcile socialist planning with individual freedom. In clarifying fully these ideas, this chapter provides a full exposition and analysis of the political economy of NED.[1] There are three parts to the chapter. As the configuration of the internal structure of the guild cooperatives draws considerably from a highly successful empirical example of cooperative labour, the Mondragon complex of workers' cooperatives, an account of the entire superstructure of the latter is provided. This serves three purposes. First, it clearly indicates that workplace democracies can, when set within a cooperative environment, not only survive but prosper. Secondly, it has developed certain structures that have been adopted in the design of NED's guilds. In the third place, the empirical inquiries that have sought to discover the extent to which these cooperatives have

1. Small passages of this chapter first appeared in the author's *Beyond Rawls* (2008). For a fuller exposition of the work of Cole and Schweickart, especially the former, see *Beyond Rawls*, chapters two and three.

negated both alienated labour and oligarchic control directly inform the analyses in Chapters 3 to 6. So at this stage, in the interests of preparatory convenience, it is worth defining the organizational content of the Mondragon complex. This is the task of Part One, 'The Mondragon Cooperative Experience'. Part Two, 'The Organisational Bases to New Economic Democracy', is purely descriptive. It introduces the organizations that constitute NED's political economy in their entirety. Part Three, 'The Plan-Market Synthesis', indicates how NED's economy will allocate goods and resources democratically. A critical evaluation of both planning and markets is presented by means of which I conclude that although each approach to running the economy will continue to have a role in NED's defetishized economy, it will not be within the frameworks established by the centralised planning of command socialism or the mixed-economy typical of social democracy. The method of planning and the delineation of the market system developed in this passage are both original, and are hence unique to NED.

Part One: The Mondragon Cooperative Experience

The exposition that follows breaks down into three sections. The first section, 'The Organization of the Mondragon System', introduces in succinct terms the key features of the Mondragon complex. A more detailed account of the cooperatives' internal structures and the banking system is reserved for further on in the chapter, where they are assimilated into NED's guilds. It is then shown in the second section, 'Efficiency in the Mondragon System', that in direct contrast to the kind of arguments that doubt the economic viability of workplace democracy, the success of Mondragon has in key respects been outstanding. The third section, 'A Note on Efficiency Elsewhere', can be seen as an additional section. It strengthens the argument that workers' cooperatives will not, inevitably, be seriously inefficient. The section concludes by returning to Mondragon; it gives prominence to the features that are suitable for export, and, by implication, used to strengthen the theoretical articulation of NED's mode of production.

The Organization of the Mondragon System

> *Taken together these arrangements [Mondragon's] are an extraordinarily subtle and imaginative exercise in social engineering which*

> *make all other attempts at industrial structure building... look like the artefacts of Stone Age workshops.*
>
> *(Oakeshott, R. 1990: 190)*

The Mondragon cooperative system is based in four Basque Provinces of Spain – Alava, Guipuzcoa, Navarra and Vizcaya – approximately 30 miles from Bilbao. It was founded in 1956 by a Catholic priest, Father Jose Maria Arizmendi.[2] There are now approximately 22,000 workers in over 160 cooperatives, each with an average membership of 225. There are seven main types of cooperative: industrial, agriculture, service-sector, educational, retail, housing and bank and social insurance. The product range consists of kitchen appliances, furniture, electrical components, machine tools, bicycles and such like. For reasons that will become clear as the chapter unfolds, the Mondragon planners limit the number of staff in each cooperative to under 500; an incomes policy of 6:1 also applies to every cooperative. At the collective level the cooperatives form part of inter-cooperative federations where they unite in what are known as cooperative groups, and subscribe to a 'contract of association' which determines cooperative structure and policy. In 1959 the first branch office of a credit cooperative bank, the Caja Laboral Popular (CLP), opened (in borrowed office space). By the late 1980s, the CLP had 1,200 staff working in 180 branches with a total of 300,000 deposit accounts; its total assets were $2.9 billion. The CLP is divided into two main divisions, finance and business; the former refers to banking, the latter to planning. Its mission is to express cooperative values, rather than impose them externally with the sole intention of improving productivity. The resources of the CLP are gained through the labour and the deposits of the associated cooperatives, some of which become collective capital which is invested in new cooperatives to keep them economically viable. This ensures the entire complex is not held ransom by the threat of capital flight. 'The CLP has taken a giant step toward demythologizing the primacy of banks and private capital in a market economy' (Morrison, R. 1997: 86, 8, 13, 19, 51, 85–6; Bradley, K. & Gelb, A. 1983: 13; Thomas, H. & Logan, C. 1982: 92, 117, 178, 181).

With the recognition that the cooperatives needed to be more tightly integrated, and the cooperatives and cooperative groups needed to be linked in more ways than just through the CLP, the Congress of Mondragon Cooperatives (Congress) was established in 1984. Its governing council

---

2. For a fascinating account of Mondragon's history and development, as well as some interesting background information on Jose Marie, see Morrison (1997: 35–59).

consists of representatives from every cooperative group; every cooperative also has representation in Congress. The Congress first met in October 1987. Although it only meets for a few days every year, its officials are active all year round. They undertake research, put forward recommendations and highlight issues for broad discussion. Not surprisingly, they have been responsible for significant structural change. The motions passed have created a 'Fund for Education and Intercooperative Development', which in effect provides aid to smaller cooperatives. They have also instigated an organization in which the cooperatives with similar productive technologies, producing for the same market, operate closely together in order to exploit economies of scale. Further, they have constructed strong base and strong support organizations that serve to link all the units. This implies that every cooperative depends, to some extent, on some of the others; and it ensures that all cooperatives contribute to the complex in its entirety. These structures reinforce inter-cooperative collaboration and monitor the growth of regional cooperative groups. So as Mondragon matured, it has become a fully integrated economy (Whyte, W. F. & Whyte, K. K. 1991: 201–3, 236; Greenwood, D. J. 1991: 76).

There are ten cooperative principles codified by the 1987 Congress – the principle of individual freedom is generally enhanced, and only limited in the wider interests of the community. They are 1), *Open admission*, entry does not depend on gender, ethnicity, religion, political beliefs or such like. 2), *Democratic organization*, the general assembly is the sovereign body, which sanctions the equality of owner-workers. 3), *Sovereignty of labour*, wage-labour is rejected, owner-workers control their cooperatives. 4), *Instrumental character of capital*, capital is actually accumulated labour; members invest financially in their cooperatives. 5), *Self-management*, an individual's development occurs with, not in opposition to, others. This involves the systematic training of members, vacant management positions are filled from within and all cooperators participate in the decisions that affect them. 6), *Pay solidarity*, this applies both internally and externally. 7), *Group cooperation*, cooperatives form groups whereby they establish supportive networks, they are not isolated entities. 8), *Social transformation*, Mondragon is a self-conscious instrument for social change. 9), *Universal nature*, the cooperators pledge their support for the wider goals of economic democracy, justice, dignity and development. 10), *Education*, cooperative principles must be taught at all levels. In addition, Congress also sought a creative resolution to the tension between centralization and decentralization/autonomy. The balance is realized through a system of democratic planning. A robust planning agency is necessary to allocate resources efficiently, and to disseminate information that would otherwise remain unavailable. Self-managed planning, however, must be distinguished from centralized planning. The former secures the participation of the institutions and people affected, and it provides a system of monitoring that can be held democratically accountable. Both the CLP and the cooperatives device annual plans, and the drafts are circulated to all the associated organizations. After the iterative rounds, a consensus on financial matters is realized (Morrison, R. 1997: 10–2; Thomas, H. & Logan, C. 1982: 186–7).

Finally, in the Mondragon system the organizational principle of *equilibrio* is one of the central defining features. It is concerned with striking a balance between interests that are liable to pull in opposite directions: between the individual and the cooperative, between shop floor and management, between the cooperative and the cooperative group, between capital and labour and between technological/economic imperatives and social values/objectives. This may be extended to ambivalence inherent in every member. As workers, they have interests in their salaries and working conditions; but as owners, there interests are in terms of the long-term stability of their cooperatives. There is, then, a need to institutionalize separate processes. Although management must firstly consider the business aspect of their cooperative, and the body concerned with the welfare of the workers must prioritize humane work,[3] they can both be pursued through the parameters established by the other. An adherence to the ethics of participation and direct democracy does not mean that every decision must be reached through consensus. It is likely that this policy would produce the kind of drawn-out and frustrating discussions which could threaten organizational efficiency. It is for this kind of reason that the Mondragon balancing principle of equilibrio is essential. Uniting a humanistic vision with hard techno-economic realities is difficult, but as I will now show, the exceptional record of Mondragon indicates it is not impossible (Whyte, W. F. & Whyte, K. K. 1991: 275, 291, 295–6, 300; Oakeshott, R. 1990: 201).

Efficiency in the Mondragon System

> *during the severe Spanish recession of the early 1980s, the CLP wrote off more than one million dollars in co-op loans and declared an*

3. This body is called the 'Social Council', and is fully introduced further on in this chapter. I will argue throughout the book that it has a central role to play in the defetishized society.

> *interest moratorium on about 40 per cent of the rest. This action was accompanied by an aggressive redevelopment plan... The cooperatives retrenched, survived, and have continued to prosper.*
>
> *(Morrison, R. 1997: 114)*

It has often been surmised that self-management will inevitably engender a loss in efficiency. Time spent in democratic assemblies is time spent away from production. One response has invoked the argument that there are social gains that more than compensate for economic losses. This is true, in a cooperative that controls its numbers, as democracy demands, members are less likely to experience their working lives as meaningless cogs in a remote and possibly hostile environment. In opposition to the standard formidable hierarchical edifices that abound in capitalist corporations, where major decisions are typically made behind the closed doors of private boardrooms, individuals in small self-directing groups are more likely to feel like valued members. But in recent years, especially since Vanek (1970), the argument that a labour-managed system would not be more inefficient has gained momentum (Jay, P. 1980: 29; Clayre, A. 1980: 4). The Mondragon experience adds credibility to this contention. Its record of economic performance is outstanding. During the first 25 years of its existence, there were no cases of involuntary redundancy, and in its entire history only 3 of the 103 cooperatives have had to close. From 1964 to 1989, total employment grew every year except two – from 3,482 to over 22,000. It is also striking that Mondragon has virtually eliminated long-term unemployment (Wainwright, H. 1994: 176; Morrison, R. 1997: 167, 172; Whyte, W. F. & Whyte, K. K. 1991: 170, 175). These astonishing facts indicate that Mondragon stands as an example of self-management with a proven record, over a lengthy time period, of economic feasibility. Thomas and Logan contend that Mondragon has achieved far more than mere survival, its pattern of growth surpass that found in private enterprise. They empirically investigated the efficiency of the cooperatives, and compared their findings with those of capitalist enterprises. Cooperative productivity, in terms of adding value, was measured through indicators that included per person (labour) and per fixed assets (capital). They found that superior efficiency lies with the cooperatives, who have put their available resources to much better use.[4] Their conclusion is that

4. See pp. 106–9 for an account of their methodology.

'without doubt' the cooperatives have enjoyed a higher profitability than the capital-controlled firms:[5]

> During more than two decades a considerable number of cooperative factories have functioned at a level equal or superior in efficiency to that of capitalist enterprises. The compatibility question in this case has been solved without doubt. Efficiency in terms of the use made of scare resources has been higher in the cooperatives; their growth record of sales, exports and employment, under both favourable and adverse economic conditions, has been superior to that of capitalist enterprises. (Thomas, H. & Logan, C. 1982: 126–7)

In light of this, Thomas and Logan assert that the Mondragon experience has 'proven conclusively' that self-management is compatible with economic efficiency (Thomas, H. & Logan, C. 1982: 109, 106–9).

Not surprisingly, the Mondragon cooperatives have attracted great interest from prospective employees. From the late 1950s onwards, more people applied for membership of a Mondragon cooperative than there were positions available. Workers also declined trade union organization within their cooperatives. 'There could scarcely be more convincing evidence that in the eyes of those working in them the Mondragon arrangements are highly valued' (Oakeshott, R. 1980: 49). These arrangements can also be invoked as a favourable response to two often-cited objections to workers' cooperatives. First, as both inter- and intra-cooperative earnings differentials are so narrow, could this act negatively upon incentives? Thomas and Logan's study on the economic performance of Mondragon revealed that, on the contrary, its record in this regard is highly impressive.[6] Secondly, could the modest income ratios be inadequate to attract high-quality managers?[7] But again, they found that this kind a disincentive has not occurred on a noticeable scale (1982: 158–61). Significantly, the much-celebrated CLP – the only successful democratic bank in history (Oakeshott, R. (1990: 165–6)) – has been instrumental in the impressive expansion of the Mondragon movement. It has an established 'management services department' which works

5. See pp. 109–12 for the figures that support this claim.

6. It is noteworthy that Bradley and Gelb's research into the Mondragon cooperatives also found that 'only 2% of cooperateurs considered themselves to be working less hard on their enterprises than they would on a conventional firm while over half considered that they worked significantly harder' (1981: 35).

7. See Part Three of this chapter.

mainly towards augmenting the cooperatives. Some of the larger cooperatives are host to a permanent CLP delegate. The financial assistance offered to the cooperatives by the CLP is a key factor why bankruptcies have been systematically avoided; new cooperatives in which losses occurred would quickly have become insolvent had the CLP not intervened. As new cooperatives do not have the financial resources to survive large losses, the CLP can help amend business plans, freeze or reduce interest payments or offer additional loans. But in the interests of efficiency, the CLP does not subsidize unproductive cooperatives indefinitely. Frequent communication with the CLP also provides for economies of scale, as the knowledge gathered in one cooperative can be circulated to all the others. These factors led Bradley and Gelb to draw an encouraging conclusion. 'It is difficult to arrive at any conclusion other than that Mondragon is a most successful group of enterprises, when judged by the usual criteria' (1981: 7). To summarize, it would appear that there are three main reasons why Mondragon has been so successful – individual workers own and control their enterprises, the cooperatives are not isolated, they form a federation and the CLP provides both financial discipline and management advice (Thomas, H. & Logan, C. 1982: 10, 66, 116; Morrison, R. 1997: 126; Clayre, A. 1980a: 172).

A Note on Efficiency Elsewhere

A solid answer to the efficiency question is absolutely crucial. If workers' cooperatives, and the environment they operate in, are in the majority of cases likely to be inefficient, the task of sketching and analysing the organizational contours of a cooperative political economy is open to critique. MaCain, however, states that when viewed through the discipline of economic theory, workplace democratic ideals actually made more economic sense than he had initially anticipated. As he 'had expected to pay an economic price for political righteousness' (2001: A2), this came as a pleasant surprise.[8] In addition, others are keen to stress that '[i]n recent years, evidence has been mounting that small-scale, decentralised, participatory, and labour-intensive organisations may be just as productive and efficient – and by some criteria, more so – as large-scale, hierarchical, and capital-intensive modes of organisation' (Rothschild & Whitt 1986: 111). In accordance with these claims, this section will show that the success of the Mondragon experience is not an isolated example. Attention is first

8. For the bibliographic references which support this, see MaCain (1993).

drawn to the plywood cooperatives of the Pacific North West, USA. I then highlight the efficiency of the building builds that existed between 1920–2. Finally, I briefly mention other examples of cooperative labour that can be cited in order to substantiate the assertion that in the appropriate environment workplace democracies will, if anything, be models of efficiency.

The plywood cooperatives are the largest and most established democratic workplaces in the USA. These firms, which range from 80–350 members, were founded just after the Second World War. They embody an enriching mixture of direct and representative democracy. The general membership meeting takes place twice annually, and is responsible for the overall governance of the cooperative. It is here that cooperative policy is determined. For example decisions regarding the hiring or dismissal of managers, the alteration of wage rates and the opening of new plants are taken here. Attendance at general meetings is frequently high; workers are well informed and there is broad participation in debate. A board of directors is elected by the workers, all of whom have a single vote. The elected board may be entirely or partially new. The board, who meet biweekly, may determine general policies in the interim between general meetings, but they must seek the permission of all members for expenditures that exceed the specified figure. In terms of income distribution, earnings are received on the criterion of work performance, not through ownership of shares. All the cooperatives have a fixed hourly wage rate, which is equal irrespective of skill level. The number of hours available for work can, however, vary from cooperative to cooperative. Annual surplus is also divided equally within each cooperative (Greenberg, E. S. 1986: 32–4).

These are the key features of the plywood cooperatives. As with the Mondragon cooperatives, there is no doubt as to their efficiency. Job boundaries are fluid, and workers generally cooperate on productive problems. Spontaneous cooperation frequently extends to an informal rotation of jobs. Formal supervision is, typically, very low. Workers manage both themselves and their associates competently. Assuming responsibility for their cooperative, they are sufficiently hard working. There is little need for extensive supervision, and what is required is provided by the fellow members acting as collective supervisors. Work is organized in such a way that individual initiatives are encouraged, and in this sense supervision is regarded as assistance-giving. Unsurprisingly, researchers have been impressed with the efficient productivity of the plywood firms. 'Without exception, studies of the plywood industry indicate that the worker-owned firms... are characterized by higher levels of productivity than are conventional firms' (Greenberg, E. S. 1986: 25); 'The American Federal Income tax officially acknowledged some years ago that... worker productivity in these enterprises was significantly higher – by an average of some 25%' (Oakeshott, R. 1980: 48). They provide approximately 10% of plywood production in their area, and there is much agreement that they supply the highest-quality product of the industry. To conclude, the literature indicates that the plywood firms can boast an impressive standard of productivity and an equally high grade of quality (Greenberg, E. S. 1986: 24–5, 41–2, 49–50; Horvat, B. 1982: 457, 637).

A similar conclusion can be reached with regards to the building guilds. Although the withdrawal of capital by a largely unsympathetic municipal government spelt their demise, during their 2 years' existence some fine work was produced. The local organizations of the building guilds were democratic. Work was carried out under self-governing conditions. Every worker was granted two votes. First, the workers on each job chose their own supervisors, who were largely thought of as co-workers. Secondly, they elected the local guild committees, who consisted of representatives from each section, bricklayers, carpenters, plasters, etc. The representatives on the committees were responsible, in conjunction with the foreman, for the conduct of their respective group of craft workers. These arrangements engendered a new form of leadership. The vast majority of men became actively interested in who they should work under and formed their opinions by observing the work in progress. An independent, experienced and skilled investigator commented how well everyone worked:

> There is a notable absence of the lethargic movements which one is accustomed to see on all kinds of building work. Everybody appears to be working with a will... On one scheme, where 236 men were employed, I took particular care to inspect places where, in normal conditions, workmen might be found 'milking', e.g., behind stacks of bricks, timber stores, sheds, etc. In no case did I discover anything of the sort. (Shelley, E. 1921: 8)

Shelley continues his glowing report by affirming that the 'experience was that, after a few weeks, two or three keen Guildsmen produced wonderful effects on a whole gang'. Work was 'of a very high standard',[9] superior to all the other contractors in the area, and one joiner with 35 years' experience proudly announced what a pleasure it was that his trade was 'honoured and

9. A Ministry of Health inspector actually described the work of the largest building guild, Manchester, as 'the best in England' (Cole, G. D. H. 1921a: 15).

not debased' (Cole, G. D. H. 1921: 14–15; 1921a: 16–18, 22–3; Shelley, E. 1921: 8–9). Although the extent of the building guilds' operations remained fairly small, Shelley nevertheless summarizes:

> 1. The guilds have proved that they are organised on business-like lines and are able to carry out building operations in a workmanlike manner.
> 2. The quality of the work produced is distinctly above the average. (Shelley, E. 1921: 11)

During their short lives, far from being incompetent, the building guilds were in both time and standard the embodiment of productive efficiency.[10]

There are also other examples that strongly indicate workplace democracies can operate with high levels of efficiently. The Metall trade union at the Uddevalla Volvo factory adopted a cooperative approach in its production. Although it closed in 1993 due to the external economic situation in Sweden, both productivity and the quality of products was of a high standard (Gorz, A. 1999: 35). Further, Horvat observes that cooperatives are, typically, more productive than their capitalist counterparts. Along with the Mondragon and plywood cooperatives mentioned above, this assertion is premised upon the example of the Kibbutzim and the French producer cooperatives. In studying 60 odd cooperatives in the Paris region, Batstone (1969) reached similar conclusions (Horvat, B. 1982: 457, 637). There are, then, a number of empirically verified examples that demonstrate cooperatives have solid, consistent track records in efficient production.

To return to the Mondragon example, perhaps the most immediate question upon which to conclude is can its experience be emulated elsewhere? That is, do the idiosyncrasies of the Mondragon complex (along with the

10. Largely due to lack of capital provision, the building guilds did not survive. This was one of the seven main reasons why the guild socialist movement lost its momentum and, ultimately, collapsed. The other six are: a), conflicting opinions within guild socialist circles about whether to condone or condemn the Russian revolution, b), reluctance of the trade unions to transfer into 'industrial unionism', c), success of the Fabian inspired labour party in 1922, d), unrealistic expectations of 'encroachment' control, e), the economic slump of the early 1920s, and finally, after the war there was a new tendency to think in terms of mass-power, placing libertarian themes like those in Cole's scheme on the retreat. It is the combination of these factors that spelt the end of guild socialism as an active political movement.

other examples cited above) mean they are poor material upon which to generalize? Thomas and Logan acknowledge that as it stands, Mondragon can only be of a 'modest significance' (1982: 188). The yields of the CLP have been impressive, but 'there is no guarantee that it would be able to secure sufficient financial outlets for much greater resources and maintain its high level of profitability' (1982: 168). There are also factors that are unique to its experience, for example the history of strong Basque Nationalism and the political oppression of Franco's fascism.[11] Nevertheless, they conclude 'that there are no *a priori* economic arguments why this model could not be experimented with in other countries' (1982: 194). Clayre highlights some of the features that are exportable: workers own and control their enterprises, lending of low interest capital by a sympathetic cooperative bank who has the same interests as the cooperatives, arrangements that ensure an adequate percentage of profit is held back for reinvestment, expert management, and federations have enough associated cooperatives to meet employment needs in response to fluctuation in demand (1980a: 172–3). These are good reasons to believe that Mondragon aspires to ideas that are ripe for adaption. Indeed:

> the structures and institutions which have been evolved at Mondragon seem so well suited to the realities and the real problems of democratic and co-operative enterprises, that it would be odd if other 'Mondragons' were to end in total disaster. (Oakeshott, R. 1990: 214)

A left-libertarian political economy which sustains non-fetishized social relations must be theoretically constructed through the best evidence available, and the Mondragon experience provides exactly that. Reference is therefore made throughout the rest of this chapter, and in the chapters that follow, to the areas where certain structures in Mondragon's superstructure have directly informed the parallel structures in NED.

---

11. Bradley and Gelb inquired into the replicability of the Mondragon complex; they rejected ethnicity, 'Basqueness', as a key reason for Mondragon's success (1981a: 10). Likewise, Oakeshott states it is not culture (Basque traditions), nor environment (market), but structural factors that have caused Mondragon's success (1990: 212). Indeed, the local conditions of Mondragon can be found throughout the Basque Country – ethnic nationalism, political oppression and isolation – but the cooperatives emerged only in Mondragon. 'This makes it difficult to invoke conditions that apply throughout the Basque Country as causes for the emergence of the cooperatives' (Greenwood, D. J. 1991: 55).

Part Two: The Organizational Bases to New Economic Democracy

In this section an exposition of NED's political economy is presented. The first thing to make clear is that the design of NED has been informed by certain bodies of theoretical and empirical literature. First, and most notably, it is the organization of libertarian socialism revealed in Cole's *Guild Socialism Restated* (1920) that informs the theoretical articulation of NED. The basic structure of society outlined here has three branches of economic and social activity that form the bases of a federal structure: a), the producers' organizations, the economic guilds, b), two distinct organizations to represent the consumers and c), the civic services, which will represent citizens' non-economic interests. This model is functional throughout, broken down into territorial units which are institutionally linked at different levels. The coordinating agency is a commune system which consists of representatives from the guilds, the consumer and the civic bodies. Secondly, NED adopts an additional structure that is invaluable to the democratization of the economy, David Schweickart's ingenious democratic investment planning. In order to assimilate Schweickart's scheme into the structure of NED's guilds, it will be subject to a thorough functional demarcation. As this forms the bases to NED's plan-market synthesis, it is fully explained in the following part of this chapter. This passage will concentrate on those aspects of NED that have been directly inspired by Cole's libertarian socialist writings. There are five sections, 'The Functional Principle', 'The Guild Idea', 'From Mondragon Cooperatives to Guild Cooperatives', 'Consumer Councils and the Civil Services' and 'The Commune System'.[12] By the end of the passage it will be clear how adopting the functional principle of democratic representation can be understood as a direct retort to the ideological significance of liberalism's separation of economics from politics. Through a politicalization of civil society and the rejection of the sovereign state, NED transcends the state-civil society dualism.

The Functional Principle

The first and most important ingredient to understand about the premises upon which NED's constitution has been built is the functional principle. Cole rejects any notion that people can be totally represented by any single

12. The expositions of the civil services and the commune system are on the brief side. This is because they both receive a more extensive analytical treatment in Wyatt (2008); chapter five part two for the former, and chapter four part two for the latter.

organization, especially the state. There is not a universal sovereign in society because individuals cannot be represented fully by any single form of association. He infers that over time the democratic ideal has been lost in an inaccurate theory of representation, a theory that holds one person can *re*present another absolutely. In contrast, the accurate principle is that only particular functions and purposes that citizens have in common are capable of proper representation. Therefore, the conditions that would produce either effective representation or misrepresentation are with the former, that representation is 'specific and functional', and with the latter, that it is 'general and inclusive'. Misrepresentation occurs when the initial reasons for granting representation lose their precision and distinctiveness. It is precisely because the state sees itself as being all-inclusive and because parliament is premised on the absurdity of universal representation that it fails. So, the concept of function is the real principle of democracy, and is consequently society's main differentiating criterion. As citizens have many different aspects to their personalities, they form an array of different associations. No particular interest can express the individual as a whole; it must be structurally possible to allow expression for a multiple of interests. It follows that there is no single general concept of citizenship. This results in the establishment of an entanglement of associations to satisfy specific purposes, each one demarcating the function of the association. Sovereignty exists only in the interaction between the various associations. Even then, communal sovereignty is incomplete because none of the groups that make up society can perfectly represent the general will of the community itself. Any obligation to the state cannot account for all the other social obligations. As the state holds no claim to superior obligations, it loses its omnipotence. 'The State, I contend, even if it includes everybody, is still only an association among others, because it cannot include the whole of everybody' (1914: 154). Any notion of state sovereignty is, therefore, inconsistent with the key defining principle upon which NED is founded (1972: 7–15; 1920: 13–15; 1920a: 47–54; Wright, A. W. 1979: 58–60). Let us now see what the functional principle of democratic representation demands in terms of organizational demarcation, beginning with the sphere of production.

The Guild Idea

The word 'guild' is borrowed from the dominant form of productive organization of the Middle Ages, the 'gild'. The idea is not to literally restore the material conditions of mediaeval production – master-craftsmanship, skilled handicrafts and town-scale production – but to breathe fresh life into the key principles that regulated their organization. In particular are security of employment, faithful communal service, mutual aid and a high value for the skilled crafts. The mediaeval gilds did not always manage to meet these demands. Cole though is not so much concerned with their actual achievement, but with the general spirit which animated them; a communal spirit that can appeal to 'the finest human motives' (1920b: 42–6). Following Cole's plea, production in NED will be accomplished through a system of national guilds. Along with the consumer councils, who in terms of importance are situated alongside them, the guilds constitute the most central organizations of NED's political economy. A guild is a self-governing association which assumes responsibility for conducting its own productive procedures. It consists of all the people working within a given manufacturing or service industry:

> A National Guild would be an association of all the workers by hand and brain concerned in the carrying on of a particular industry or service, and its function would be actually to carry on that industry or service on behalf of the whole community. (1920b: 46–7)

For example the railway guild will include managers, porters, technicians, engine cleaners, signal-men, etc. It is assigned by the community the job of administering an efficient railway. So long as it fulfils this task, its internal democratic arrangements like choosing its officers and its methods of administration will remain its own business.[13] There is no need to specify the exact number of guilds, or draw distinct lines of demarcation between them. As Cole points out, railway and road transport may be run by distinct guilds, or by one guild with internal divisions. These are matters of convenience, rather than principle. But what is clear is that, in accordance with the functional principle, every guild equates with and expresses a defined and coherent group of services (1920b: 46–7).

For democracy to be real, every member of the guild must exercise it directly. The freedom of the small unit is therefore vital. The guild cooperatives are the principle component of industrial democracy. With the workplaces mostly conducting their own affairs, the larger guild organizations will coordinate production to match supply with demand, supply

13. The details of the guild elections are clarified in more detail in Chapter 5, where they are analysed.

raw materials, sell products that were not directly sold from the factories themselves, establish general regulations of organization and productive methods and represent the guild in its external communal relations – such as other guilds and consumer bodies. The district committees will represent the various factories and different classes of workers, and the national committee will represent the district and sectional interests. So, the guilds are structured with an organizational complexity, but as they have been functionally demarcated, they do not constitute huge conglomerates. In this sense, they cannot be considered mini sovereign statelets. The guilds will be coordinated through the Industrial Guilds Congress (IGC). This will be the ultimate representative confederation on the productive side. It will act as the guild legislature, and on solely guild matters, adjudicate in its capacity as a final court of appeal. It will also interpret the basic principles of guild practice, as well as determining the pay to the different grades of workers in and between the guilds. Like the guilds, the IGC would have guild councils at the local and regional levels (1972: 60–5; 1920b: 43–54, 59–62, 69–73). This, in brief, is the bases to NED's guilds. Although they are inspired considerably by Cole's guilds, there have been certain revisions. Cole sees the organization of the guilds as being elastic enough to allow a variety of factories.[14] In NED, this translates into a variety of semi-autonomous cooperatives. The guild cooperatives follow the same format in terms of organizational design, and the larger guild structures provide the inter-cooperative linkage. The inter-relations of NED's guilds differ from what Cole had in mind; part three of this chapter explains and analyses these qualifications. In order to prepare the way for these and other discussions that follow, it will be informative to first include a preliminary account of the internal structures of a typical guild cooperative.

From Mondragon Cooperatives to Guild Cooperatives

> *Mondragon is a source of excitement and optimism... because it represents the emergence of a transcendent and accessible model that allows us to make constructive use of the energy of the great transformative forces at work within industrial modernism.*
>
> *(Morrison, R. 1997: 225)*

---

14. For a fuller account of Cole's guilds and how he hoped they would come into being, see Wyatt (2008: 34–7).

As the political constitution of the guild cooperatives draws substantially from the Mondragon cooperatives, this section introduces the essential features of the latter. This will inform the analyses that follow in the remainder of this book. The democratic principle of the Mondragon cooperatives is that authority is conferred via the sovereign body, which is constituted through every member. The ballot box is used at general assemblies of all the members, each with a single vote, to elect the control board (the 'junta rectota').[15] Usually the board is made up of 9 people – a chair, a vice-chair, a secretary and 6 other members. They are elected for a 4-year period, and half the board is required to vacate their position every 2 years, whereupon they may stand for re-election. The general assembly meets at least annually, and examines matters like accounts and balance sheets, amendment to internal rules, modification of administrating norms and such like; crucially, it also reviews the conduct of management and approves management plans. The control board meet at least monthly, among its competences are the appointment of management and the nomination of department heads. They also prepare internal rules for submission to the general assembly. Management assumes the executive role of ensuring their cooperative functions as a productive unit. Along with appointing candidates for middle management and subordinate roles, managers are responsible for the same tasks undertaken by managers in private enterprises – commercial performance, execute production plans, coordinate programmes between departments, etc. It is also designed to accommodate suggestions from all departments and to make informed recommendations. To summarize, management is responsible to the control board, who in turn are accountable to the general assembly. Mondragon enterprises, therefore, distinguish between policy and management: policy-making is determined through the elected control board, while more daily management tasks are carried out by the appointed management team (Thomas, H. & Logan, C. 1982: 26–8, 40; Morrison, R. 1997: 76, 82; Clayre, A. 1980a: 172).

There are three other internal bodies to mention, the management council, the Social Council and the watchdog council. The former is made up of experienced executives. It serves advisory and consultative functions, and is responsible to management and control boards. The Social Council has prescriptive powers and monitors management and the control board. Its decisions determine matters like safety and hygiene at work, and the administration of welfare payments. It can also propose additional items

---

15. The Control Board is also referred to as the 'Supervisory Board', or the 'Governing Council', depending on the researcher.

for the general assembly agenda, and if an item is endorsed by 10% of the cooperative's membership, it becomes mandatory. The Social Council members are elected for 3-year periods, on the condition that a third vacate their positions every year. Workers elect their representatives from their sections, with whom they meet weekly. Each cooperative holds a meeting every 3 months of their entire Social Council. Finally, the watchdog council consists of 3–7 members elected by the general assembly for periods of 4 years. It provides the ultimate security for the smooth running of its cooperative. Its purpose is to control the general behaviour of management and the control board, and to ensure the management and Social Councils are operating sufficiently.

It is important to appreciate that the guiding principles of the Mondragon cooperatives are intended to implement decentralization. Centralization increases the likelihood that their organizational structures would succumb to oligarchic control. The growth of administrative apparatus threatens the cooperative spirit as face-to-face intimacy starts to decline. Bureaucratization has, however, been avoided and self-management upheld through a decentralized strategy. So rather than centralized cooperatives with satellite departments, there are autonomous cooperatives associated into groups. The policy has been that as soon as developing cooperatives reach a certain size, they divide into two, rather than remain as one large institution. The Mondragon planners prefer cooperatives to be no more than 350–500 people. This is in line with past experience, which indicates that the workforce of a cooperative should be no more than 500, otherwise the democratic process becomes obstructed; large numbers jeopardize meaningful participation. At the same time, 500 has been shown to be large enough to accommodate industrial realities. Mondragon's size restriction has been much admired. 'The small size of each particular Mondragon enterprise is no doubt one of the reasons for the harmony and constructive enthusiasm that impress most of those who visit the place' (Clayre, A. 1980a: 172). The delineation of new enterprises helps prevent large concentrations of power in markets (Thomas, H. & Logan, C. 1982: 28–9; Morrison, R. 1997: 76, 81, 127).

These, then, are the internal structures that constitute the Mondragon cooperatives. As experience has proved them to be highly successful, they will be adopted by the guild cooperatives almost in their entirety. The only difference of any note is that in the latter, there is a far more extended role for the Social Councils. The reasons why are fully explained in Chapters 3 and 6. A significant point on which to conclude is that these arrangements overcome a common objection to market forces economies. The argument that markets promote self-reliance ignores the unequal access to the material resources required to realize self-reliance. By placing the responsibility of controlling the means of production into the hands of the guild cooperatives, which ensures an egalitarian dissemination of material resources, NED cannot be charged with this critique.

Before we move on, there is one final issue I would like to briefly address, production through units which are too small to constitute a cooperative. Where associative effort is required, which is the majority of cases, production will take place predominantly in the guild cooperatives. Beyond this, NED has no objection to self-employed individuals, freelance writers and artists, and small work teams. Nove infers that producing privately for sale is acceptable if it is just one individual. He would also allow a private entrepreneur to employ a small team of workers and profit from their labour. For example a family farm can employ a few labourers, and a small restaurant may hire seasonal kitchen staff. The key point for Nove is that in these cases the entrepreneurs are themselves working, there is no unearned income from mere ownership rights. They could be limited by the number of workers employed, or by the value of capital assets (1983: 121, 206–7). Nove's suggestion makes good sense, and a similar reasoning will be adopted in NED. True to its libertarian spirit, NED will accommodate any number of small businesses and sole traders. This is not in any sense at odds with NED's cooperative ethic. The guilds still have regulatory and advisory functions; they are also responsible for setting standards of excellence. This implies that where individual artisans and small work teams remain, a looser membership to a guild is still obligatory. Self-employed tradesmen and women would have served an apprenticeship in a guild cooperative, and they will be dependent on a guild for the supply of raw materials and parts. They will also be accountable to the guild in terms of annual health and safety assessment, in much the same way heating engineers do at present with the Gas Board (in NED for Gas Board read authoritative department in the building guild). As such, some affiliation to a guild is unavoidable. In all instances, therefore, the guild and their cooperatives are the central component of NED's mode of production. With the form of organization on the productive side now established, let us now turn to a sphere of equal importance, consumption.

Consumer Councils and the Civil Services

In NED, relations at the workplace are not the only social bond; the consumptive sphere will also seek to integrate. Cole sees consumption as possessing a principle of differentiation analogous to, yet different from, production.[16] It has two main divisions. First, household that includes individual choice; he calls this 'personal and domestic consumption'. Secondly, where consumption and use is undifferentiated and supplied in mass, which he calls 'collective consumption'. Separate organizations are needed, and Cole names them the 'cooperative council' to represent the former consumption, and the 'collective utilities council' to represent the latter. Their function is first to safeguard consumer concerns like the quantity and quality of production, the prices charged, the variety of need and, secondly, to protect them from the producers. To be genuinely democratic it is essential that, like the guilds, these organizations are decentralized and local. This, in brief, is how Cole proposes to formally organize consumer interests. He takes the ideology of consumer power and choice that is normally used by apologists of capitalism, and puts it to work for very different ends. Cole's model undermines capitalist social relations by de-coupling consumer choice from individual income, and by making consumer representation a right of citizenship rather than a privilege of the wealthy. This is an ingenious argument. As such, consumer councils will be central to NED's mode of consumption. We shall return to them in the chapters that follow, especially in part three of Chapter 3 (1920b: 79–92).

Finally, self-government must also apply to the civil services. He sees the need for an education guild, a health guild and a guild for every non-economic civil service such as drama, music, medicine and sanitation. Along with the consumer councils, every locality needs a council to represent citizens' general interests in education and health. Not surprisingly, he calls these bodies the 'cultural councils' and the 'health councils' respectively. Their role is to articulate the civil point of view and cooperate with the relevant guilds to ensure supply meets demand. In choosing their consumer and civil council representatives, citizens will vote by way of wards within the town (1920b: 101–10, 123–6). In Cole's work it is unclear how the consumer and civil councils will be funded. In NED the financing of the consumer and civil councils may proceed through two sources. First, an income tax taken directly from local citizens – possibly in line with a moderate progressive scale in accordance with the 6:1 incomes ratio (see Part Three of this chapter). Secondly, a purchase tax on products brought. With regards to the goods required to satisfy basic needs, this can be minimum, if at all; it can be higher with regards to luxury items. This kind of purchase tax may be applied differentially on products so that consumption

16. This distinction is not one of individuals, for the differentiation is – as with producers – between interests.

will be in line with the social concerns brought to light by the consumer councils. To conclude, these – the producer, consumer and civil services; all demarcated via the functional principle – are the three main branches of economic and social activity. The final task is to indicate how they will cooperate as part of a single system.

The Commune System

The coordinating agencies will be the local, regional and national communes. The national coordinating body, the national commune, will consist of representatives from the industrial and civil national guilds, from the economic and civil national consumer councils and from the regional communes. A local commune would be mainly a coordinative, and not an administrative, body. The guilds would manage their services, and their cooperation with the relevant councils would largely determine their policy. The communes will act as courts of appeal in disputes between the different types of functional bodies. In this sense they retain a sovereign power. But as they do not hold arbitrary powers of intervention in cases that are not brought before them, the substance of sovereignty has been redefined. The self-governing bodies will, through mechanisms of consultation and negotiation, be the means by which democratic social governance is realized. Administrative apparatus is, concurrently, diffused into the demarcated spheres of democratic authority. Government functions are, therefore, devolved to and carried out by these bodies. The commune will unite these groups, coordinating the producer, consumer and civil elements, which together constitute the totality. The private sphere is now one of cooperation and collective governance. It is this sense that NED transcends the doctrine of state sovereignty. The division is transformed by circumscribing the central powers of the state, and by increasing the powers of the middle-range functional institutions. So while a civil society consisting of self-governing associations needs a genuine yet secondary public power to regulate their interactions, its role is mainly to coordinate and to protect associational rights. NED's communes do not determine all the activities in their territories, and herein lays the repudiation of the sovereign state[17] (Cole, G. D. H. 1972: 36–8; 1920a: 124–7; 1920b: 127–9, 35–41; Hirst, P. 1994: 103–4, 167–8).

---

17. See Wyatt (2008: 90–102) for the argument that NED's commune system cannot in any way be associated with the modern liberal state. This argument contains an important clarification of why functional democracy is incompatible with state sovereignty.

Summary

In this passage I have laid out the organizational bases to the political economy of NED. It can now be appreciated that the re-politicized civil society, adopting the functional principle of democratic representation as the demarcating criteria, is hostile to any notion of a sovereign state. The guilds and consumer councils are the democratic institutions that will bring politics closer to the hearts of localized citizens. This provides the essential premise upon which to embody defetishized social relations. As yet though, little has been said about either the actual method of democratic planning or the role of a market mechanism. This is the subject of the next and final part of this chapter.

Part Three: The Plan-Market Synthesis

This passage addresses the structural tensions that are likely to emerge when the attempt to transcend fetishized forms is set forth. In recent years, arguments within socialist circles have raged about the most appropriate way to manage the economy, the most tenacious of which is whether either a centrally planned or a market economy, or a combination of the two, can realize socialist goals. NED offers a genuine third way.[18] Drawing from the literature in which alternatives to capitalism and radical political economy are discussed, I will show why planning of some description is the key prerequisite to the defetishized society. Attention then turns to a further issue that is indispensable to the democratization of civil society, 'democratic investment planning'. Participatory democratic planning is used for purposes of allocation, rather than reliance upon expert state planners or recourse solely to competitive markets. Here it is shown how NED can approach the vital but potentially hazardous issue of how to finance its industries and services democratically. It is then indicated that planning is not suitable for the entire economy. A market sector regulated by an appropriate body is, therefore, unavoidable. The passage clarifies why the planning process must subordinate the market mechanism. So while commodity relations will remain, strict limits are placed upon their scope. This passage breaks down into two divisions, 'Social Planning' and 'Markets'. The former has three sections, 'The Call for Planning', 'Participatory Planning'

18. Neither market socialism nor centralized planning is critiqued here to any significant extent. This task was undertaken in Wyatt (2008), chapter three, where I argue that NED offers solutions to the shortcomings of these other two socialist approaches.

and 'Democratic Investment Planning'. The latter also has three sections, and will be introduced at the time.

Social Planning

> *The life-process of society, which is based on the process of material production, does not strip off its mystical veil until it is treated as production by freely associated men [sic], and is consciously regulated by them in accordance with a settle plan.*
>
> *(Marx, K. 1977: 442)*

The Call for Planning

Liberating labour in a socialist society was often thought by Marxists to involve the total abolition of the commodity form. Marx writes in chapter 1 of *Capital I* on the contrast between mystified commodities and 'a community of free individuals, carrying on their work with the means of production in common, in which the labour power of all the different individuals is consciously applied as the combined labour-power of the community' (1976: 79). Yet with regards to both the particular appearance of commodity relations and the fetishism of forms in general, the task is infinitely more complex. Brus for example infers that the attitude which assumes a socialist society will have no commodity production is 'primitive'; it is merely a 'substitute for an appreciation of the contradictory aspects of reality a verbal resolution of a closed circle of definitions' (1973: 48). It will become clear why continuing with a curtailed production of commodities may, when set within a radical framework, facilitate the development of left libertarianism. As explained below, commodity relations have positive effects in certain areas. But on the negative side they escalate the isolation of economic actors, ensuring personal interests are often realized to the detriment of social interests. Brus recognizes this can impoverish the social consciousness, over-commercialize human relationships and weaken solidarity. He therefore arrives at a compromised position:

> A society which consciously constructs a mechanism for the functioning of its economy chooses between different combinations of direct and market forms of allocation, and subordinates commodity relations to autonomously defined goals and criteria of rationality. In this way, society can overcome commodity fetishism... without losing the opportunity of employing commodity relations in areas

where...they will assist in the attainment of social aims. (Brus, W. 1973: 55)

A non-market satisfaction of needs expresses solidarity. Non-market forms are not only concerned with social philanthropy and mutual assistance, they also uphold collective social life. Some needs must be financed via the social fund. Otherwise the areas that bring social benefits but may not attract individual investment, either because likely profits margins are low or the outlays are beyond personal resources, will remain underfunded (Brus, W. 1973: 50–2, 59–61). These are solid reasons in support of planning.

Horvat states there are four key functions of a social plan. 1), it is a 'forecasting instrument'. It analyses economic trends in order to provide producers with knowledge of probable economic changes. 2), it coordinates economic decisions. As it is formulated in a participatory manner, it represents a projection of mutually agreed change. 3), it guides economic development. Through coordinating the initiatives of the economic decision-making bodies and affected social agents, it determines the changes that will be optimal for society in its entirety. 4), an obligation for the bodies that implement it. Policies formulated by work organizations and consumers must be carried out by the body politic.[19] Horvat proposes that these functions of planning must be participatory. Although plans should be framed and developed through expert as well as social components, the overall plan is formulated through an active procedure of consultation and negotiation (1982: 333–4). This suggestion makes good sense. I would only add that social planning through consultation and negotiation is best realized through a system of functionally demarcated organizations operating in a thoroughly democratized civil society. The aim is to generate changes in the composition of consumption patterns so that they are compatible with a left-libertarian society, a task not easily engendered by the market mechanism. This may affect individual consumption at the luxury end of the market scale, but it does secure consumption to social groups who would otherwise be denied. Participatory planning of some kind then is the first ingredient to the defetishized society. The following two sections show, in terms of price fixing and investment, the method through which participatory planning proceeds in NED.

---

19. As will now be clear, in NED this last point translates to the policies formulated by the guild cooperatives and the consumer councils must be adopted by the commune.

Participatory Planning

The fixing of prices is to be determined by the guilds in conjunction with the corresponding consumers' council. For illustration purposes, Cole considers the example of a single commodity: milk. The distributive guild is to deliver milk, which it will buy from the agricultural guild. The consumers have the cooperative society to deal with the milk question. The distributive guild will combine the amount it gives to the agricultural guild with its own distribution costs and will then propose a price to the cooperative society. If they concur, this becomes the selling price. If not, negotiations between all three bodies begin until an agreement is reached. Only in the case of impasse does the matter go before the appropriate level commune. In one of these ways, through consultation and open discussion, Cole is sure a just price will emerge (1920b: 88, 141–2; 1920c: 1). So, the regional and national representatives of the relevant guilds, the distributive guild, the collective utilities and cooperative councils provide an inclusive forum through which just prices will be determined. NED adopts this approach to price fixing. It will not, though, apply to the whole of the economy. It is neither necessary nor desirable to plan the entire economy. Only the prices of the goods and services whose supply is essential for the satisfaction of physiological needs like hunger will be determined in this way, and even then only in the cases where NED's functionally demarcated market system cannot be expected to satisfy basic human needs. But where price fixing is required, it will be through this method. In NED the use of market criteria in productive decision-making will continue to have a role, especially when demand is in relation to personal wants, desires and tastes. But in the case of catering to needs, participatory planning will be the norm. It can now be shown how NED aims to subsidize the products that will be sold below their cost price. Cole stresses that it will often be desirable to sell certain commodities below their natural prices, that is, the cost of their production (1920b: 142–3). MaCain clarifies and expands the issue:

> The determination of prices may lead to operating cross-subsidies…This involves a system of direct lump-sum transfers among the guilds, to cover the costs of production of some goods for sale below their 'natural' prices. These transfers are decided like other economic magnitudes under guild [libertarian] socialism – by direct negotiations among the guilds with arbitration by the next, more inclusive body in the case of impasse. (MaCain 2001: B4)

In brief, the Industrial Guilds Congress, both through its own deliberations or in the last resort through the direction of the commune, will tax at source and draw the agreed amount from the labour-power of the guilds. This is the first and most fundamental aspect of NED's social planning. It is, however, not the full story. To complete the picture a more detailed account of the planning of investment is required.

Democratic Investment Planning

This section introduces David Schweickart's ingenious approach to how investment can be planned democratically. This will inform the discussion that follows in the next section. Schweickart is a market socialist whose model of 'economic democracy' (ED) prioritizes worker self-management. Although cooperatives will compete, competition occurs against the backdrop of a democratic investment plan. This constitutes a second dimension, which is to complement workplace democracy. In ED the totality of productive assets is collectively and publicly owned, with each firm paying a tax for their use. *New* investment is financed externally, through a national investment fund that is bankrolled by the capital asset tax. 'Economically this tax functions as an interest rate on capital... The proceeds of the capital-assets tax constitute society's investment fund, all of which are ploughed back into the economy' (1998: 17). The entire capital assets are regarded as collective property, although they are utilized by the various work forces that control them. There is not a money market that unites private savers and private investors. The capital assets tax generated funds for new investment are dispersed through democratic channels. It is important to emphasize that it is not the entire economy that is planned; it is only new investment, which is investment that is not financed through depreciation set-asides. Firms are free to spend their depreciation reserves on any capital improvement they see fit. This spending is considered ongoing investment, and is distinguishable from the bank financed new investment. Established firms will only be affected by the planning if they seek to expand operations which cannot be supported by their depreciation funds. Schweickart states that social control over the supply of decentralized investment funds will be realized by interconnected plans and banks. Decisions about which projects to favour will be taken democratically at three general levels by elected legislatures. Here investment hearings will occur where expert and popular opinions can be expressed (Schweickart 1993: 68, 71–4; 1998: 16).

To begin with, the national legislature will determine how much is to be set aside for national projects (pollution control, transport maintenance, etc.). It can also mandate the encouragement of certain types of projects by making suitable funding available. The rest is distributed to the regions on a per-capita basis: if a certain region has 8% of the national population, then it receives 8% of the investment fund. Regional legislatures will do likewise. Now only the decisions about where to channel public capital and which particular projects to encourage are made on a regional basis. The regional authorities will receive the former sums and the remainder will go to localized communities. For their part, these communities will also decide how much is to go into local public investment and, secondly, how much is needed to finance their own encouragement grants. Finally, communities will allocate funds to the banks in their localities. Every bank will get a portion of the investment fund received by the community; the exact amount will depend on how many firms are affiliated to it and by its record at making sensible grants in the past. Every enterprise within this area chooses one of these banks to affiliate too.[20] The selected bank will not only render the usual services of holding the firm's sales income and providing it with working capital, it will also, significantly, retain its depreciation reserve. Banks are free to make grants (note grants, not loans) as they please, charging a basic use tax in the majority of cases, although this rate may be reduced for encouragement projects. As per their criteria, they will use a 'projected profitability and employment creation'. It is to these banks that enterprises will appeal for new investment capital (Schweickart 1993: 74–6). To summarize, in Schweickart's scheme of democratic investment planning funds are dispersed to regions, from regions to local communities and then to local banks.

This is the bases of Schweickart's proposals. The market would still set prices, but there is no incentive to invest in the firm in the hope of extracting profits. In contrast to capitalism, the course of investment is not under the command of the market. The manner in which funds are returned to communities is democratically planned. This investment mechanism is preferable to unrestrained market forces. Workers, acting as citizens, can help determine the formation of the investment fund, and in this sense participate in directing the economy. There is not the dichotomy between owners and non-owners of wealth stemming from property ownership. These measures are intended to limit inequality. While a given firm could secure a higher profit than others, it is divided among the firm's workers. As profits cannot be converted into capital wealth, firms cannot make money just by having it. In regards to political equality, individuals will not have either so much or so little that they will be in a dominant or subservient

20. Community banks will have a cooperative nature. Their governing councils will be made up of representatives from their own work forces, from the community planning agency and from the firms affiliated to it (Schweickart 1993: 75).

position (Schweickart 1998: 16–18; 1998a: 127; 1998b: 171; Howard 2000: 14, 107, 156). Along with the approach to democratic planning outlined in the previous section, the method of democratic investment planning explained in this section can embody the four key functions of a social plan put forward by Horvat. In particular, it can coordinate economic decisions and it can guide economic development. Schweickart's strategy will be assimilated into NED's political economy; I will shortly indicate how. As this will take us into a discussion of the use of a market mechanism in NED, I will first state how the following passage breaks down.

Markets

Neo-liberals believe that market prices coordinate economic actors in a way that is more efficient than deliberate attempts to coordinate economic behaviour through planning. This, apparently, ensures that consumers dictate production and guarantees the efficient allocation of resources. The argument is that markets show a tendency to self-regulate. As competing producers need to satisfy consumers, they have to provide value for money. By realizing their own self-interests, producers necessarily produce the goods that consumers desire. The opportunity for consumers to exit, that is change supplier, effects producer self-interest. Interventions, it is claimed, undermine the workings of the 'free market'. Even if producers have little interest in the welfare of their customers, their personal interests are still best met by producing the goods that are in short supply, thus benefiting consumers. This, in brief, is the bases to the 'invisible hand' thesis. Since its first articulation in Book IV of Adam Smith's *The Wealth of Nations*, it has attracted a variety of critical responses; the most immediate of which are clarified below. As NED has a subordinated role for a market mechanism, it is legitimate to ask first whether invisible hands are invoked as a coordinating criterion, and secondly whether it is susceptible to the critiques of the invisible hand thesis. There are three sections in this passage. The first two, 'Beyond Invisible Hands in Production' and 'Beyond Invisible Hands in Consumption', highlight the insufficiencies of the invisible hand argument; they then show how NED responds to them from the perspective of both production and consumption. It is shown that although a social (non-private) market system is retained in NED, invisible hands are not relied upon to coordinate supply and demand. But although they do not have a direct application, the critiques of the invisible hand thesis are used as a springboard upon which to ground the analytical defence of NED's market system. Leading on from this, the third and last section,

'Centralized Bureaucracy or Decentralized Social Planning', demonstrates, through a discussion with a maverick quasi-contemporary socialist, that NED represents a genuine third way; here the argument that planning will inexorability give rise to a huge centralized bureaucracy is refuted.

Beyond Invisible Hands in Production

This section will show how NED moves beyond the need for invisible hands in the sphere of production. It begins by clarifying that neither a capitalist class nor actual capital has any role in NED's political economy. I then explain how, in response to Sayer's discussion on networking, the models of democratic planning devised by Cole and Schweickart can be synthesized. In the process, it is shown how a certain level of competition will be monitored by politico-economic bodies operating in a democratized civil society, the guilds, rather than through a dichotomized state. For reasons that will become clear as the section unfolds, particular attention is paid to the organization of inter-guild cooperation, income differentials between and within the guilds and the guild banking system. In order to add substance to my argument, the Mondragon complex is drawn from as we proceed.

The invisible hand thesis claims that consumer spending provides signals to motivate producers. Sayer stresses that this assumption overlooks who receives the profits. Although employees may receive bonuses in line with sales, as it is the capitalists who appropriate the gains, the employee–consumer relation is indirect (1995: 115–19). In NED's market system, the producer–consumer relation is more direct. NED's publicly generated capital does not, unlike capitalist privately generated capital, move geographically to where it can secure the highest returns. The investment fund is mandated to return to the communities where it initially originated. Capitalists are no longer indispensable. In democratic investment planning:

> there is no 'privileged class'... i.e., a stable class of people with more power than the combined power of the elected officials... there are no capitalists, nor is there any other set of non-elected officials who possess anything like the power of the capitalist class under capitalism. (Schweickart 1998a: 127)

Once capitalist ownership has been replaced with workers' cooperatives, as there is no longer a capitalist class extracting a surplus value, capitalism will be abolished. With the capitalist class now obsolete, markets can be reshaped in workers' interests (Schweickart 1998: 19–20). Neither is there any significant role for capital as it is typically understood. Capital is not merely wealth, it has a self-expanding value; it is wealth invested in the hope of securing greater wealth. This inherent expansionary tendency guarantees wealth will be self-centred; it becomes obsessed with its own growth. Schweickart infers that within democratic investment planning, capital, as self-expanding value, will not exist. New investment, it will be recalled, is funded by the capital assets tax-generated investment pool. Although there is capital assets, the material means of production each cooperative control, there is not the kind of capital which defines capitalist societies (1998b: 169–70). Capitalists may be compelled to reinvest their profits to increase the value of capital, but the guild cooperatives are not subject to the same unremitting pressure to expand. The latter are restrained from reinvesting their profits; they are distributed among the work-force. This ensures that in NED consumer spending can provide clearer signals to the guild cooperatives because profits are not appropriated by a capitalist class; producers have more to gain by responding to the latter. So, supply and demand in NED can be coordinated between producers and consumers more directly than through the supposedly invisible hands of capitalist economies.

Continuing his critique, in a discussion on networking through which information is exchanged for mutual benefit, Sayer makes the following claim:

> Contrary to the fiction of markets as a self-contained mode of coordination needing only price information, actors cannot rely on merely 'going to the market' to see what is on offer and to see who will buy their wares; groups with common interests – especially producers – need to share information, negotiate, form common views about the future and harmonize plans. (Sayer, A. 1995: 109)

But although networks can partially supplant 'arm's-length' market exchanges, members are still separated through ownership and they still engage mostly in commodity exchange. This indicates that networks only supplement markets, rather than replace them. Networking also has its own shortcomings. They can only function properly with small numbers and with straightforward goals. Further, although networks share information and collaborate, members are not always equal in power. Neither are network relations necessarily democratic. It is not always easy for firms to network with those who are equal in power. Firms are less likely to share information with competitors, especially when it threatens self-interest. Individuals will be disinclined to share mutually beneficial information on the (quite reasonable) assumption that competitors may not reciprocate. As such, Sayer infers that networks need an outside body like a state or an industrial association to override individualistic pressures (Sayer, A. 1995: 109–11).

Sayer's appeal for producers 'to share information, negotiate, form common views about the future and harmonize plans', and his call for an external body to negate naked self-interest, are especially pertinent. They both directly prefigure NED's guild system. In NED the latter task is undertaken by industrial associations, the guilds, and not a state. Likewise, it is through the guilds that the former function will be realized. My position will now be substantiated by demonstrating how competition will be monitored by the guilds. This is followed by discussions of the twin need for inter-workplace collaboration and an apposite incomes policy; both are reinforced by reference to the Mondragon complex. Together, they go a long way towards negating the difficulties of networking noted by Sayer. We will then be in a position to realize how Schweickart's scheme of democratic investment planning has been adapted in its assimilation into NED's mode of production; this is most prominent in the banking system at the local level. The conclusion reiterates that in the sphere of production, the invisible hand thesis has no application in NED.

In Cole's libertarian socialism extra profits simply return to the local commune, which will facilitate further deliberations about future allocation and reinvestment, while in Schweickart's scheme they are disseminated between the cooperative's work-force. As with the guilds in Cole's scheme, Schweickart's workers control their firms, they do not own them; but unlike Cole's guilds, the worker-governed enterprises will be in open competition. It is on this question, whether a competitive ethic should be sanctioned in a democratic socialist society, that a compromise between the positions of Cole and Schweickart can be sought. NED sheers a path between the extremes of competition and coordination. Even with a restricted role for competition, NED sustains the communal structures which are a prerequisite to the encouragement of cooperation, reciprocity and mutual respect. First, competition between the guilds themselves will for the most part be virtually non-existent. The car manufacturing and the building guilds are both in service to the community; they are not in open competition to design new engines and construct housing. How then might a measured degree of competition be implemented? The answer lies in *intra-guild* competition. In NED the guilds will consist of an association of quasi-autonomous cooperatives operating at the local levels. Each individual national guild would be responsible for overseeing competition in its own domain. The guilds will retain a percentage of their profits, and the distribution to the guild cooperatives will include a performance criteria. So in contrast to Cole's guilds, the guilds in NED have licence to return a percentage of their profits to their workers. Although everyone will be guaranteed a standard income, the cooperatives with higher sales will be rewarded accordingly. Cole is sceptical about the profit motive being the only incentive to incite adequate standards of efficient production. He is not alone; the critique that capitalism nurtures greed and selfishness has a long history. But in a cooperative environment which embodies an inclusive social ownership of productive assets, a closely regulated profit motive can provide a stimulant to innovate without jeopardizing community and altruistic values.

There is good reason to believe the guilds can perform this balancing act. As the Mondragon system has formalized channels for inter-cooperative communication, it can be referenced in order to support this claim. Mondragon's cooperatives collaborate within their respective industries, where they collect and share information on their markets, finance and research. Their property relations are based on self-management, and as we have seen, they have strict guidelines which prevent cooperatives expanding beyond a given size. Wainwright stresses both arrangements 'mitigate against the emergence of economic inequality and hence antagonistic competition, atomization of decision making, secrecy and economic opacity' (1994: 175). Federations of cooperatives – in NED for cooperative groups read guilds – will, in their organization, mirror the structure within the individual cooperatives from which they are comprised. Policies are determined via the general assembly – an assembly which expresses the collective desires of its members. The assembly is constituted through the control boards and the managements of the component cooperatives. These social mechanisms seek to self-consciously preserve a balance between the personal needs of cooperatives and the wider goals of the community. Market success is important, but it does not subordinate democratic communication. For inter-cooperation to have any substance certain conditions must hold – that personnel must be transferrable, that the appropriation of surplus be subject to democratic adjudication and, crucially, that competition be regulated stringently (Wainwright, H. 1994: 175; Thomas, H. & Logan, C. 1982: 38). The guilds are ideally suited to serve these functions.

With regards to the latter, as the guild cooperatives will often be competing in the same market, this will inevitably introduce a competitive ethic into the internal relations of the guild. A failure to keep ahead of intra-guild competitors could, in a sense analogous to capitalist firms, be detrimental to business. The question then emerges as to whether this would duplicate capitalist sentiments? There is good reason to doubt this. The cooperatives will enjoy sympathetic relations of reciprocal benefit. Within the structures of mutual aid, in the interests of engendering technological innovations there will be limited competition to attract consumers. The regional and national committees within the guilds, who are constituted jointly through representatives from all the cooperatives, are responsible for closely monitoring the competitive ethic within their industry. It will be their role to ensure that competition is equitable. Guidelines would be imposed by ensuring that advice flows to every locality equally, that material on markets and research is shared, that cooperatives adhere to a policy of open-books, and that no single workplace comes to be in an advantageous position whereby it can exploit its market position to further its own self-interests. In other words, an egalitarian dissemination of information will prevent the more successful cooperatives from commanding the power to exert a disproportional influence upon future rounds of market transactions.

This tendency will be further enhanced through the implementation of a suitable policy of income differentials. In NED labour-power is not a commodity; this implies that its value is not decided exclusively through the market, it will also be determined through planning. In addressing the question of what measure of inequality should exist, Nove remarks that income differentials are the only real alternative to directing labour politically. He infers that material incentives cannot be avoided. But the differentiation level necessary to attract voluntary labour should, he adds, be decided democratically. 'I do not mean that "the people" would determine the income of Bloggs the pilot…But the principles and limits of income differentiation can and should be decided by elected representatives at some level or other' (1983: 52). Inequalities between senior officers and their juniors are needed to elicit the required response, yet this does not need to justify capitalist differentials. For Nove the required incentive need only be a 2:1 or a 3:1 ratio between the highest and lowest earners. With an appropriate minimum wage, he believes this is not a 'fantastic prospect'. In the competitive sector of Nove's feasible socialism, a modest bonus scheme, corresponding to profit, would also exist (1983: 215–16). Horvat also considers the determination of labour incomes. He divides the economy into 'techno-economically homogeneous industries' (what I call guilds). Within every industry, individual cooperatives will perform with different degrees of efficiency, and this will be reflected in differentiated dividends. Yet the overall incomes for all industries must remain consistently the same. The average incomes, corresponding to a skills ratio, should be approximately the same across every industry. This will call for 'appropriate policy instruments' like taxation concessions (1982: 268–9).

At the empirical level, Mondragon implements an average earning scale that applies to every cooperative in all sectors. Large differences between industries are routinely avoided and intra-cooperative earnings differentials are regulated by a strict principle. Their incomes policy dictates that the pre-tax differentials between the highest paid manager and the lowest paid worker is not above 6:1.[21] Without this guideline, market pressures would render cooperative principles mere hollow sound-bites; the inevitable huge differentials in income would quickly erode inter-cooperative solidarity. Equity rules are fairly complex. Net profits are assigned first to individual accounts; and secondly to two collective accounts, a 'collective reserve' and a 'social fund'. The former receive up to 70% of profits, the social fund 10%, although the sum given to the collective reserve goes up as profits increase. From the 70% that is allocated to individual accounts, the dividend is based on time spent at the firm. This ensures that the longer a worker is a member of the cooperative, the larger the share received. This kind of income policy has produced positive results in the Mondragon complex. Indeed, the remarkable record of its success can be explained partly by the appreciative attitudes of their cooperatives; appreciative attitudes that in a large part spring from minimum pay differentials (Bradley, K. & Gelb, A. 1983: 17–18; Thomas, H. & Logan, C. 1982: 131–3). Following the reasoning of Nove and Horvat, and the empirical example of Mondragon, the Industrial Guilds Congress (IGC) in NED will set the basic salaries for all the guild cooperatives within every guild in line with the 6:1 skills ratio, supplemented by a bonus scheme for successful innovations and productive efficiency which will again be uniform across all the guilds. In light of this, together with the equal dissemination of information discussed above, some of the problems of networking captured by Sayer – unequal power relations between network members, disinclination of larger firms to share information and the difficulty of sustaining a democratic spirit within network links – will be negated in NED's guilds.

With this in mind, I now wish to draw this chapter to a close by clarifying the way in which Schweickart's model of democratic investment planning has been incorporated into NED's mode of production. As an appropriate

---

21. The ratio changed from 3:1 to 4.5:1 in 1982 (Bradley, K. & Gelb, A. 1983: 17), and then from 4.5:1 to 6:1 in 1987 (Whyte, W. F. & Whyte, K. K. 1991: 45).

banking system is the means through which social plans are implemented at the local level, particular attention is paid to their organization. At the national and regional levels, the IGC would appear to be the appropriate body to determine the funds required for national and regional projects. That is, the guilds would be designated assignments by the elected investment fund legislatures, who will be integral to the IGC at the three general levels. But at the local level, the investment fund will be subject to a more defined functional demarcation. Cooperatives would, in accordance with Schweickart's suggestion, be affiliated to community banks. They would now, however, be organized along guild lines. Community banks would therefore be guild banks, and the firms connected to them would be of a similar industrial type. The benefit of grouping cooperatives together is that investment decisions can be made in accordance with the interests of the guild cooperative groups. The opportunity for the two consumer councils to monitor investment decisions at all three levels applies unreservedly. The following section discusses the role of consumer councils in NED's economy; at this point it is opportune to establish in brief the organization of a typical guild bank.

An insight can be gained, again, by referring to the fine example provided by Mondragon. The role undertaken by Mondragon's bank, the CLP, has been instrumental to the success of the complex. The sovereign authority in the CLP is the general assembly, which meets at least annually. The general assembly is made up from staff of the CLP itself and proportionally elected representatives from the associated cooperatives, one for every 20 cooperators. The idea is to formulate a general assembly that cannot easily fall under the domination of a particular constituency. The CLP's control board, which is responsible for appointing management, is elected by the general assembly for a 4-year period. It has 12 members, 8 from the associated cooperatives and 4 from its own owner-workers. This ensures the cooperatives retain some authority over the bank, and a system of rotation restricts the likelihood of monopolization. The internal structure of the CLP is virtually identical to the organization of the cooperatives – a watchdog committee, management and social advisory councils, a control board and management. The CLP shares the interests of the cooperatives in the sense that staff salaries are in proportion to the average profits of the federation, and not on the fortunes of the branch itself. A mutually supportive and responsive relationship between associated cooperatives and the CLP is installed by a 'contract of association', which provides the basic organizational guidelines that inform cooperative activity and establishes suitable conditions through which cooperatives can, and have, operated efficiently (Thomas, H. & Logan, C. 1982: 77, 119, 179; Clayre, A. 1980a: 171; Morrison, R. 1997: 92, 97). The CLP stands as an empirically verified example of an efficient and successful cooperative bank. As such, the internal structure of the guild banks will, characteristically, share the essential features of the CLP. Once again, there are very good reasons for claiming that NED represents far more than a quaint pipe-dream.

This, then, in terms of production is how NED puts to good use what is best in both the theoretical and empirical literature. The seminal theories of Cole and Schweickart, together with the superb example of the Mondragon complex, have all been instrumental in the construction of NED's political economy; and the latter, I conclude, is all the better for that. Finally, it can now be appreciated that in the manner in which information will circulate equally to every cooperative within a guild, supply can be arranged through an extended use of networking and without resort solely to market signals. The harmonizing of productive plans and the exchange of knowledge between the cooperatives, along with a quasi-egalitarian incomes policy, are intended to enhance cooperation; there will be no commercial secrecy within NED's guilds. Further, in the absence of capital, as it is understood in classical political economy, inequalities are non-cumulative. Hence, the resulting mutual benefit within a guild, as it neutralizes in a large part the need to compete vigorously in the desperate scramble to satisfy consumer needs, transcends the invisible hand thesis.

Beyond Invisible Hands in Consumption

Continuing with this theme, this section will show why the invisible hand thesis has no application to NED's mode of consumption. First, certain critiques of invisible hands are introduced. I then respond to these critiques through a discussion on value-relations in NED. It is shown why use-value must subordinate exchange-value. The consumer councils will first be instrumental in sustaining the seniority of use-value. Secondly, where exchange-relations remain, the consumer councils will, in constant dialogue with the guild cooperatives, help regulate them. My conclusion is that in both cases, supply and demand will not be coordinated through invisible hands.

Horvat exposes imperfections of supposedly invisible hands. He stresses that consumers' choices can be incorrect, they can be irrational, informed by custom and frequently lack adequate knowledge. The continuing popularity of tacky items indicates that consumption habits are often trivial. In this respect what is consumed frequently gives no lasting satisfaction. The likelihood is that individuals continue to consume as they do because they are all too easily taken in by slick advertisements and/or ideologies. This suggests the relevance of a familiar contention; meaningful consumption choice is dependent upon adequate education and less-imperfect information, the implications of which are clear. 'If our choices are socially determined, then we had better consider how to control the forces responsible for this determination and stop flattering ourselves as to how much individual sovereignty we enjoy' (1982: 330; 329–32). Uncertain consumption habits also mean producers' responses will be equally unstable. In addition, Sayer adds that markets in which prices are volatile are less common than fixed-price markets. The latter is where producers respond to low sales by holding out for custom, rather than lowering the price. Placing quality and reliability before price provides a stable environment for organizing production. He then highlights the difference between standardized goods brought 'off-the-shelf', contracting in which only information on the price is given, and those 'made to order', 'relational contracting' where producer–consumer relationships are more than minimal. The latter involves the sharing of information and the enhancement of trust. Sayer contends that liberals tend to overestimate the accuracy of information displayed via prices. Non-price information also needs to be exchanged, usually free to consumers, and is hence outside market exchanges. And even when information provided by markets is accurate, productive units may not be in a position to take advantage of it. In these cases markets are anything but self-regulating; extra market modes of coordination are needed to uphold them. It cannot be contended, then, that supply and demand will be coordinated sufficiently by invisible hands (Sayer, A. 1995: 84–6).

It is in response to these critiques that consumer councils offer a real improvement to the way markets operate. This claim will now be substantiated through a discussion of value in NED. Consider first the distinction between use- and exchange-value. As Sayer explains, under-market systems productive goals are expressed in terms of exchange-value. Use-value becomes merely the means to an end. The provision of use-values is subordinated to the imperative of maximizing sales. It is possible that competition may inadvertently improve use-values, but where exchange-value is the chief regulator of economic behaviour, irrational outcomes are frequent. 'It is therefore common to find unused labour power (unemployed bricklayers) and resources (surplus bricks) which cannot be deployed to satisfy unmet needs (houses for the homeless) because the exchange value conditions are not right' (1995: 179). In light of this, it is legitimate to ask how products are ascribed value in NED. The form of work is not wage-labour, it is creative labour;[22] this is partly what gives commodities their exchange-value. An embodiment of creative labour is what gives products value from the productive side. It is not by simply invoking the labour theory of value uncritically (neither does it place the determination of value in the hands of state planners), but as NED has no *a priori* objection to the production of surplus-value, and as labour is still a key variable in its determination, it does adhere to labour values. Products have value as the outcome of creative labour. This though is only half the story. The democratization of production is an indispensable step towards defetishization. Yet by itself, it remains incomplete. A corresponding democratization of consumption is of equal importance. So in NED there is in addition a second sense in which products are ascribed value – through the democratic input of consumers. In the needs sector, the items produced are mainly determined directly by the two consumer councils. In the wants sector, although the guild cooperatives are free to respond to market fluctuations, the consumer councils are empowered to veto products that invoke significant criticism. This is not the task of the Commune. Every product, therefore, will be realized through inclusive democratic means, or by satisfying the conditions determined by the consumer councils. This is what gives them value from the consumption side of NED. In a line, value relations in NED are premised upon creative labour and producer–consumer dialogue.[23]

It can be appreciated that exchange-value is not the centrepiece of NED's mode of production. The functionally demarcated market system is subordinated to the democratic planning process; and the latter will prioritize the satisfaction of citizens needs over and above their wants. It is true that the guild cooperatives will compete for grants, but the awarding criteria – determined jointly through the guilds and consumer councils – will not be 'profit conscious', it will be 'social benefit conscious'. It is in this sense that use-value can take precedence over the expansion of exchange-value. In capitalism, only the use-values that are expected to expand exchange-value get produced. On fear of bankruptcy, the market imperative to maximize exchange-value must be obeyed; a use-value with little exchange-value will not attract investors. Yet in NED, the guild cooperatives are not motivated by the relentless drive to expand output. New productive projects are not only financed through increased sales. Cooperatives who wish to expand into wider fields within their functionally demarcated domain are required

22. Chapter three analyses this claim extensively.

23. To do it justice, an analysis of value in NED would take up the volumes of a separate book. But the general idea, I think, clear enough.

to apply to the investment fund of their guild. Commodity production is not the dominant economic form. This does not imply that competition will be totally abolished in NED. But it does imply that competition – together with its inevitable companion, advertisement – will not take the same form they do in market forces economies. This puts me at odds with other thinkers who have proposed alternatives to contemporary capitalism. Nove for example stresses that competition/advertisements have some positive features. They are both a prerequisite and a consequence of free choice, and as they provide a stimulus they can ensure improvements in quality and service. The aim of advertising is to attract customers, without it there is the danger of indifference to their needs. He acknowledges that this can degenerate into the undesirability of 'pseudo product innovation and differentiation' and 'excessive expenditure on garish packaging'; but without competition, technological breakthroughs may be infrequent. So in Nove's feasible socialism, glossy catalogues will continue to excite potential customers (1983: 38, 41–2, 205).

In my opinion, this is an inappropriate way to entice the interests of consumers. It is precisely this kind of marketing strategy that directly gives rise to fetishism. It is also a prerequisite for and a consequence of an economy that is dominated by exchange relations. Exorbitant competition engenders gimmicky advertising, sales-pitch promotions, commercial blurb and such like. It also obscures the difference between necessary products and the triviality of tasteless items. What critics of capitalism generally dislike is the excessive drive towards what often amounts to scruple-less advertising, especially for goods that only differ in label – coke, coca-cola, pepsi, pepsi-cola, dr. peppers and so on. These are evidently not conducive to the defetishized political economy. So in contrast to Nove's feasible socialism, superficial 'garish packaging' will be discouraged in NED. But if, following Nove, a degree of competition is the most optimal method by which to stimulate technological innovations, then a check on how producers attract consumer interest becomes crucial. Exchange relations cannot be subordinated while, simultaneously, producers have no other means by which to commercialize their goods than through aggressive advertising. NED's solution is in part, as the last section makes clear, to organize production along guild lines where advertisements can be monitored closely by a body constituted through representatives of all the cooperatives involved. In order to supplement this process, NED provides social forums, the consumer councils, who will, in constant dialogue with the guild cooperatives, also subject product promotions to scrutiny. Crucially, their seal of approval will send clear signals to consumers of the quality and quantity of given products; and if the same products can be determined methodically and disposed off openly, there is not the same need to advertise. So through the data purveyed by the consumer councils, producers can be responsive to consumer needs in the absence of cut-throat competition. It is in this sense that the consumer councils will act as educational forums, providing less imperfect information. This suggests that in the sphere of consumption, irrational choice will be less frequent than in an unshackled market forces economy where marketing departments have greater licence to publicize, perhaps through deceit, their firm's products. Hence, NED's consumer councils offer far more than just a palliative.

To summarize, markets typically operate with information that is limited and/or imperfect. The consumer councils offer the necessary corrective. Their task is, fundamentally, to subordinate at all times exchange-relations. Expressing productive goals in terms of use-value reduces irrational outcomes. This is the basic reasoning behind the appeal to satisfy human needs before wants. Further, where exchange-relations remain, consumer councils can help advance rational economic behaviour. Although in any economy that values freedom of choice consumer preferences may not always be based upon good judgement, through the extra-market information supplied by the consumer councils, consumers in NED will lack adequate knowledge less often than their counterparts in capitalist economies. By providing an outlet for the sharing of non-price information, producer–consumer relations can wherever possible be determined through relational contracting. Following Horvat's appeal, consumer councils can control the forces responsible for the social determination of consumer choices; they also constitute the extra-market modes of coordination Sayer calls for. As such, the consumer councils can gauge demand and ensure that standards of quality and reliability are maintained in the absence of invisible hands.

Summary

As the above discussion on markets has raised and responded to a number of contentious issues, before we move on to the next and final section of this chapter, it will be instructive to briefly summarize the key points of my argument so far. This passage has, following on from the previous passage on social planning, established the organizational bases to the defetishized political economy. I have contended that a market sector cannot be the dominant mode of production and distribution. But as markets do serve certain functions well, a market mechanism of some description is a necessary requirement of a modern complex economy. So while participatory planning is the first ingredient, exchange through the medium of a market can assume its role only within the parameters specified by the former. We have seen, however, that although a combination of planning and markets will be upheld in NED, both are unique in substance. Planning proceeds through the functional bodies in civil society; these bodies will also monitor the subordinated market sector. Neither task falls to the state. As NED retains a role for functionally demarcated markets, it was important to indicate how supply and demand can be coordinated efficiently without recourse to so-called invisible hands. Indeed, there is nothing invisible in the way supply and demand is coordinated in NED. Due largely to the insufficiencies of supposedly invisible hands, markets must be monitored by bodies that are far closer to producers and consumers than the modern state. In NED this translates into guilds who, in conjunction with the consumer councils, will determine social plans. This suggests that supply and demand in NED will be coordinated with more transparency than in capitalist markets.

Centralized Bureaucracy or Decentralized Social Planning

Having established the organizational bases to NED's political economy, I would now like to complete the analysis in this chapter by clarifying the uniqueness of the market system in NED. In order to achieve this, it is necessary to pick up once again the democratic determination of the product mix and return to NED's original method of social planning. The main task is to indicate why NED's planning will not give rise to an immense bureaucratic structure. In NED, economic rationalization does not point towards centralization. Through an engagement with Alex Nove (1983), who presents a forceful argument for why planning should be circumscribed, I will distinguish NED's planning from the centralized planning typical of command socialism. Nove argues that a modern economy can be organized only through commodity production or by means of instructions from a centralized planning bureau; and although the two extremes may be compromised, there is no (independent) third way. He also suggests abolishing market relations will inevitably lead to a giant state bureaucracy. In contrast, this section shows why NED's planning will not engender a commanding centralized bureaucracy. In the process, I indicate that NED's plan-market mix moves the debate on political economy in a direction beyond market capitalism and state socialist planning. NED, then, stands as a genuine third way.

Nove does not dispute the need for a degree of planning; neither is he an advocate of an untrammelled free market. Rather, in his feasible socialism there is a combination of planning and markets. He stresses that in centralized systems of planning state planners can perceive the overall picture, but they cannot comprehend the finer details of the localities. Decentralization through market transactions can ensure transparency in the latter, but it cannot fully appreciate the effects at the macro level. The solution, Nove suggests, must be a compromise. His position is that as some decisions are more appropriately freely negotiated, and others are more suitable to administrative instructions, a mix of plan and market is an 'essential ingredient' of a socialist economy. For Nove, the most democratic way to empower consumers is to allow them to influence production through their voluntary purchases. He denies the possibility of a direct political alternative. What for example would happen to minority rights in consumption? Is it right that a majority should vote not to allow the production of an item desired by a minority? Nove's answer is that the intensity of desire for any item is only measurable by the amount people are prepared to pay for it. Cloths and food products come in many variants. That a central authority cannot plan these items quantitatively is, he states, 'the beginning of wisdom'. With a suitable incomes policy, and the elimination of large unearned incomes, the best method to identify consumer choice is to provide consumers with the opportunity to choose by means of their purchasing power (Nove, A. 1983: 42–4, 225–6). Nove is aware that orthodox Marxists will claim this is merely commodity production, a 'species of market economy', but:

> in a complex industrial economy the interrelation between its parts can be based in principle either on freely chosen negotiated contracts (which means autonomy and a species of commodity production) or on a system of binding instructions from planning offices. *There is no third way.* (Nove, A. 1983: 44)

This, then, is the bases to Nove's argument that there is not a third way. Echoing Nove, NED does combine planning and markets, but as the previous five sections of this part of the chapter have elucidated, the content of both are unique, and therefore very different from that upheld in feasible socialism. I will conclude that NED's original political economy does represent a third way. The issue I now wish to address is can NED avoid the entrenchment of a huge and intimidating bureaucracy? Nove's reasoning on allowing the market to determine microeconomic consumer choices can be applied accurately to luxury items. Markets though have a poor record of meeting human needs.[24] It is true that with an appropriate

24. See Wyatt (2008: 48–9).

incomes policy, and in the absence of huge inequalities, this problem may be partially negated. But it is not eliminated. The basic goods that everyone needs should, as argued above, be provided for collectively, irrespective of the prerogatives of personal wealth; and this can only be met through social planning. Nove recognizes there are real problems with markets – cyclical fluctuations, huge inequalities and the entrenchment of giant corporations – but, he insists, there is no alternative:

> it is clear that someone (some institution) has to tell the producers about what the users require. If that 'someone' is not the impersonal market mechanism it can only be a hierarchical superior. There are horizontal links (market), there are vertical links (hierarchy). What other dimension is there? (Nove, A. 1983: 226)

In answer to this question, yes, there is another dimension: place the responsibility of planning into the hands of organizations that have decentralizing as well as centralizing structures; organizations that will exist in a thoroughly democratized civil society. The information that producers need in order to respond to consumer demand will not, in NED's needs sector, be provided solely by the impersonal market mechanism; neither will it be dictated by a hierarchical superior. This task falls to consumer councils. In this sense there will be horizontal non-market links between producers and consumers. Nove does not allow for the possibility of this method of planning. He argues that the Marxist doctrine points to centralized and extensive planning. The elimination of commodity production makes, he infers, decentralization almost inconceivable. A local authority only has knowledge about its own domain. Producers will not know what to produce, who it is for and when they need it unless planners decide on their behalf. In the absence of the market, Nove concludes, production for use can only be installed through a 'centralising logic' (Nove, A. 1983: 29–30).

Nove is casting doubt over the possibility of eliminating market relations without simultaneously engendering a colossal and inefficient bureaucracy. A dominant bureaucracy, he contends, can only be evaded by reducing its functions, and this involves enterprise autonomy and commodity production. Given the experience of centralized planning in command socialism, his fears are well founded. But I think he is wrong on this point. A dominant and inefficient bureaucracy can be avoided in a democratically organized political economy without granting commodity production an excessively high status. State socialism fell into error by centralizing economic power in the hands of state planners.

The solution is to decentralize to the greatest possible extent the organizations responsible for determining the plan. For this to be inclusive and participatory, decentralization must be combined with functional representation. If it is only undifferentiated decision-making that is decentralized, then all the perplexity that exists generally at the national level will merely repeat itself at the local level. It is more important to disentangle problems and to secure direct representation of every person's relevant interests. Individuals are only free when they have a different representative for every interest. Freedom by devolution does not imply absolute freedom, but freedom from a distant central body (Carpenter, L. P. 1973: 257). NED replaces the omnipresent state with numerous different electoral agencies, as many as there are essential social functions. Functional representation allows people to become active citizens by providing them with the chance to express their opinions on public policies. It is unrealistic to suppose that NED's functional organizations will transcend bureaucratic structures completely, no modern complex industrial society can do this, but a plurality of smaller and less intense bureaucracies does not pose the same threat to the individual's liberty as an immense state bureaucracy does. It is only within this setting that the market mechanism can serve the valuable functions Nove ascribes to it.

So in NED's unconventional mixed economy, participatory planning subordinates a market system. The former is a precondition for the latter's efficiency; planning can perfect market choices. Planning though will not advance through the state, but as we have seen, through the guilds and consumer councils. Some items are, as Nove indicates, suitable for centralized planning. Water, electricity, gas, health care, public transport, education, the key food groups and personal items like basic clothing all fall within the needs category. In these cases, the committees within the higher echelons of the guilds and consumer councils will oversee the planning procedure. They will facilitate referendums on broad issues, determine the priority of policies and arbitrate the fixing of prices. The planning of some of the above, however, can wherever possible be arranged on decentralized bases. In direct contrast to centralized command planning, basic needs can be articulated democratically from below through negotiation and consultation between the cooperating functional bodies. On a closely related issue Martell points out:

> market research needs to be carried out in order to identify needs which are distorted or unrepresented in patterns of consumer market demand. Such mechanisms can be sensitive to the diversity of needs

> as they are defined by people themselves, resorting to neither the statist imposition of preferences nor the distorted perceptions of market forces. (1992: 159)

The consumer and civic councils are ideally suited to undertake the market research that will enable them to supply the guild cooperatives with the necessary information. As decentralized functional organizations, they would only need to articulate local information to the corresponding workplaces. They are well placed to respond to the particular knowledge of local circumstances, and would not have to comprehend and accommodate the ramifications of national plans. If mediated contracts between producers and consumers at the local level decide this element of the plan, the guild cooperatives will retain a degree of autonomy and the economy will not be administered entirely from the centre.

By way of summary, I do not mean to imply that the market mechanism will play no role in the satisfaction of people's basic needs. Where markets work well in this regard, they should be retained. A complete abolishment would also result in administrative chaos. As Nove has shown, there are numerous goods and services on offer, with infinite permutations; subjecting microeconomic consumer choice to the ballot box is, as he puts it, 'unthinkable' (1983: 42–4 or 225–6). But I do mean to imply that consumer councils have a far greater aptness to correct market failures than the state. And I imply further that the direction asserted by the consumer councils will take precedence over the dictates of the market. Beyond this, the market mechanism can be left to determine supply and demand with a lesser degree of regulation – the main qualification being that the consumer councils will hold the power of veto in highly controversial cases, for example in the case of externalities. So in NED, the context is a far cry from the one typical of both capitalist market and state planned economies. This, then, is the political economy through which NED will determine the product mix without engendering a formidable bureaucracy.

Conclusion

This chapter has argued that NED represents an authentic third way; a third way through which the defetishization process will advance. I have attempted to synthesize what is best from cooperation and competition. It is NED's pluralist mediation of state and civil society that can make the best use of participatory planning and markets. It can now be appreciated how NED responds to the liberal separation of politics and economics. NED harbours both a self-governing civil society and a pluralized state. Crucially, in democratizing and unifying both domains it moves beyond the state-civil society paradigm. That is, government functions are delineated and entrusted to the functional agencies for their execution. In this sense, a vast and daunting centralized bureaucracy is averted; simultaneously, the doctrine of state sovereignty is repudiated. In making this argument, it was important to indicate where NED stands on the continuance of exchange-relations. As the subordination of use-value to the expansion of exchange-value is a key characteristic of capitalism, in post-capitalist society exchange-value must be suppressed so that it no longer regulates the social organism (Cohen, G. A. 1978: 297–8). NED accepts and responds to this statement through its unusual approach to determining the plan-market mix. In NED, socially predetermined use-values circulate democratically. In accordance with its libertarian spirit, NED does not produce use-values through a centralized plan; neither does it regulate markets through the state. As will now be clear, both tasks are realized by virtue of democratic organizations in a re-politicized civil society. Use-values in NED pass from producer to consumer in the absence of market exchange because they are the result of distributive planning. And in contrast to both *lassie faire* capitalism and the command planning of state socialism, the exchange-value of the market sector is regulated by functionally defined bodies – and not by the state or by a body politic analogous to the modern state. Yet even here NED does not invoke the invisible hand thesis to account for market coordination. On the contrary, in the way the direction of the economy is determined through open dialogue between organized production and organized consumption, coordination of supply and demand could hardly be more visible.

I have also indicated that NED will not succumb to aggressive advertising. Rather, it will instigate – through methods that will engender sympathetic inter-cooperative relations in the federations of cooperatives – schemes of networking in which information is disseminated equally to all the cooperatives within every guild. NED's demarcated markets will not be overly competitive. While a limited scope for the commodity form remains, it is embedded within a system of pluralist planning. This implies that an inclusive approach to planning will subordinate exchange-relations. Commodities are no longer the centrepiece of economic life, and their production and distribution will only proceed through the parameters established by the democratic method of planning. Although it is a planned economy, the emphasis is on dialogue and negotiated coordination between the delineated interests of all those affected. In this way people's material relations will not, as the following chapters will argue, be externalized in the exchange-relations between things; exchange-relations will not, then, conceal the social relations of production. Only in this left-libertarian scheme can the positive aspects of commodity production remain without being burdened by the tendency to fetishize.

SECTION II

DEFETISHIZATION IN THE ECONOMY OF NEW ECONOMIC DEMOCRACY

3

Superseding Alienation

This lengthy chapter argues that alienated labour can be superseded in NED. The key contention is that the internal political structures within the guilds, and their external relations with the consumer and civic councils, are arranged in such a way that the guild cooperatives will have every opportunity and every incentive to provide the material conditions through which creative labour can be sustained. There are three parts to the chapter. Part One, 'Alienation and Dealienation', establishes what Marx means by alienated labour. Then, in response to the claim that it cannot be negated, I provide a rational for what I have termed the organizational solution. Part Two, 'Creative Labour in New Economic Democracy', is the longest part. It addresses both the macro (external to guild cooperatives) and the micro (internal to guild cooperatives) divisions of labour in NED's political economy. I argue that creative labour can be embedded within this material system. Finally, Part Three, 'Dealienated Consumption', highlights the role played by consumer councils in NED's dealienated mode of consumption.

Part One: Alienation and Dealienation

There are four sections to this first part. The first, 'Marx and Alienation', provides an exposition of his critique of alienated labour.[1] The second, 'Alienation and Fetishism', reaffirms the connection between alienation

1. As dealienation is my primary interest in this book, I will here only summarize the key characteristic points of Marx's theory of alienated labour in fairly succinct terms. For a more detailed and fascinating, though challenging, exposition, see Meszaros (1975), especially on Marx's conceptual framework (pp. 99–114), and on alienation and the division of labour (pp. 140–50).

and commodity fetishism. The third, 'Alienation Unavoidable', introduces the argument that due to the complexities of the division of labour in all advanced economies, alienation is inescapable. In the fourth, 'Realizing the Impossible: The Organizational Solution', the productive conditions that are a prerequisite for engendering creative labour are laid-out.

Marx and Alienation

The young humanist Marx argues that human nature is twisted negatively by the structures within capitalist society. It is this distortion that he calls alienation. Marx holds that human essence is more than just thought; it is, more fundamentally, creative activity – the many aspects of labour. Consciousness can only be considered one feature of humanity. It is practical, creative activity that is the focal point of his alienation theory. This theory is not so much related to the subjective experience of workers, but to the structure of the commodity economy. In the social class structure of capitalism, one class, the non-owners of the means of production, have no choice but to sell their labour power to another class, the owners of the means of production. It is this central social relation in capitalism, wage-labour, that is the bases of alienation. Marx, then, locates alienation at the base of capitalist society (1977: 85). To help explain why 'the more powerful the work the more powerless becomes the worker' (1977: 79), he invokes a religious analogy. The maker of a product, Marx suggests, undergoes a similar experience to the maker of god. In both cases, the more energy people put into god or a product, the less they retain in themselves (1977: 79). As Part One of Chapter 1 explained, in the actual process of producing workers externalize basic human attributes, thereby objectifying humanity. The laws of political economy are not directly willed by the workers they regulate, which implies the latter cannot be considered free. The workers, having no say in the direction of their work, are transformed into a thing due to the dependence on capital. That is, Marx identifies an inversion between appearances and what really is. As capital, which is produced by human endeavours, is an estranged being that rules people via its economic laws, there is an inversion between the person–thing relation. The society of alienated labour, as with the society of commodity fetishism, has no autonomy. People are not masters controlling their own fates, but slaves to the economic infrastructure they have brought into existence. In this self-contrived inverted world, capital appears as a thing dichotomized from the people who created it and who in turn are ruled by it. Individuals' lives are progressively determined unintentionally by the collective activity which is structured by impersonal exchange relations (Marx, K. 1977: 79, 85; Howard, M. W. et al. 1985: 18; Fromm, E. 1992: 49–50; Perlman, F. 1972: xiii–iv; Ritzer, G. 1992: 57).

In the *Economic and Philosophical Manuscripts (EPM)* (1844) and the *Notes on James Mill* (1844), Marx argues that a person's subjectivity is a function of his or her relationship with external nature (essential to which is the means of production) and with others. It is this subjectivity which is alienated by wage-labour. Alienation from human essence therefore means people's subjectivity – their physical and intellectual energies, or work capacity – is removed from them. In this separation material objects are not merely things, they become incorporated in the objectification of human subjectivity. When they produce just to exchange, people do not relate to each other's objects as human beings because they themselves do not relate in a human way to those they produce (1977: 114–15). Workers exchange labour power for wages, and in the process alienate themselves from their producing activities. The labour of workers becomes something external to them, something to be appropriated by others. Alienated labour becomes a commodity, its price determined by market factors. As a corollary, workers are alienated from the products their labour produces. Labour is embodied in an object. As soon as labour is sold, it follows that the goods produced by that labour, including the exchange-value of these products, also belong to the employers. Further, workers become alienated from others, who come to appear as egoistical competitors, and from their own social being because they do not contribute in any significant or meaningful way to the planning of production. Consequently, they do not come to identify with universal interests. So in estranged (wage) labour, the labourer's 'essence' is objectified and alienated. The key point in the *EPM* is that the workers' estrangement is the separation of social relationships from themselves. Marx's argument is that workers transfer to something else (god, political state or in *Capital* the inhuman power of commodities and capital – all of which assume an independent entity) that which is essential to their nature, to control their own activities and hence initiate historical processes. It is important to add that for Marx, the process of objectification is a universal feature of all societies; and it may be a positive or negative experience, depending on the particular social relations of production in which it occurs (Marx, K. 1975: 282–7, 295–303, 327–30; 1977: 80–3, 114–15; Colletti, L. 1975: 50–2, 54; McLellan, D. 1986: 34; 1995: 110, 242; Howard, M. W. 2000: 77).

It is evident that Marx dislikes markets because commodity exchange in capitalist society alienates people's human existence from their essence. His concept of work attempts to capture this essence, or 'species' being. According to Marx, people have both a 'natural' and species being. They are natural beings in the sense that they share a number of physical features with other species – the need for food, water and to reproduce through sexual selection. As a species being, people can be distinguished from other living things, for they now possess qualities which are uniquely their own, and can only be known by their own species. Like human's natural power, their species power implies particular relationships between them and nature, including other people as parts of nature. The importance for Marx is that humans manifest themselves as a species being through activity that can only be done by human beings. He proposes that in the appropriate productive process, people's creative and free activity, in cooperation with their fellows, could be given expression in the goods they are producing; and how genuine control over the process of self-creation can be initiated. People act as a species being when they produce for others in order to satisfy their needs, so consciously directing labour. In this cooperative process of creative self-activity, when they see others appreciating their products, work becomes a fulfilling experience. A conscious understanding of the needs of others is generated. This, as Marx puts it, is to produce in a 'human manner' (1977: 121–2). Under the system of private property, exchanges are conditional, individuals expect something in return. Here there is no personal use-value; that is, a person produces something s/he does not want, it is only a means to other goods. Alienated labour, so understood, is to produce something of no interest to oneself. Relations are based around private property owners, not as species being. Products are in private hands, the exchange is one of private properties. So although exchange (or 'interchange') is our species activity, all the time it takes place within the framework of private property, it is alienated species activity. The gap between individual and the general interest increases when the chief aim is to collectively exchange commodities in an impersonal market, which is the domain of profit-seeking egoism. So for Marx, in capitalist society workers are denied an expression of their species being, or communal creativity, who, as such, experience lives of misery, un-fulfilment... alienation. He concludes that in order to realize their species being people must end the system of commodity exchange in a distant market (Marx, K. 1977: 82, 114–18; Ollman, B. 1971: 76, 82–5; McLellan, D. 1986: 34; 1995: 110, 242; Howard, M. W. 2000: 77).

In summary, an alienating context exists wherever the social relations of production prevent, by a fragmentation of the natural interconnectedness (of people-to-people and people-to-nature) that is essential for a human life to reach its potential, the development of the full range of human capacities. Marx's alienation thesis is commonly broken down into four aspects. First, workers are alienated from their *productive activity*, and thereby from the essence of humanity. The seller of labour power relinquishes control of productive decision-making. Once the process of production is under the direction of the capitalist, labour, subject to minor restrictions, cannot be self-directed. Discipline is typically enforced by close supervision, which severely undermines the enthusiasm for workers to develop their creativity and autonomy. The loss of freedom is further enhanced by the dictates of technology, which is frequently employed in the capitalist enterprise to deskill and intensify a minute division of labour. Secondly, each person is alienated from the *product*. It follows that if workers are alienated from their productive activity, they must also be alienated from the goods their productive activity produces. The worker has no control over the determination of what gets produced, nor how it should be disposed. In the third place is alienation from *fellow workers*, who are likewise alienated from human life. Where everything is a commodity, individuals are forced to compete with each other. Cooperation (which for Marx is, as clarified above, our natural inclination) becomes less prevalent, and people come to see each other as means to their own ends. The resulting interpersonal hostility ensures workers are alienated from their associates. Finally, in the fourth place is alienation from *oneself*. Self-alienation refers to the separation from what it means to be human: to produce through creative, purposeful and rational activity. Workers are alienated from their own potential, and cannot express their human attributes. These, according to Marx, are the four forms alienation takes in capitalist society. The crucial point is that the labour process is outside the direct control of disempowered workers (Marx, K. 1977: 80–3; Ritzer, G. 1992: 57–9).

Alienation and Fetishism

Before moving on to address the argument that alienation is unavoidable in any modern economy, it will be helpful to reconfirm the interrelation between alienation and commodity fetishism. McLellan (1971) stresses that Marx's theory of fetishism recalls clearly his earlier writings on alienated labour. To briefly reiterate, in *Capital I* Marx demonstrates that in commodity societies the products of labour generate an independent and anti-human power. As with alienation, the fetishism of commodities emerges when products are exchanged through an impersonal market.

Marx states that a commodity is a very mysterious thing because the social character of labour that it embodies appears to the workers as an objective character. These commodities, which have only achieved their status through complex social relations, then appear to interact with each other and with people, whereupon they seem to have values and a life of their own. People's values become largely centred on appearances, things and what they are worth. The relations of producers to their own labour appear in their eyes as a social relation existing between independent products, and not between themselves. The result is that individuals, vis-a-vis the theory of alienation, remain separated from each other and from the general interest. As in capitalism the chief forms of social relations are based around commodities. Marx concludes the tendency to fetishism is hardly surprising. But it does mean that the real social processes, including the manner in which labour is exploited, remains concealed and unrecognized. Geras (1971) offers a similar insight. He states that in Marx's thesis, fetishism inflicts itself upon people as mystification and domination. Mystification was covered in Chapter 1, it is the dominating aspect of fetishism I now wish to draw attention to. In contrast to former modes of production, in capitalist society the domination is disguised, and it is impersonal. Domination is a reoccurring theme in Marx's writings. It first appears in the *EPM* (1844) in his discussion of alienation, and is present in *Capital 1*.[2] Interestingly, Geras stresses that the role of alienation in the latter is that its roots are in specific social relations, not in a negated species-being. It is this, he suggests, that separates *Capital* from *EPM*. 'In place of a concept of alienation founded on an essentialist anthropology, we have one tied to the historical specificity of forms of domination' (1971: 3; Marx, K. 1977: 435–6; McLellan, D. 1971: xxxvii, xli; Howard, M. W. 2000: 77–9, 82).

Others, too, have drawn attention to the general unity in Marx's thought. For Perlman (1972) and Rubin (1972) Marx's concept of alienation and his theory of commodity fetishism are, along with the theory of value, formulations which address the same issue: how working activity is determined in capitalist society. In the *EPM* Marx explains alienation in a way that will reflect his later account of commodity fetishism. The more effort workers put into their product, the more their lives are displaced in it; in proportion, the poorer their inner lives become. Likewise, the more value workers create, the more worthless they become. For Marx, this impoverishment

2. To cite just one example from *Capital 1*, the division of labour in manufacturing 'produces new conditions for the domination of capital over labour' (1976: 486).

is a 'contemporary fact of political economy' (1977: 78–9). As labour is embodied in an object, the later appears as an objectification of labour:

> The externalization [alienation] of the worker in his product implies not only that his labour becomes an object, an exterior existence but also that it exists outside him, independently and alien, and becomes a self-sufficient power opposite him, that the life that he has lent to the object affronts him, hostile and alien. (Marx, K. 1977: 79)

'This passage', Perlman concludes, 'seems, in retrospect, like a summary of the theory of commodity fetishism' (1972: xxix). Alien objects stand opposed to labour as an independent power because the labour embodied in the product is appropriated by the capitalist. It is in this sense that both fetishism and alienation are inherent in the social relations central to commodity-producing societies. The capitalist class appropriates the labour which the working class alienates. So by its very definition, wage-labour is alienated labour (Marx, K. 1977: 78–9, 84; Perlman, F. 1972: xvii–iii).

In his later writings Marx abandons terms like 'human essence'. He now considers human nature to be conditioned by material factors which are constantly changing. So rather than human nature in general, Marx now bases his analysis on human beings producing in a given historical setting. This enables him to make a new claim: the essence of human beings cannot be separated from their historical existence. People create their material conditions, not by way of an ideal society, but through the limits laid out by the existing forces of production. Rubin captures the transformation in Marx's thought neatly:

> In order to transform … [his] theory of 'alienation' of human relations into a theory of 'reification' of social relations (i.e., into the theory of commodity fetishism), Marx had to create a path from Utopian to Scientific socialism … from negating reality in the name of an ideal to seeking within reality itself the forces for further development and motion. (Rubin, I. I. 1972: 57)

Marx's 'progression' from utopian to scientific socialism involved a change in how he conceptualized alienation. The contradiction between alienated workers producing in capitalist society and their unalienated species-being, or human essence, is now dropped. The opposition between the social relations and their material base is no longer treated as an opposition between what actually is and what ought to be; both opposing factors are now located in existing reality. But although Marx came to abandon the word alienation, he continues to develop its content. And it is this development that occurs in the new formulations of commodity fetishism and value. 'The link between alienation and commodity fetishism is the concept of "reification" (materialisation or objectification) of social relations' (Perlman, F. 1972: xxiii; Rubin, I. I. 1972: 57–8).

Chapter 1 explained that the term reification refers to a mistaken interpretation of an abstract entity (god, state) or concept as concrete. To briefly reiterate, Marx uses the term mostly to explain how commodities, money, capital, etc., are given the status of things when they should more accurately be treated as social relations. The work process causes labour to be objectified. People appropriate the natural world, and, through their labour, objectify themselves in it. When this objectification occurs under alienating conditions, it may be termed reification. Reification, so understood, describes a situation in which the social relations between people appear as the relations between things. The reification of productive relations is supplemented by the personification of things. People come to evaluate others just as they evaluate things. Crucially for Marx, they do not perceive this as abnormal, but as natural. With intensified commodification, the market becomes the only standard of evaluation. Impersonal market forces come to dominate human relations. It is this fundamental aspect of reification that Marx labelled commodity fetishism. Behind the veil of commodity fetishism, the market is experienced by alienated people as an impersonal force. In *Capital 1* the reification of social relations is explained as not just the result of the thinking process of commodity producers, as Marx had suggested in 1859 where he refers to reification as a 'mystification', it is located in the internal structure of commodity-producing society. It is the capitalist economy that causes fetishism; capitalist social relations necessarily lead to reified social relations. Reification is a consequence of capitalism, but it is more than that, it is inseparable from it. Hence, fetishism, as an objective feature of commodity-producing society, is a phenomenon of social being (Rubin, I. I. 1972: 58–60; Horvat, B. 1982: 97–8).[3]

---

3. With regards to the young versus the old Marx debate – that is, whether or not Marx underwent a radical epistemological break in his reasoning as he matured – Meszaros responds with an unambiguous no. He stresses that Marx dropped neither the word alienation, nor the concept itself. He provides references from the following texts, in chronological order, to make his case: *The Holy Family, The German Ideology, The Communist Manifesto, Outline of a Critique of Political Economy, Theories of Surplus Value* and *Capital: Volumes I, II and III.* Unsurprisingly, Meszaros concludes that 'the concept of alienation is a vitally

In sum, it is apparent that Marx's account of alienation is expressed in his theory of commodity fetishism. In both critiques the properties conferred upon commodities are uncontrolled by human beings; labour is expressed as an objective property of the items it produces. Human beings are rendered subject to the commodity-producing process and to the attributes bestowed, falsely as natural, onto the commodities themselves. The point to stress, then, is that domination is central to the understanding of the critiques of alienated labour and commodity fetishism. The solution for Marx is a radical retransformation of economic relations.

Alienation Unavoidable

This section introduces the arguments that alienation is unavoidable in all modern technological economies, and that every attempt to eliminate it through conscious planning will inevitably fail. Attention is drawn to the critics who assert that the complexities in the division of labour ensure alienation is inescapable. Coupled to this is the claim that there are inherent inconsistencies in Marx's reasoning. Marx argues that an advanced division of labour results in alienation, and that it is possible to transcend the division of labour. For Marx, communism would indeed realize this without returning to primitive modes of production. As I will indicate, it is this assertion that has been dismissed in the literature. In order to achieve this, it will be helpful to begin by summarizing Marx's discussion in *Capital 1* chapter 14 on the division of labour and manufacture.

Marx distinguishes between two broad divisions of labour, one within the workplace, what he calls the division of labour in manufacture – and as manufacture has a technical character (1976: 480), it may be called the *technical* division of labour; and the other in society taken as a whole, he refers to this as the *social* division of labour (1976: 471). The former is rationally designed to ensure optimal efficiency, and reflects the capitalist's production plan. The latter emerges spontaneously, unintentionally, the result of market transactions; it is complex as there are literally millions of competing plans. These two divisions of labour are distinct in terms of degree and kind (1976: 474). The former is enforced upon the workers by the despotic authority of the capitalist. The latter is imposed upon everyone by the market mechanism; here independent commodity producers, who as Marx puts it only

---

important pillar of the Marxian system as a whole, and not merely one brick of it' (1975: 227, 221–7).

acknowledge the authority of competition, are brought into contact. In the technical division of labour, fragmented workers do not produce commodities; it is the finished product of their combined efforts that becomes a commodity. This implies that it is only the social division of labour that is mediated via the exchange of commodities; the technical division of labour arises when a number of workers sell their labour-power to a single capitalist. In the latter, the means of production are owned by the single capitalist, whereas the former presupposes a widespread dispersal of these means among a multitude of independent commodity producers. So the workers are confronted with alienating conditions within the workplace, whereas both the workers and the capitalists are faced with the un-designed and uncontrollable social division of labour. That is, with the latter the variables of chance and caprice cause a motley distributive pattern of productive assets (Marx, K. 1976: 475–7; Prychitko, D. 1991: 15).

Marx draws particular attention to how manufacture isolates the various stages of production and ensures their independence from each other. The speed at which articles can be produced gathers pace as the content of tasks performed by separated workers is increasingly narrowed. This means that skills are split-up into various isolated yet mutually interdependent operations. As handicrafts are decomposed into different partial operations, so each worker is riveted to a sole aspect of the work process. So although the technical division of labour is a particular method of generating surplus-value, for Marx it does this at the expense of subjecting the dependent worker to the unrelenting commands of capital. In the manner in which manufacturing furthers only one particular skill in each worker – and often only a very basic skill – while suppressing a whole range of productive inclinations, the worker is converted into a 'crippled monstrosity':

> Not only does it increase the socially productive power of labour for the benefit of the capitalist instead of the worker; it also does this by crippling the individual worker. It produces new conditions for the domination of capital over labour. (Marx, K. 1976: 486)

Finally, while Marx does infer that the social division of labour 'can exist in the most diverse economic formations of society', he immediately adds that the technical division of labour 'is an entirely specific creation of the capitalist mode of production' (1976: 480, 455–7, 463–4, 480–1).

With the key claims Marx puts forward in his discussion of the technical and social divisions of labour now established, the critical responses it has invoked can now be introduced. For Andrew Sayer (1995), an advanced economy without a marked division of labour, and therefore alienation, is unfeasible. He stresses that the division of labour is not only 'remarkably complex', but also 'intrinsically intractable'. He suggests that radical political economy has not paid enough attention to the division of labour. This leads it to underestimate the intractability of all advanced economies. Within a division of labour individuals perform differentiated and often highly specialized tasks, a process that creates inter-dependency. Following Marx, Sayer also draws attention to the fundamental difference between, on the one hand, producing a given commodity through a technical division of labour, and, on the other hand, coordinating a social division of labour. The latter, Sayer contends, has features that have an 'irreducible material character' which will remain regardless of relations of ownership and modes of organization. The coordination of an advanced economy is a function of the material make-up of a complex division of labour. He states that 'the vast range of different production units in a social division of labour requires different forms of organisation', and that 'Marx fails to see the material divisions of the social division of labour as an obstacle to the socialisation of the means of production' (1995: 69). His point is that the development of the forces of production does not just incorporate increases in science and technology; it also engenders an increasingly differentiated division of labour. In which case, the opportunity to socialize control, contra Marx, decreases (Sayer, A. 1995: 43–4, 57–8, 68–70).

Sayer infers further that alienation would not decrease under democratic planning. Work does not simply increase in meaning just because it is determined through plans rather than market criteria. In advanced economies substituting market coordination with planning does not, he argues, ensure transparency in producer–consumer relations. It actually makes it worse because the plan needs to be centralized, it is forced upon both producers and consumers, vital feedback through prices is removed and producers are accountable to planners rather than consumers. Production is valorized through the plan, and not by the market behaviour of consumers:

> Alienation in Marx's sense is unavoidable in an advanced industrial society, whatever the social relations of production, since economic processes necessarily become ever more specialized…more routinized and rationalised, as a condition of the possibility of high levels of material development. (Sayer, A. 1995: 39)

So for Sayer, the critique of alienation no longer carries much force. He concludes that individuals cannot participate in all the decisions involving the numerous differentiated tasks through which commodities are produced. And, he asks, would they really want to? He states that he does not wish to consume items produced by exploited workers, or those that harm the natural environment. In these cases, he would like the opportunity to question concealing divisions of knowledge. But other than this, he has no desire to get involved about what should get produced. He reiterates that the effects of the division of labour – he cites uneven development and anarchic coordination – cannot be reduced to the social relations of production. His aim is not to dismiss radical political economy's explanations, but to correct an existing imbalance (Sayer, A. 1995: 78–9, 173–4).

Others offer a similar line of reasoning. David Prychitko (1991) calls for a postmodern analysis of Marx's work. By this he means an approach that recognizes the limits to Marxist-humanism. He too draws particular attention to the inherent difficulties in planning. There will, he insists, emerge in a comprehensively planned modern technological economy an organizational logic that points towards centralization, and away from democratic and participatory ideals. He identifies what he terms an 'essential tension' between Marx's humanistic vision of the ideal communist society, on the one hand, and the organizational realities of a rationally planned economy, on the other hand. Prychitko argues that Marx underwent an intellectual struggle. Marx visualizes a decentralized system of workers' cooperatives in order to eliminate economic and political alienation. However, with regards to the social division of labour, Prychitko infers that the eradication of both commodity production and a market device engenders centralization and hierarchical organization. His argument is that plans administered from a centralized bureau will negate democratic life in workers' cooperatives. Non-market socialism, however decentralized in theory, will in practice inevitably centralize and quickly evolve into statism. So for Prychitko, centralism, and by implication totalitarianism, is the price to pay for the abolishment of the market. Unsurprisingly, he concludes that a largely unhampered market, in which voluntary transactions are decentralized, is indispensable to a corresponding decentralized political system (Prychitko, D. 1991: xiii–xvi, 10, 33, 53).

So, Prychitko is adamant that all attempts to combine socialist planning with markets will, inexorability, run into grave difficulties. For example he charges Horvat, an advocate of planning who acknowledges the need for a market to secure the autonomy of producers and consumers, with inconsistency. Markets and planning will, Prychitko contends, pull in opposite directions. The market will be antagonistic to planning because market decisions are coordinated *ex post* (based upon the past; rather than *ex ante* – based upon anticipated change) through an array of price signals. Models of self-managed socialism like Horvat's (and NED) cannot sustain workplace autonomy because the means of production are socially owned, and they can only be coordinated through rational planning. This relates to what Prychitko terms the knowledge problem in self-managed socialism. Private production plans have effects that go beyond the context that the workplace can be expected to command. Market prices signify the various and often disparate plans of producers. An enterprise can integrate its production plan within a diversity of other producers' plans. Some plans will be in conflict, and after marketplace negations enterprises alter their personal plans. The outcome is an undersigned yet integrated pattern. Prychitko's point is that the market coordinates *ex post*:

> Horvat apparently fails to understand that the attempt to duplicate…the complexity of the market order through *ex ante* planning requires that the necessary knowledge that is distributed throughout millions of individual minds cannot be effectively concentrated in the offices of a planning bureau. (1991: 90)

In contrast to planning, spontaneous market prices serve to guide producers more efficiently. Producers in open competition, Prychitko concludes, are more likely to discover improvements in productive methods than a planning bureau (Prychitko, D. 1991: 85, 89–90).

In sum, Prychitko identifies a tension in Marxist thought between, on the one hand, an impetus towards decentralization that stems from Marx's insights into alienated labour and the exploitative nature of capitalist production, and, on the other hand, the inclination towards centralization that derives from his critique of the fetishism of commodities. Marx was very much in favour of abolishing commodity relations, he also believed socio-economic relations should, and could, be made transparent. But for Prychitko, due to the complexities of modern economies this in effect is to prescribe a command economy; such economies must, of necessity, sanction expert rule at the helm, and will inevitably be authoritarian. 'Neither Marx himself nor his contemporary followers could overcome the tension between comprehensive planning and self-management, centralisation and decentralisation' (Prychitko, D. 1991: 117).[4]

4. Nove and FitzRoy raise similar concerns. They both infer that the choice between decentralized-markets on the one hand, or bureaucratic-administrative allocation on the other hand, is inescapable (Nove, A. 1983: 46, 50, 56; FitzRoy, F. R. 1978: 26–7).

There is, then, a consensus of opinion among these critics that alienation is, to a large degree, unavoidable in any modern technological economy. They share the view that not only will all attempts to eradicate it through rational planning fail, the plans will inevitably centralize. These claims are reinforced by the actual experience of socialist centralized planning. The prediction that any attempt to implement creative labour universally will necessarily end in futility is informed by the historical record of centralized planning. On this point, Howard stresses that alienation exists, inevitably, in command socialism. Rather than alienation between the workers and the capitalists, it remains between the workers and the representatives of the state. A commercialization of interpersonal relations is, he justifiably infers, replaced by a dependence on connections (2000: 86–7). As such, the contentions covered in this section serve as a sober reminder of the intricate difficulties involved in theorizing a dealienated constitution. Nevertheless, in what follows I will show why these positions can be called into question. Alienated labour can, although not easily, be avoided.

Before we leave this section, I would like to highlight one particular response to Prychiko's work. Hillary Wainwright (1994) regards his argument, and by implication all of the above, as powerful. She offers, though, a different interpretation of transparency, one which revolves around *accessibility*. Crucially, transparency understood as the general availability of knowledge requires the eradication of inequalities in power and wealth. Knowledge may then be distributed evenly and used in common, rather than being usurped by private economic agents and used mainly to further self-interests. This recognizes economic knowledge to be both socially produced and transformable, which in turn allows it to be democratized and socialized. In this way, social objectives can be fulfilled through the course of economic coordination (1994: 183–4). Through extra-workplace democratic structures, self-management can exist in the firm without collapsing under the predatory dictates of the market or the commands of a centralized state:

> Organised democratic networks, supported by the state and the self-managed enterprises, can investigate the expressions of taste and demand indicated by market trends, can gather knowledge of social needs, and environmental costs, and share tacit skills in ways which turn relations of economics – including those of buying and selling – into transparent relations between people. (Wainwright, H. 1994: 183)

Wainwright's argument that knowledge must be made widely accessible has a direct relation with NED. For organized democratic networks read consumer and civil councils, for the state read the commune and for self-managed enterprises read guild cooperatives. Wainwright recognizes the need for political agencies to express and represent the economic knowledge gained through production. In NED this task falls to the guilds, in continuous dialogue with the consumer councils. It is within this basic structure that alienation will be eradicated. The remainder of this chapter will analyse this claim.

Realizing the Impossible: The Organizational Solution

The task of this section is to explain how NED implements yet simultaneously moderates Marx's pre-eminence of productive factors. My contention is that placing both organized producer and organized consumer interests on an equal footing in the absence of both capital and state sovereignty is the most suitable mechanism for cooperation, and forms a valid response to the claim outlined in the previous section that planning will, inexorably, intensify alienation. This discussion is centred on the democratic relations that determine and continuously revise the plan, and in a sense prefigures NED's *social* division of labour.

Marxist-humanism would organize work relations in order to realize human excellences. The particular way of life encouraged is a free and creative productive sphere, in which self-realization is achieved through cooperative labour. For Marxists, this ideal can be satisfied by socializing productive assets and eradicating wage-labour. Joyful creative labour is regarded as the fundamental end, the highest human want. It is evident that Marx regards the appropriate transformation of the productive sphere as humanity's prime objective. As explained above, his view is that people share an innate need to express their creative capacities freely in their place of work. In the appropriate circumstances labour becomes a fulfilling and rewarding experience. NED is sympathetic to the general spirit of Marx's early writing, while, simultaneously, softening the endorsement of the productive realm. It is true that Marx's creativity value is highly distinctive, the imperative to create is held above non-productive values. But an endorsement of the former does not need to go this far. A moderated usage of this premise constitutes a necessary revision to his theory.

In a just society all, or nearly all, citizens will be producers or will provide a service, and, equally, all will obviously be consumers. NED democratizes this relationship by providing structural spaces in which dialogue between the two demarcated interests is sanctioned. This is the fundamental criteria with which the scheme is formulated. Labour is fundamental, no society can exist without it; and in this respect, labour is unique. As such, the idea that production should be organized so that it becomes to the greatest possible extent a creative and uplifting experience for all citizens, with the communal appreciation of each other's products, holds, once it is placed on an even par with consumer interests, enormous intrinsic appeal. To overcome the problems of alienation and commodity fetishism, producers must be in a position to democratically control their working environments. Social relations must be prevented from falling into relations between commodities. For Marx this involves rational planning. NED's planning also aims to fundamentally transform the worker to worker and worker to nature relationships. Although commodity production will continue in the wants sector, the opportunities to engender creative labour are maximized. Citizens will meet each other in capacities other than merely exchangers of products in an impersonalized market. Democracy in the workplace and democracy over investment planning will help eradicate alienation and commodity fetishism as there will be direct relations both within organized groups of workers, and between workers and consumers. Here relations are not just through commodities, and producers will not be transformed into 'things' due to the dependence on capital. Recall the exposition in Chapter 2, in NED capital, understood as a self-expanding dynamic, does not exist. That said, NED does not prioritize the productive sphere. Part of the role of the consumer councils is to maintain an adequate standard of material consumption. Production is not the primary domain of fulfilment. Although no other set of values is ranked higher, consumption is, in terms of importance, situated alongside it. This is how NED softens its commitment to Marxist-humanism. Marx's argument that creative cooperative production is the key *single* characteristic to human excellence is not fully endorsed. Production is not elevated at the expense of non-productive values. But as work is clearly a part of life, and for most of us a central part, I do claim creative labour is an important, even necessary, component to a decent life.

Although the bodies that will engender the conditions which are able to sustain creative labour in NED's cooperatives are the guilds, it is important to re-stress that they will be in continual communication with the consumer councils. This is the mechanism for cooperation. It is essential to understand the significance of this structural arrangement in determining production. Cooperation is often looked upon favourably by socialists. Yet for Sayer, the division of labour is simply too complex and diverse to permit this. He argues that Marxism's elevation of the productive sphere gives it a bias view of cooperation. Instead of an even-handed cooperation between producers and consumers, cooperation between producers runs the risk of engendering a producer monopoly over consumers. Reducing inter-producer conflict increases the chances of producer–consumer conflict. All workers produce only a small range of commodities, or help produce just one, yet consume numerous different commodities. As such, producer–consumer interests are often liable to diverge (Sayer, A. 1995: 60). NED's democratic institutionalization of producer–consumer dialogue provides a response to Sayer's argument.

In NED it is highly unlikely that producers will be in a position to exert a monopoly over consumers; or for that matter the other way round. NED eliminates alienation not through an equal ownership of private productive property, but by socializing the instruments of production. Note, however, the specific way it does this. Producers are sovereign over the labour process, yet consumers are sovereign over the items produced. This constitutes an alternative interpretation of, and makes an important amendment to, Marx's theory. It was explained above that in Marx's thesis there are four main forms in which human beings are alienated from their most distinctive characteristics, their species life: 1), from *productive activity*, and therefore the essence of humanity 2), from the *product*, 3), from *fellow workers* and 4), from *themselves* – their species-being, what it means to be human. Marxist-humanism pictures a society of cooperative production in which productive assets are socialized, and workers freely produce to meet each other's needs. Insofar as it establishes a system of productive democracies whereby workers will be able to control the dynamics that give rise to the above four forms, alienated labour will no longer endure. In terms of the power it grants to labour, NED does not go this far. Although workers will take control over the work environment, they do not determine the items and commodities produced; this task falls to the consumer councils. Workers of course can contribute in this respect, but it is not through the organizations of the workplace; rather, it is in their capacities as consumers, first by virtue of the consumer councils and secondly through their purchasing power in relation to the guild regulated markets. Under these conditions it is difficult to see how, contra Sayer, producers could command a monopoly over consumers. The recognition that both productive and consumptive interests are equally valid implies that neither sphere should take precedence in constitutional design. This, it seems to me, is the correct starting point.

As we saw in the previous section, Sayer and Prychitko both insist that planning will not transcend alienated labour as the plan will need to be centralized. But if the plan is determined through continuous dialogue between organized producers and organized consumers, rather than being forced upon both, ensuring that producers are directly accountable to consumers, rather than state planners, then producer–consumer relations can, as far as possible, be transparent. So in contrast to centrally planned economies, production in NED can be valorized chiefly through the non-market (and only then in a secondary sense the market) behaviour of consumers. The task is to devise a democratic approach to planning which minimizes to the greatest possible extent economic and political opacity, hierarchy and bureaucracy; while simultaneously institutionalizing the accessibility, democratization and socialization of economic knowledge that Wainwright calls for. NED, I contend, does precisely that.

Part Two: Creative Labour in New Economic Democracy

> *Within the co-operative society based on common ownership of the means of production, the producers do not exchange their products; just as little does the labour employed on the products appear here as the value of these products, as a material quality possessed by them, since now, in contrast to capitalist society, individual labour no longer exists in an indirect fashion but directly as a component part of the total labour.*
>
> *(Marx, K. 1977: 567–8)*

For Marx, the elimination of alienated labour requires – along with an increase in productivity so that material scarcity can be overcome, otherwise people will continue to struggle for access to scarce resources – the abolishment of the technical division of labour, the capitalist market system and the private ownership of the means of production. As we have seen, his solution is to socialize the means of production. But for Gouldner (1980), how exactly this would transcend the alienation that is based within the division of labour is unclear. He claims that Marx's view of the division of labour is ambivalent. 'If, on the one side, specialization dehumanizes men, on the other, the increased productivity which it produces was also believed necessary for eliminating want and thus class domination' (1980: 185, 185–7). NED overcomes this contradiction. There are very good reasons for assuming the guild cooperatives will be highly efficient in their productivity, this was explained in Part One of Chapter Two. This section will show how NED humanizes work to the greatest possible extent; in the process it will become clear how the above three criteria are met. Gouldner is right, however, that Marx's discussions on the negation of alienation are incomplete.

Marx's writings on the cooperative nature of communism are brief and scattered. Quotes like the one above though clearly indicate that although he did not (deliberately) address the question at length; he nevertheless believed that a communal ownership of productive assets would put an end to the domination of exchange-relations. For an example of common ownership, or 'directly associated labour' as Marx sometimes calls it, he cites medieval Europe. As in all other previous historical epochs, the social relations of production were characterized by personal dependence, and hence domination. Yet here both labour and its products need not display a 'fantastic form different from their reality'. The immediate social form of labour is its particularity, not the universality of commodity production. He observes that 'the social relations between individuals in the performance of their labour appear at all events as their own personal relations, and are not disguised as social relations between the products of labour' (1977: 440). The corn and cloth produced by rural peasant families confront them as products of their collective labour, not as commodities. Rather than objectify the social characteristics of labour, as in the world of commodity production, their labour contains its social character (1977: 440). This, though, sheds little light on how the products of labour can assume a form consistent with their essence in advanced modern economies. That is, how the social characteristics of labour in mass societies may appear objectively in the goods it produces without being distorted and mystified by passing through the medium of exchange-relations. The challenge is to visualize individual labour existing 'directly as a component part of the total labour', and within this to show how, as the previous section makes clear, to overcome alienation within a complex division of labour. Marx frames the question brilliantly, but to find a solution we must move beyond his work.

This section argues that creative labour can be sustained within the guild cooperatives. In the interests of analytical convenience, I adopt the social/technical distinction of the division of labour covered in the first part of this chapter. First, in regards to the *social* division of labour, the immediate question of what is the most optimal role for markets is addressed. Attention then turns to the structures within the guilds. In the sense that they are internal to each guild, they fall under the heading of the technical division of labour, but as they are still external to the guild cooperatives they are, from the perspective of the members of the latter, also subject to social process. For convenience sake, I will refer to these wider guild structures as an *intermediate* division of labour. I argue that they are sufficiently vigorous to maintain the conditions for creative labour to thrive. Finally, the internal arrangements of the guild cooperatives themselves, the *technical* division of labour, are theorized in order to show how they may also sustain creative labour. There are, accordingly, three headings in this section, each one concentrating on one of the divisions of labour.

The Social Division of Labour

This section addresses the role of a market in NED, or more specifically the means through which it is best monitored. A survey of the literature reveals that for most authors a market of some description is unavoidable in any modern economy:

> The most elementary lesson of socialist economics tells us that the idea of millions of 'associated producers' collectively controlling an advanced economy *ex ante*, without recourse to *ex post* regulation through markets and without needing prices to assess allocational efficiency and relative scarcity is a quaint pipe dream. (Sayer, A. 1995: 58)

It will be recalled from the second section in Part One of this chapter that Prychitko also asserts this position forcefully. Horvat, too, recognizes the need for a market; in terms of alienation though he reaches an entirely different conclusion. 'If commodity labour is eliminated, other commodities may remain and the market may be used as an allocational device without at the same time being an institution that causes alienation' (1982: 90). So for Horvat, the solution to alienated labour may be found within an appropriately organized market economy. It is my argument that NED's functionally demarcated markets constitute such an economy. In NED, the organizational distributional formula is not wage-labour; labour is not treated as a commodity. Command is not the natural right of the capitalist class. Democratic control not only involves participation in management, it also demands the deconstruction of capital. Only when the market is monitored by the institutions within a re-politicized civil society, rather than the modern state, can it live up to Horvat's expectation. This statement will now be defended by engaging with the work of the market socialist Michael W. Howard (2000).

The argument has been made, typically by market socialists, that it is the market in capitalism, and not the market *per se* that is responsible for problems like commodity fetishism and alienation. In discussing these matters Howard acknowledges that if a socialist society has a substantial role for commodity production it is confronted by an immediate difficulty:

> a society of worker-owned cooperatives, exchanging their products in a market, could still be an alienated society. The workers might still be egoistic, mainly concerned with profit and consumption, alienated from other cooperatives and from the general interest, relating to each other indirectly through a direct relationship to things, commodities exchanging for prices in the market. (Howard, M. W. 2000: 77)

The correlation between alienated labour and the phenomena of commodity fetishism is immediately apparent. So how can producers control their products and relate to one another directly? For Marx, rational planning is the answer to alienation and commodity fetishism. Yet Howard believes market socialism can go a long way towards approximating a solution. He distinguishes structural fetishism from psychological fetishism. The former refers to the way economic relations are organized so that no one person, or group, assumes responsibility for exchange-values; they are determined by the market laws of supply and demand. The latter is the 'egoistic disposition' that fails to recognize the unintended consequences of economic agents, and not to see beyond exchange-values. It is the mystification that is generated by the production of commodities that Howard calls psychological fetishism (Howard, M. W. 2000: 77–9, 85).

Marx held that structural commodity fetishism cannot be separated from commodity production. In their market transactions, people behave as 'utility maximizes'. In addition, if profits are believed to be of greater substance than people, if workers do not envisage alternatives to wage-labour, if consumers seek the cheapest prices irrespective of market externalities and if this kind of reasoning (or lack of) determines their behaviour then their consciousness is driven by market considerations. This is what is meant by psychological fetishism. Howard points out that it was Marx's belief that structural fetishism inevitably gives rise to psychological fetishism, a belief he calls into question. For Howard, structural and psychological fetishism are not inseparable. 'To subjectively raise oneself above the social relations that shape one is to overcome commodity fetishism in the psychological sense' (2000: 83). Commodity producers may then grasp the true nature of commodity fetishism and, accordingly, seek appropriate remedies. He cites welfare benefits and rights (including democratic) within the workplace; socially yet unprofitable labour can also be subsidized by progressive taxation. These restrictions on the market will, he hopes, be acknowledged by everyone as desirable:

> They [producers] are no longer 'ruled by their products' but have agreed to let their products rule them within a limited domain... They have agreed not to agree beforehand on a central plan about such things as prices of products or labour or types of goods to be produced. Thus, the discipline of the market is a self-imposed one. (Howard, M. W. 2000: 80)

Producers are still profit motivated, but they are aware that this is not the only rule of the market game. Production for profit is retained because it ensures a high productivity of labour, it allocates resources efficiently and it endorses the claim that the consumer is sovereign (Howard, M. W. 2000: 80, 83, 85).

Howard suggests a market socialist society may compensate for structural commodity fetishism by democratizing both the workplace and the investment plan. This can also engender an ethic of justice capable of neutralizing the tendency towards psychological commodity fetishism. 'My hypothesis is that the widespread overcoming of psychological commodity fetishism... depends upon substantial opportunities for meaningful democratic participation' (2000: 82). For Howard self-management can minimize structural fetishism and negate psychological fetishism. Structural and psychological commodity fetishism can be divided; the latter may then be eradicated via mediating institutions like the state. So Howard's position is that commodity production need not entail commodity fetishism, and by implication alienation. He does not deny that commodity production generates a tendency to fetish. But in the domain between capitalism and post-capitalism, alienation may be abated, even if it cannot be abolished completely. A market economy constituted through workers' cooperatives, with the socialization of productive assets and democratically planned investment, provides workers with the opportunity to control their products directly. Although the market does exert certain constraints on workplace humanization, alienated labour can be overcome (Howard, M. W. 2000: 81–2, 85, 87).

This argument has real strengths. I too believe that 'the widespread overcoming of psychological commodity fetishism... depends upon substantial opportunities for meaningful democratic participation'. As I will now show, however, it prefigures NED, not market socialism. Although NED does have a subordinated role for markets, they are functionally demarcated. This represents the most significant distinction between Howard's market socialism and NED. In the former, it is the state that enforces restrictions upon the market, and through their citizenship producers meet each other in an extra-market capacity. Howard argues that the state ceases to be an instrument of class domination if inequalities are tightly regulated and limited, and if restrictions (like democratic elections) are imposed upon those who control productive assets. In Howard's market socialism, then, it is through the state that commodity producers overcome commodity fetishism. Under these circumstances commodity production remains but, Howard contends, psychological commodity fetishism will no longer exist. Workplaces exert a relative autonomy and consumers enjoy freedom of choice. But it is a freedom that everyone recognizes as subordinate to the limitations laid down by the state (Howard, M. W. 2000: 80–1).

In NED's mode of production, the guild-regulated markets that supply consumers with their 'want' items are subordinated to the 'needs' sector which is determined through democratic planning via the guilds and two consumer councils. In the latter, consumers themselves decide what their needs are and the goods required to satisfy them. The consumer councils are the forum through which this occurs. As such, in this sphere producers do not, in their capacity as producers, determine what gets produced. Of equal significance, profit interest is, as Chapter Two Parts Two and Three explained, not the sole motivational criteria. It is in this sense that producers are not 'ruled by their products'. Only when producers act in response to organized demand which has been established by open market research and through non-discriminatory channels of consultation, rather than simply respond to the blind dictates of the 'free market', are they overcoming structural, and so psychological fetishism. It is within this system of democratic planning that a (functionally demarcated) profit motivated market economy can assume its place and fulfil the functions Howard ascribes to it: high productivity, efficient allocation of resources and consumer sovereignty.

To 'subjectively raise oneself above the social relations that shape one' in order to transcend psychological commodity fetishism does, as Howard suggests, require both democratic rights within the workplace and a collective democratic control over investment planning. But if producers agree 'to let their products rule them within a limited domain', as they do in NED's wants sector, then the guild to which they belong is a far more suitable regulating authority than the modern state. Howard is probably right that in a genuine egalitarian economy, the state may lose its function as an instrument of class domination. But the state is too distant as a decision-making body, certainly too removed from the workplace, its bureaucracy is too formidable, and it cannot possibly prevent the entrenchment of oligarchic structures. It also adheres to an undifferentiated ethic of representation; and hence its claim to be a democratic institution is highly suspect. It is worth reiterating this key difference between Howard's market socialism and NED as it captures the latter's stateless administration of society. In the former, it is through state-imposed restraints upon the market behaviour of economic agents that commodity fetishism is transcended; that is, the autonomy of workplaces and the freedom of consumers exist within the parameters established by the state. In NED, the task of regulating the market is realized through the democratic institutions of a re-politicized civil society – the guilds and consumer councils, organizations that citizens are more intimately involved with. As this chapter is making clear, it is NED that offers the best hope of embodying creative labour.

The Intermediate Division of Labour

Gorz (1988) offers a theoretically sophisticated discussion of alienation. He captures neatly the immediate problems that are likely to be encountered if creative labour is to be successfully installed. Engaging with Gorz (in this and the next section) provides a sound framework of analysis in which to show how creative labour in NED can be upheld. In this section I will consider two interrelating issues raised in his work, the restricting power of capital and the arena best suited for the determination of societal goals.

To understand Gorz's discussion on the requirements for labour to assume a non-alienating character, it is first necessary to highlight what he means by 'heteronomy'. The sphere of heteronomy is the combined total of distinctive activities which are undertaken by individuals, yet are coordinated externally by an established organization. The manner in which tasks are determined ensures that individuals operate like cogs in a large machine. Specialized tasks are accomplished in isolation. This ensures that workers in capitalist societies cannot coordinate their own activities through procedures of self-management. Gorz recognizes that the key conditions for superseding alienated labour were, for example, partly met in the Metall trade union at the Uddevalla Volvo factory, but he adds that a key 'insurmountable barrier' remained, only the representatives of capital defined the goods that were to be produced. Although the quality of product involved the workers, this was premised upon decisions that were taken one-step removed from the workers, who were consequently unable to question. Gorz's point is that the goal was imposed, the 'optimum valorization of capital'. He warns that autonomy in work will be incomplete if it is not extended into the cultural and political spheres. The crucial task, therefore, is to create the cultural and political mediations which can challenge productive methods and outcomes. Production must be organized so that autonomy is realized both inside and outside the workplace (Gorz, A. 1988: 32, 40, 78).

Moving on to the second issue, where to locate political decision-making, Gorz believes it cannot occur within the workplace. He argues that the work of maintenance workers cannot be likened to those who perform a trade in the 'full sense'. A 'fully rounded' trade permits control over the entire product:

> Thus skilled workers, manufacturing clothes they have designed themselves on programmable textile machines they have tinkered with... are practising a fully rounder trade... The same skilled workers, maintaining and programming a battery of such machines in a textile factory, are not practising a fully rounded trade... they have no control over the product and none, therefore, over the use to which the machine is put. (Gorz, A. 1988: 80–1)

Although the tasks of the latter can involve the same technical skills, they still have an alienated character. The fully rounded trade of craft-workers, who are in control of both their productive assets and the goods produced, can appreciate their technical culture as well as the 'culture of everyday life' as Gorz calls it. The skills of the maintenance worker are restricted to the former. Computer-based systems operators, as an example of the latter, are employed in discontinuous labour, interchanging periods of activity and inactivity. Gorz claims these workers cannot assert a political responsibility at their place of work. This can only happen if the function and societal consequences of their production can be divulged to workers through their internal work processes. At present, all the facets of production procedures are not transparent to everyone involved. So for Gorz, the effects of production methods and the determination of societal goals are political tasks. Such tasks, he proposes, fall to trade unions because the information they have access to provide them with a richer knowledge of social processes. This is to be used publicly to debate various technical issues and question production goals. Crucially, these social matters cannot occur within the work context. Technical and political responsibility, he contends, cannot coincide; this indicates a gulf between the culture of occupation and the culture of daily life. Technicians cannot be citizens in their workplace. The argument here is that political responsibility involves a detachment from work. A capacity for political questioning presupposes a culture in which activities transcend solely occupational roles; it denotes a life not utterly immersed in work. The need is for a framework in which workers 'can publicly debate, in their capacity as citizens, the societal repercussions of decisions it will be their function to implement' (Gorz, A. 1988: 83, 80–4).

The members of the guild cooperatives, as I will show here and in the next section, will be craft-workers in the fully rounded sense, and will therefore possess knowledge of the culture of everyday life. But following Gorz's logic, it is the structures of the guild (external to the cooperatives yet internal to the guild) that can reveal the social consequences of their productive methods. This is in a big part due to the role of consumer councils in determining and overseeing the goods that the guild cooperatives produce. Gorz insists political decisions about societal goals are a matter for trade unions. In my opinion they are a matter for guilds, in constant dialogue with the consumer councils. In NED, each guild has internal committees who are responsible for regulating the supply side of their demarcated markets. Overseeing the parameters within which a competitive ethic is legitimized is a central aspect of this. The committees' task is to ensure that no single cooperative can gain an advantage by returning to a (possibly) more cost-effective production method which neglects creative labour. There are good grounds for assuming that the cooperative material context in which creative labour can be upheld is, all things considered, no less efficient than the private property regimes which give rise to alienated labour. Indeed, the argument that cooperative workplaces are inefficient is seriously challenged in both the theoretical and the empirical literature. This point was emphasized strongly towards the end of Part One of Chapter 2. It is, nevertheless, conceivable that rigid automated labour can also produce high output. As a corrective, the guild committees will protect an equal footing by elevating creative labour as the standard competing cooperatives must inspire too.

There are other important functions that fall to the guild committees. Although a surplus is created, and the guild cooperatives can reinvest in their existing enterprises, they may only expand into other projects – within their functionally demarcated domain – by appealing for a grant. The democratic investment planning committee at the local level within each guild will look favourably on the cooperatives that prioritize appropriate productive techniques. As Chapter 2 made clear, the opportunity for the two consumer councils to oversee investment decisions at all levels applies unconditionally. Along with low pollution technology and high employment prospects as their criterion for awarding funds, the guild grant administrators will also give preference to the value of creative labour. Cooperatives who wish to expand into new ventures will be required to have put into effect creative labour. Successful cooperatives will be those who have a congruous track record. Items produced through conditions detrimental to meaningful work will not make it onto the market. This is by no means all; the same reasoning applies with the financial assistance offered to poorly performing cooperatives. Here NED can adopt procedures designed by the Mondragon planners. The funding of Mondragon's cooperatives proceeds through a series of stages. Firms can be rejected for a failure to implement cooperative values, the production of unsuitable goods or an inability to carry-through their business plan effectively. In NED, the guild banks will add to this list the cooperatives who fail to prioritize creative labour. Morrison stresses that Mondragon's filtering process is key to why incompetent cooperatives are so impressively rare (1997: 118). There is no reason why this cannot apply to NED. Not only will careless risks be avoided, creative labour will be institutionalized universally. In these senses, creative labour is enshrined in the constitution of NED.

It can be appreciated that heteronomy will be minimized to the greatest possible extent as tasks are not carried out in isolation. Gorz, though, offers a word of warning. He acknowledges that autonomous work groups who produce creatively, which will involve taking responsibility for organizing their work and for the control of product quality, reduce the degree of heteronomy significantly. But, he adds, they do not eliminate it. Although the individuals who make up the group enjoy the autonomy to execute complex tasks, the tasks themselves are predetermined, and along with the tasks of other groups are coordinated externally. The main difference is that it is not individuals but groups who function as cogs. The work undertakes a specialized task that acts within the material system in which it is embedded. As such, limiting autonomy to a group's internal labour relations cannot equate with full sovereignty (1988: 78–9). In response to this, all I can say is that the tasks must be predetermined as openly as possible, and the agencies responsible for planning must themselves be inclusive and democratic. A material system constituted through workers' cooperatives must also be doing everything it can to uphold and universalize creative labour. If these conditions hold, as I believe they do in NED, then the problem posed by heteronomy will be reduced significantly.

Indeed, Gorz stresses that in a complex society, autonomy cannot replace heteronomy completely. But if work tasks are re-skilled and restructured through workers' self-management, the degree of autonomy within the sphere of heteronomy can be enlarged. So, autonomous activities have repercussions on the structures of heteronomy, even if they cannot subsume them thoroughly (1988: 93). NED is a society of workers' self-management, this claim is substantiated in Chapters 5 and 6, and it is shown immediately below how work will be re-skilled in NED's guild cooperatives. Of equal significance, the insurmountable barrier of the dominance of capital does not apply in NED. As will now be clear, capital understood as the self-expanding tendency of value has no place in NED's economy; neither is there any role for the capitalist class. This point cannot be overemphasized. The cultural and political mediations that help determine production will be realized through the consumer and civic councils. These coordinating bodies, which are not external in the same sense that capital and the state are, will not be compelled to impose the 'optimum valorization of capital'. In this way, autonomy can be maximized both within and beyond the workplace.

The Technical Division of Labour

I now wish to consider the structural arrangements that may enable the guild cooperatives to preserve creative labour, the technical division of labour. Hitherto, the analysis in this chapter has been largely at the theoretical level. This is because there has never been a society that resembles NED. There are, however, significant similarities with the Mondragon complex. As such, the design of NED's guild cooperatives has been informed markedly by the Mondragon cooperatives. The argument that follows is therefore reinforced by considering the empirical inquiries into real existing workers' cooperatives. Along with Mondragon, the literature on the plywood cooperatives is consulted. I start by summarizing the findings from this empirical literature. This will serve to inform the discussion that follows.

One significant empirical enquiry into alienation in the plywood cooperatives was conducted by Greenberg (1986).[5] He found that dealienation

5. Greenberg's research places much emphasis on the subjective experience of workers. While this is perhaps largely unavoidable in inquiries of this kind, it is not, strictly speaking, where Marx locates the phenomena of alienation. Nevertheless, Greenberg's work still constitutes the best empirical evidence available.

is realized only incompletely. He concentrated on the four aspects of alienation explained in section one of this chapter: from *productive activity* (understood in terms of productive decision-making and the work itself), from the *product*, from *fellow workers* and from *oneself.* Starting with the product, he discovered that workers decide not only what to produce, but also how to produce it. As they freely decide whether to produce things like construction graded plywood or more specialized marine plywood, or the quantities of exterior and interior panelling, workers are not separated from their products. They understand the products and how they are produced, they are aware of where they go once they leave the workplace and they know the ways they are used by consumers. There is, therefore, a qualitative difference from the constraints experienced by workers in the capitalist enterprise (Greenberg, E. S. 1986: 74–5). In NED workers control over the product is qualified; all productive property is considered social, although it is in the temporary care of the guilds. The guild cooperatives are not entirely at liberty to produce whatever takes their fancy.[6] They will operate within certain constraints. They must respond first to the consumer councils and secondly to guild regulated market signals. But even if the initial choice of product is not entirely in their hands, once the quantity and quality of a given product has been democratically decided, as they know their products and for what purposes they will be used, there is still a sufficient control to ensure this aspect of alienation typical of wage-labour will be negated.

The next aspect of alienation Greenberg considered was from productive activity (or the process of production as he refers to it), captured first in terms of worker participation in productive decision-making. He found that 90% attend the general meetings and that they were often vocal during the proceedings. He also found that they discussed the board's decisions with each other frequently, and that this increased over time. So in respects of dealienation from the product and productive decision-making, Greenberg's inquiry adds empirical substance to the argument that alienation is not inevitable in modern industry. But in terms of alienation from the work itself, the expectation in the theoretical literature is not supported:

> The production process in cooperative and conventional mills is indistinguishable; it is universally noisy, dirty, dangerous, monotonous,

6. This, though, applies to producers in all modern economies. The social relations of production can be private, state-centred or socially orientated (cooperative, as in NED), but in all cases producers respond to external information. See Wyatt (2008: 114).

> and relentless. Production workers in both types of firms are appendages of the machine process. Workplace democracy in the co-ops has not made a dent in this reality. (Greenberg, E. S. 1986: 81)

The work in the plywood cooperatives did not even remotely develop the creativity and autonomy Marx held to be the principle capacities of our species essence. Skill content was scant, most jobs being easily mastered in a couple of days. Workers did little more than form links on the automated process. As such, they seemed to be resigned to the technological imperatives that render creative labour unlikely. The results were also disappointing in regards to alienation from others. Dealienation involves transcending a competitive consciousness in which others are seen as a means to personal ends. In the plywood cooperatives a sense of community remains elusive. Cooperative members did not socialize beyond the workplace anymore than conventional workers, and they behaved as social isolates while in the workplace. Solidarity was not enhanced by self-management in the plywood cooperatives. Finally, Greenberg addressed self-alienation by considering the subjective psychological orientations towards job satisfaction, conceived broadly as an affective attitude with regards to their work. He found that there was a relation between decisional participation and work satisfaction. But as the difference between cooperative and conventional workers was not as large as might be expected, he concludes that decisional participation does not counterbalance the dull repetitive nature of plywood production (Greenberg, E. S. 1986: 76–8, 81–4, 88–9, 91–3, 96).

So, dealienation in the plywood cooperatives is partly met. As workers control their products and the productive decisional process, the causal relation between workplace democracy and dealienation *is* established. But as alienation from others and the work itself remains, it is *not* established in terms of the technical division of labour and the relationships between associates. It seems that the linkage between workplace democracy and dealienation can only be seen as tenuous. The cooperatives are, though, in the US plywood industry, a nation not known for its sympathy towards workplace democracy. Greenberg therefore completes his analysis by considering friendlier environments and comparing his findings.

Disposition of the surplus is part of alienation from the product. In the Mondragon system this, with some qualifications, is largely in the hands of cooperative members. But with regards to alienation from the process, understood again first in terms of decision-making, Greenberg found that the Mondragon cooperatives operate as conventional enterprises do with managers giving orders. This is reflected at general meetings in which the agenda is largely under management control. He infers that as participation is so minimal there are only annual 'plebiscite-style elections'. Few members speak at general meetings, and few have regular contact with management.[7] Turning to the second aspect of alienation from the process, the work itself, Greenberg stresses that work in the Mondragon cooperatives was the same as it was in the plywood cooperatives, dull and boring. At the level of the work group, far from controlling technical production, workers remain objects in the process of production, in much the same way workers with no ownership rights are. There is an extensive division of labour, and a highly routine assembly-line. But with regards to alienation from others, Greenberg highlights that unlike the plywood cooperatives, the Mondragon workers appreciate and take pride in their community.[8] Finally, in terms of job satisfaction, self-alienation at Mondragon has been reported to be less than is typical of conventional enterprises (Greenberg, E. S. 1986: 103–4, 107–11).

In conclusion, the question whether workplace democracy engenders a dealienation from the four key aspects of alienation: product and control over the surplus, from the productive process (captured in terms of decisional participation and the work itself), from others and from self, the answer is not straightforward. To repeat, the plywood and Mondragon cooperatives have not diminished alienation in every respect. On the one hand, they have not – at the time of Greenberg's study – changed significantly the forms of alienation that relate to the work itself, the technical division of labour and hierarchy and specialization. As the technical process of production is just as important as participation in decision-making in harbouring job satisfaction, this is a serious drawback. On the other hand, the plywood cooperatives have made significant inroads into the decision-making process, and the Mondragon cooperatives have decreased alienation from others. Moreover, both have partly negated self-alienation

7. Although as we shall see, this was to change significantly as the role of the Social Councils became more extensive.

8. Morrison also states that life in the Mondragon complex is gregarious. 'After work, it is usual for people to socialise in bars and clubs…there is strong community feeling: an assembly worker will sit and chat with the general manager' (1997: 70). Further, Bradley and Gelb found that the lack of a significant gulf between work-teams and management is paralleled by an absence of any large social divide beyond the workplace. 'Only 18% of cooperateurs perceived a substantial social divide; 45% saw no division at all' (1981: 28).

and, crucially, they have both accelerated appreciably the dealienation process in terms of controlling product and profit. All the cooperatives Greenberg directly or indirectly studied achieved, 'without exception', real advances in these regards. Seen in this light, cooperative workers have put a considerable distant between themselves and the alienated conditions typical of wage-labourers. So although workplace democracy is, as it stands, a 'limited instrument of dealienation', it is far from ineffectual (Greenberg, E. S. 1986: 113–14).

The indications that dealienation can manifest in NED are then, up to a point, promising. But it is clear from the empirical studies that the aspect of alienation that is most in need of theoretical review is the nature of the work itself. It is this issue that is now addressed. I will first illustrate what dealienation in the workplace requires. I then summarize how the Mondragon cooperatives have responded to this kind of challenge. Finally, the discussion is completed by clarifying how alienation in the technical division of labour can be negated in NED's guild cooperatives.

Gorz suggests that work can be an autonomous endeavour, devoid of alienation, only if certain conditions are met. He stresses it must be organized by the workers themselves, and that they see the product as the outcome of their collective activity. It will be clear from the previous section how NED accomplishes these tasks. The other key condition Gorz highlights is the one I now wish to concentrate on: the mode of work must develop skills and faculties, and it must ensure work is to the greatest possible extent an interesting and fulfilling experience for all workers (1988: 32, 40). For labour to be less tedious and repetitive, work needs to be enriched. Isolated subordinates working under autocratic management should be superseded by cooperatives run by participative management. On the production line, fragments need to be reintegrated. Assembly lines should be reassembled into separate teams who would complete the entire task. Clerks can take responsibility for whole accounts, and not just single parts on each one; piecework must be replaced with teamwork, and hourly wage with weekly salaries. As Horvat explains, in this way workers, whether blue or white collar, can take control of product assembly. The idea is that equal amenities for office and workbench workers will eliminate status differences (1982: 89–90, 433–6). So, given that an uncompromising division of labour restricts greatly the opportunity for job inter-changeability, how exactly can fragments be reintegrated to ensure work is enriched by becoming less tedious?

An empirical example Gorz highlights is the Metall trade union at the Uddevalla Volvo factory. One of their demands is of particular significance.

'Work cycles' had to be at least 20 minutes long...which meant that each worker was responsible for a varied and complex set of operations on each vehicle. Work was thereby to become much less repetitive and monotonous' (1999: 32–3). Further, the indirect labour commonly associated with foremen was to become part of the workers remit, a remit that included preparing parts, quality control, final adjustments, apprenticeship training, etc. The idea was to enable workers to reflect upon their work. Each group of workers had to master a certain range of operations. This meant that each worker was interchangeable and the group could function if some members were absent (Gorz, A. 1999: 32–3).

Along similar lines, at the theoretical level Albert and Hahnel (1991) put forward the idea of what they term 'balanced job complexes'. They argue that the opportunity to develop skills in decision-making must be egalitarian. When work is mundane and repetitive self-esteem is depressed, when work is stimulating and appealing self-esteem is enhanced. Creative labour is, therefore, a prerequisite to the survival of workplace democracies.[9] Accordingly, Albert and Hahnel propose the structural device of balanced job complexes. As its name suggests, this procedure refers to a workplace democracy in which every member enjoys a job complex constituted through 'comparably fulfilling responsibilities'. Work duties are thoughtfully combined so that diverse job complexes are equally empowering. Although this does not imply everyone does everything:

> [i]t does mean, however, that the half dozen or so tasks that I regularly do must be roughly as empowering as the different half dozen or so tasks that you regularly do if we are to participate as equals in council decision making. (Albert, M. & Hahnel, R. 1991: 19)

Rather than organize work tasks into the same levels as wage-labour does (the organization of jobs with similar qualitative features into homogenous groups), the suggestion is that tasks may be combined into job complexes which contain an equal mixture of responsibilities. So instead of office workers operating the phone-system and typing standard letters, some would mix the former with a more stimulating task, while others would do the same with the latter. One person's work complex may include both extremes of exciting and tedious tasks, while others may be more uniform. But in all cases it would not be possible for a worker's job complex to include

9. This point is taken up again in Chapters 5 and 6, where it is analysed in more detail.

only one end of the continuum – aesthetic, repetitive, responsible, subordinate, etc. The idea is that through comparable circumstances everyone's work has the same qualitative impact; this secures an equitable influence in decision-making processes (Albert, M. & Hahnel, R. 1991: 19–21).

This, along with the more familiar proposals of role rotation and task sharing, together with the Uddevalla Volvo-style work cycles, appears to me to be a sound suggestion. Consider the robotized factories in which workers only manufacture semi-finished products. Autonomous skilled work groups are, typically, only responsible for singular sections of the production line. For Gorz, this is a far cry from non-alienated work. The only contact skilled workers have is with the machines that transform actual materials, not the materials themselves. They do not specialize in making products, they specialize in operating machines. Even then, they only make sure the robots function correctly and the machines obey their programmes. Gorz's point is that here workers are not performing fulfilling labour as their work is uninteresting and uniformed (1988: 78–80). It is productive relations such as these that balanced job complexes can change positively. If the operation of robots constitutes a mundane task, this will be considered in the design of job complexes. It will not be the case that only one team of workers will carry out this or similar assignments. It will, along with the other boring and repetitive tasks, be regulated along egalitarian lines. This is a consummate way of institutionalizing dealienation. As Gorz rightly insists, a general social knowledge is a prerequisite for self-management in production. Workers must understand the manufacturing process as an intelligible whole in order to command its workings. They must reflect upon how to improve product design, how to engage in discussion and how to express and question themselves. The worker must be a multi-skilled individual – designer, fabricator, manager, etc.; and workers in collective bodies must take control of their communal endeavours. Along with working on production directly, intellectual skills like consultation, communication and the pooling of knowledge need to be enhanced (1999: 30–1).

There is empirical evidence which indicates that this kind of positive response to technological imperatives is not in any sense unrealistic. Modern technologies like the computer-integrated-manufacturing (CIM) systems require small teams of skilled workers. Capital investment in this technology can result in job losses as it allows a smaller workforce to increase production at a lower cost. As Mondragon has adopted the CIM systems, they are confronted with the job eradicating and deskilling aspects of automation. The cooperative members are, however, involved at every level of production. The new technologies are used not to deskill, but to develop the workers' abilities:

> At Mondragon...the operators of numerically controlled machine tools are trained to program them. Persons who study machining...first learn the classic manual techniques, then are introduced to the use of the numerically controlled machines...Workers are retrained, not de-skilled. (Morrison, R. 1997: 215)

It is clear that new technologies are only developed if they are consistent with cooperative values (Morrison, R. 1997: 214–17). Even here, balanced job complexes can still serve to ensure the more unpleasant tasks are rotated on an egalitarian bases. So, balanced job complexes can only help in all regards. They will be sanctioned in NED's guild cooperatives and, further, upheld by the guild committees in the way suggested above in the discussion on the intermediate division of labour.

The next task is to show how this will be achieved. Recall briefly the exposition in Chapter 2 of a typical guild cooperative. The sovereign body is the general assembly that elects the Control Board. For their part the Control Board appoint management who oversee the accounts/finance, production, marketing and personnel departments. There are three other important internal bodies. First there is the Management Council, which is responsible to the Management and Control Boards. Secondly the Social Council, which is elected by all members via their work sections, monitors the Management and Control Boards. Thirdly, the Watchdog Council provides the ultimate security for the smooth running of the cooperative. Its purpose is to control the general behaviour of management and the Control Board; it also ensures the Management and Social Councils are operating sufficiently. Whyte and Whyte (1991) offer a useful point of clarity. The primary interest of the governing councils is to represent members in their capacities as *co-owners*, while the Social Councils are chiefly concerned to represent them as *workers*. This dual structure has real strengths. As members, cooperators have interests in the long-term survival of their cooperatives. As workers, their concerns are based around income and attractive working conditions. The required balance is achieved by having two official bodies (1991: 230). In keeping with Mondragon's initiative, it will be the responsibility of the Social Councils in NED's guild cooperatives to organize balanced job complexes.

In the Mondragon complex, the role of the Social Council is to integrate the interests of workers into management decision-making. But in 1975 an internal review reported that it only passively transmits information, it merely rubber-stamps management decisions, and highlights effects while neglecting causes. Participation of workers in the Mondragon complex was restricted to governance. In addition, the Social Councils were not involved in the design of new work forms to any great extent. An uncertainty about their position prevented them from taking a leading role in the reconstruction of work. This amounted to a contradiction between, on the one hand, democratic self-governance and, on the other hand, a Taylorist authoritarian and inflexible approach to the organization of work relations. Accordingly, in 1982 the scope of the Social Councils was extended to engage with management on issues like the organization of work, internal structures and managerial leadership. Acting upon this, the CLP stated in 1986 that the functions for the Social Councils, now seen as deliberative bodies, were to include an evaluation of experiments in work redesign programmes. New forms of work organization are intended to transcend the dependent relations of Taylorism, and to endorse participation in self-managing. The idea was to enhance the social values that underlie cooperative governance. This involves removing the old long assembly lines and implementing a new socio-technical system. It was hoped that this could make work tasks more socially rewarding by increasing job satisfaction. The first experiment occurred, naturally, in a manufacturing cooperative, Copreci. The lengthy conveyer belt was removed and replaced with much smaller work tables. Workers could now establish a work rhythm that suited them. As there were more tasks than workers, they all had to move freely around the table:

> All workers were expected to perform all the tasks and could rotate tasks as they themselves decided. As they gained skill and confidence in this new way of working, the workers began to take over such supervisory and staff functions as requisitioning tool and materials and recording their output. (Whyte, W. F. & Whyte, K. K. 1991: 116)

Other work group programmes followed rapidly. The groups assumed additional responsibilities like identifying the causes of defects and then rectifying them. At the work tables, the workers organized and monitored their own work. Important lessons were quickly learnt. Plans do not need to be minutely detailed, they can be left open. In this way the integration of work processes can run more effectively; productivity can be increased as idle waiting time is decreased. And with the production of complex products, quality improves as information about the work can be freely exchanged (Whyte, W. F. & Whyte, K. K. 1991: 103–7, 113–17, 123–4).

Whyte and Whyte investigated the effects of work group redesign projects, and this point is of the highest importance, they found that work was greatly enriched. Production and assembly were placed side by side so that operations were efficiently coordinated. This enabled workers to grasp the real significance of their work, giving them a sense of how they were contributing to the whole product. Unsurprisingly, both managers and workers overwhelmingly supported the new approach to the organization of work. Workers felt great relief that the 'terrible monotony' of the assembly line was finally over. A growth in self-esteem was attributed to the work groups, within which individuals felt valued members. There was a feeling throughout the cooperatives that the programme had definitely improved both productivity and quality. It was not long before other cooperatives began to follow Copreci's work redesign programme. The rate of progress differed between them, but Copreci remained the most successful. In Fagor, where work groups rotated tasks and organized their own work, workers expressed a greater job satisfaction. As with Copreci, far from inhibiting efficiency, this actually increased both quality and productivity. When Ulgor opened a new factory from scratch, with a new design of work, the results were positive. Rather than instil assembly lines, they introduced a system of work stations, with work teams situated at each one. Groups planned the rotation of tasks themselves, and there was no foreman as such. The new role for supervisors was not to dictate detailed instructions, but to take ultimate responsibility for the forming of groups. Again, this proved very popular with the workers. The implementation of work redesign programmes was, however, not without its difficulties. The experience of Arrasate indicates that a loss of productivity may occur while the reorganization of production takes place. Due to work space restrictions, when Ulgor tried to create work groups, the changes were not extensive. Here the work groups could not be coordinated easily with the main assembly line. Work groups also failed in Lenniz, but this was due largely to an insufficient knowledge of the technical personnel. Likewise, a lesson drawn from Ederlan is that the changes must be reinforced by the re-education of managers and workers. Technology and an adequate technological training, it is now clear, must help facilitate the formation of work groups (Whyte, W. F. & Whyte, K. K. 1991: 117–22).

Balanced job complexes will be a valuable addition to these kinds of work redesign projects. Where the projects are enjoying success, they may only need to be implemented loosely; they may also help overcome some of the difficulties mentioned above. Whyte and Whyte conclude that the introduction of new work forms is a 'socio-technical' issue. All parties in the cooperative need to understand the human, technical and organizational aspects of the work. There are examples where the introduction of new technology did not yield the desired outcome as the designers did not fully comprehend the social aspects and the organizational features of the work. Conversely, as Lenniz shows, new work forms can run into difficulties if managers and workers have an insufficient knowledge of the technology. So one of the key lessons learnt is that the socio-technical design of new work forms requires changes in the overall system of the firm (1991: 126–7). Balanced job complexes provide the means by which this can be put into effect. A socio-technical competence can be achieved as every member of a cooperative will be entrusted with comparably fulfilling responsibilities, ensuring their work exerts a similar qualitative impact. As mentioned above, it is not necessary for everyone to know everything about their production, even if this were possible. But as balanced job complexes can be arranged so that both social and technical knowledge will be disseminated on an egalitarian bases, technical designers will have a greater understanding of the social nature of the work, while workers will have a deeper insight into its technical aspects. Balanced job complexes, I confer, can meet the educational requirements highlighted in the experience of Ederlan.

Creative labour can only be engendered in multi-skilled work teams; it cannot possibly develop alongside the utter drudgery of the old style assembly line production, with its rigid division of labour. This is because for labour to be creative, certain conditions have to be satisfied. Work tasks must be enriched and rotated. On the assembly line fragments need to be reintegrated, providing workers with the opportunity to reflect upon their work. Crucially, as Gorz has rightly stressed, the mode of work cooperation must develop to the greatest possible extent skills and faculties in all workers. The tedious nature of some of the work in the actual existing cooperatives indicates that role rotation is, on its own, insufficient to implement dealienation. It has to be a role rotation of jobs that have high skill content, so that skills are continuously developed. An enrichment of work requires balanced job complexes and technical processes in which the enhancement of human capacities can be maximized. Only in these productive surroundings can work be a rewarding and fulfilling experience. This is a demanding criterion, and due to the need to institutionalize balanced job complexes it prefigures a more substantial role for the Social Councils, but as the Mondragon experience indicates, it can be met. It is important to reiterate that most of the difficulties Mondragon experienced were not so much due to the nature of the new work groups. Neither was the uneven progression of new work forms caused by a lack of value commitments; management of the cooperative group was thoroughly committed to their implementation. Problems were encountered as the new work forms could not be easily assimilated into the existing structures which were organized through conveyor-belt production lines (Whyte, W. F. & Whyte, K. K. 1991: 125–6). The establishment of a system of new cooperatives would not be faced with this problem.

To summarize, the empirical literature indicates that dealienation has clearly occurred in terms of workers' control over their products. There has, to a lesser extent, also been success with both input into decision-making and a connection with others. In the absence of work redesign projects though, the nature of the work remained a monotonous and tiresome affair. But since the instalment of new work programmes in the Mondragon complex, the signs are auspicious that workers are finding their work more fulfilling and rewarding. This has been realized through an enlarged role for the Social Councils in the cooperatives. In NED's guild cooperatives, the Social Councils will also assume responsibility for this role; a role that will include the design of an additional structural device, balanced job complexes. I have argued that in the sense that complex processes will not be broken down into their most basic components as they often are in the typical capitalist enterprise, this device is indispensable to dealienation. Balanced job complexes, inevitably, bring with them their own dilemmas and hurdles to overcome, some of which are considered in the following chapters. But they do provide a firm premise upon which creative labour can be brought to fruition.

Part Three: Dealienated Consumption

> *Any distribution whatever of the means of consumption is only a consequence of the distribution of the conditions of production themselves... If the material conditions of production are the co-operative property of the workers themselves, then there likewise results a distribution of the means of consumption different from the present one.*
>
> *(Marx, K. 1977: 569–70)*

As the idea of consumer councils will be new to most readers, this third and last section of the chapter clarifies some of the immediate benefits they are likely to secure. It is shown how superseding alienation in the productive sphere may impact positively on the purchasing behaviour of consumers. As a corollary, it then reveals why NED's mode of consumption is, in terms of negating alienation and commodity fetishism, superior to market forces and centrally planned economies. In keeping with the previous section, my argument is again substantiated by reference to empirical literature.

Consumer Councils and Non-Alienated Consumption

Treating the above accounts of the social, intermediate and technical divisions of labour generically, it can be appreciated that consumers in NED will be able to purchase their products and commodities in the safe knowledge that they were produced through creative labour in democratic cooperatives. As well as having evident benefits for producers, this can also instigate significant changes in the behaviour of consumers. In capitalist society, work is often (usually) repetitive and meaningless. It has little intrinsic reward. As a result, people commonly attempt to derive self-determination as consumers through an increased acquisition of things. Expensive commodities are brought not so much to satisfy needs, but to impress others. Likewise, the possession of works of art becomes a status symbol. Horvat uses the term 'alienated consumption' to refer to the satisfaction of imposed and artificial needs; the satisfaction of greed, rather than authentic need. The goal is to accumulate, not to create, but to have (1982: 98–100). NED can restrict the tendency for consumption to assume an alienated character. In any modern economy the interests of producers and consumers can clash, hence the need for the differentiated representation of principal interests. But it is still, obviously, the case that the vast majority of consumers will be, or have been, producers or providers of a service. Individuals have innate interests as producers, and the same in their capacities as consumers. In a real democracy, both require separate representation. But they are still inherent to the same person; the two sets of interests feed into and impact upon each other. The whole idea is to engender not just an advanced mode of production, as vital as this is, but also to instigate a corresponding renewed mode of consumption. It would be rather pointless if people worked in a left-libertarian character yet continued to purchase as if in capitalist society. It is a closely held belief on the Left that the face-to-face decision-making common to participatory democracies may invoke an efficacious citizenry. To participatory theorists, participation in self-direction is the principle by which ordinary people are moulded into whole and integrated citizens. As a direct consequence of their participation individuals will, the argument goes, be equipped to participate in extra-workplace social spheres (Greenberg, E. S. 1986: 17–19), such as consumer councils.

So, can workplace democracy foster values that can help revitalize a political life that may replace the distant and impersonal system of representative politics that at present passes for democracy? It has been suggested that the experience of life in a democratic workplace realizes these salutary effects as it teaches the skills and knowledge a real democracy requires. The hypothesis is the more workers participate in their immediate surroundings, the greater their familiarity with the attributes of citizenship. Greenberg notes that with regards to workplace democracy and participation in other social institutions, the empirical literature supports the claim that participation is habit forming. It has been satisfactorily demonstrated that self-determination and self-governance in the workplace correlate positively with an increase in activity in other social institutions outside the enterprise. This held true for all the cases studied. Although he found that there was not the degree of participatory spill-over effect in the plywood cooperatives anticipated in the theoretical literature and verified in empirical research, *social* participation outside the workplace did increase the longer members worked there. The educational benefits of cooperative life can hardly be trivialized. 'Rather than distracting from outside involvement, democratic activity in the firm does serve to enhance democratic citizenship away from work' (Greenberg, E. S. 1986: 121, 115–21).

The empirical literature reviewed by Pateman (1970) and Mason (1982), and the empirical inquiry of Elden (1981), supported the linkage between workplace democracy and *political* efficacy. Greenberg's study, though, does not reinforce the consensus. 'Egalitarian and democratic life in the plywood cooperatives does not seem to contribute significantly to growth in a sense of personal mastery in the political realm' (1986: 122). But in terms of workplace democracy and political participation, his data is consistent with the theoretical expectations that experience in the former increases involvement in the latter. Political participation was measured in terms of voting, campaigns, community affairs and such like. He found that cooperative members did participate to a greater extent than conventional workers.[10] As such, he concludes that when individuals experience direct democracy in their working lives they are indeed more likely to participate in the social and political institutions beyond the enterprise. This was 'strongly supported' by his evidence. Further, the gap between cooperative and conventional workers in this regard increased over time, which indicates a process of political education (Greenberg, E. S. 1986: 128, 124–5,

10. See Greenberg (1986: 125–8) for supporting data.

131). It would, therefore, seem highly likely that workers in NED producing through creative labour will be changed by their experience, and it is just as probable that this will induce a 'knock-on' affect in their behaviour as consumers.

This has important implications, and when compared with the typical conduct of consumers in market forces and centrally planned economies, becomes hugely significant. Consider the following argument from Sayer. Consumer spending causes inequalities. When the majority of consumers buy from certain producers, inequalities will emerge in producers' incomes. This is the unintended consequence of the freedom of consumers to choose, and is how the invisible hand discussed in the previous chapter is supposed to operate. In the absence of inequalities, the argument goes, there is little incentive for producers to respond to consumer demand. Market logic implies that economic actors are only interested in what they sell and can buy. If this is all they respond to, they will remain neutral to the attributes of other actors. Neutrality stems in part from ignorance; consumers know little about the circumstances through which their goods were produced. It is here that the phenomenon of commodity fetishism is directly encountered. The social relations of producers remain indiscernible to consumers. Yet for Sayer, ignorance is not unique to markets:

> 'It is partly a function of the fact that products rarely bear the mark of their producers' character, and that where the division of labour is fairly developed, producers and consumers are likely to be distant from and unknown to one another, regardless of whether they are coordinated by a market or some other means.' (Sayer, A. 1995: 126)

Sayer's point is that there is nothing to say that an individual who receives an item either freely or at a subsidized rate will know any more about the social relations through which it was produced than if it was purchased through a market. If so, the capitalist economy is not the only one to engender commodity fetishism, 'a pot of paint brought from a state store under communism and one brought in a market may be identical and each will tell us equally little about its producers' (Sayer, A. 1995: 126, 123–6).

It is true that both capitalist and command socialist economies are plagued by ignorance, and as such both stand about as much chance of abolishing commodity fetishism as they do alienation, which is virtually nil. Sayer's argument, however, cannot be applied to NED. It must be remembered that NED's functionally demarcated market system is set within, and is subordinated too, a democratically planned economy. Here market logic does not dictate that consumers are only interested in what they can buy. Through open communication between their councils and the guild cooperatives, they will not be ignorant about the productive conditions through which their goods were produced. In NED, as all (or the vast majority) of goods are produced in democratic conditions through cooperative labour, they can 'bear the mark of their producers' character'. And as they have been determined socially – through the two consumer councils and the guild regulated markets – thus rendering the social relations of production visible, consumers will not be overly distant from producers, even if they will often be unknown to them. This is a key benefit of the guilds-consumer councils approach to coordination.

In market forces economies consumers can only choose from what is on offer, which may be at odds with their true preferences. By way of contrast, in NED the consumer councils provide consumers with the opportunity to participate meaningfully in what should get produced, irrespective of their personal bank balances. This does not imply that every single item produced must be subject to the veto of a consumer council. In a society where literally millions of items are produced daily, this would be unworkable. But it does give consumers the power to block particular products, or certain methods of production, that have been shown to be detrimental to the community interest. As mentioned above, Sayer states that for the most part he has no desire to get involved about what goods are suitable for production. Fair enough; but, however, he understandably does not want to consume items that are either produced by exploited workers or harm the environment. Neither do I. So what room for manoeuvre is there in market societies? Organize boycotts, participate in demonstrations, lobby the state, etc. These are all laudable actions, but they are all too easily frustrated by the power of capital. NED has a more radical, yet more favourable solution. Consumer councils are the political structures through which discontent can be channelled. As legally empowered decentralized bodies they can, on the mandate of local consumers, prevent a product from going to market. There may on occasions be fierce debates within these inclusive social forums. This is to be welcomed, for in the process of discussion socio-economic relations are rendered visible, and transparency plays a central role in negating the mystification and concealing aspects of commodity fetishism. One final point, Sayer believes that ignorance of the social relations of production is not necessarily a bad thing. The low informational requirements of markets save much time. Even if the behaviour of economic actors is uninformed, opacity only becomes problematic when what is being concealed is of an exploitative nature (1995: 126).

But if opacity remains, how is anyone supposed to know whether what is being concealed actually does involve either social or natural exploitation? Ignorance of the social relations of production is, to my mind, very much a bad thing – hence the need for the transparency role of the two consumer councils.

Conclusion

After consulting the literature on the plywood and Mondragon cooperatives (as well as the Israel Kibbutz and the old Yugoslavia systems), Greenberg draws this conclusion. 'The specific linkage between workplace democracy and dealienation seems to be dependent not only upon the specific form of workplace democracy but upon the political, cultural, ideological, and economic setting within which democratic workplaces operate' (1986: 113). In citing the main reasons why cooperatives have failed, Oakeshott stresses that over the last 150 years they have been mainly producing independently, usually in a hostile environment (1980: 50). The plywood cooperatives exist within a free-market environment. Their survival depends on profits gained through the market, which engenders a possessive individualism hostile to and largely incompatible with workplace democracy. This is why Greenberg calls for an increased sensitivity to context. In a more hospitable environment, one in which cooperatives are united in mutually supportive groups (like guilds), there is every indication they will flourish. The remarkable history of Mondragon has shown this is not in any sense utopian fantasy. Despite being restricted by a largely unshackled market economy, there is also much in the plywood cooperatives that is reproducible. They demonstrate that ordinary people can manage a modern advanced industry. Modern organizations can be run along egalitarian and non-hierarchical lines even in a hostile context. They also strongly indicate that alienation can be negated, in particular with regards to the product and productive decision-making. The goal must now be to universalize these fine achievements. In order to implement dealienation more fully, it must be invigorated by a supportive economic and political environment, fully committed to participatory democracy. The analyst, Greenberg concludes, is obligated to provide an account of the system within which workplace democracies will function (1986: 113–14, 167, 170–1).

This chapter has attempted to do precisely that. Neither market nor centrally planned economies stand much chance of eradicating alienation. NED provides the necessary corrective. This chapter has argued that creative labour can be successfully institutionalized in the guild cooperatives.

I have rejected the assertions that alienation is inescapable in all complex economies. Sayer is right that a complex division of labour is indispensable to any modern economy. But in terms of the supposedly inescapable alienating character of labour, this does not entail alienation is intractable. Marx found it bizarre that '[t]he same bourgeois consciousness which celebrates the division of labour in the workplace...denounces with equal vigour every conscious attempt to control and regulate the process of production socially' (1976: 477). By way of contrast, NED pays great attention to how democratizing the social relations of production affect the details of the social, intermediate and technical division of labour. This has been a pivotal task. In NED a social division of labour will remain, but the crucial point to re-emphasize is that it is embedded within a politically organized civil society. It is in this sense that NED responds to the critiques of Sayer and Prychitko that planning will inevitably centralize. They all assume that planning will proceed through a bureaucratic centralized state. With regards to NED's democratic approach to social planning, this could not be further from the truth. The effects of the difference between the former and the latter will, I have suggested, be considerable. In addition, the technical division of labour can, through balanced job complexes, be notably weakened. Democratizing the social relations of production in the unique way NED does, institutionalizing continuous dialogue between organized producers and organized consumers (the correct mode of coordination), unifying the state-civil society paradigm without creating a leviathan, democratizing investment planning and establishing a fair criterion for surplus appropriation provides the most desirable socialization of productive assets. It has been shown throughout this chapter that this affects positively and in a creative direction the division of labour in NED.

Finally, it can now be appreciated that workers in NED, as they sufficiently control both the process of production and the entire product, perform a trade in, to use Gorz's phrase, a 'fully rounded' sense. And through their joint membership of a guild cooperative and consumer/civil councils, they will possess knowledge of the 'culture of everyday life'. This, though, comes at a price. Although the divisions of labour in NED are constituted in such a way that creative labour can be upheld, the structural mechanisms through which they are realized take time to establish. It is probable that this will result, initially, in some loss in productive efficiency. For example work cycles of no less than 20 minutes demand that every member of a work team is competent in a range of activities. This may require extra time and resources to train apprentices and retrain skilled workers. Likewise, designing enrichment projects like balanced job complexes and installing role rotation structures will, probably, be time-consuming affairs. I shall return to this salient issue in the following chapters on organizational democracy. The point I wish to conclude this chapter on is that the real question is not whether creative labour can be sustained universally; technological imperatives can fall within the range established by social objectives. The issue is whether the advantages of doing so outweigh the disadvantages. The reasons why they do are central to the argument of this book.

4

Towards a New Economic Democracy Critique of Oligarchy

When democracies have gained a certain stage of development, they undergo a gradual transformation, adopting the aristocratic spirit... against which at the outset they struggled so fiercely. Now new accusers arise to denounce the traitors; after an era of glorious combats and of inglorious power, they end by fusing with the old dominant class; whereupon once more they are in their turn attacked by fresh opponents who appeal to the name of democracy. It is probable that this cruel game will continue without end.

(Michels, R. 1999: 371)

the effect of real democracy will be an immense liberation of social and individual energy... [I]t is not because they worship organisation for its own sake that Guildsmen build their plans for a new social structure: it is because they believe that this structure will liberate energy and promote happiness and achievement in countless directions which it is impossible to foresee.

(Cole, G. D. H. 1920b: 158–9)

Along with the next two chapters, this chapter argues that the productive organizations in NED will not yield to the oligarchization process Michels believes inevitable. It is shown throughout why functional democracy is, suitably developed, the premise upon which to construct a viable participatory democracy. The first step is to lay out the theoretical positions of Michels and the leading advocate of functional democracy, G. D. H. Cole. In order to show why the essential component of Michels' organizational theory covers NED, particular attention is paid to his brief but definite remarks on the inevitability of oligarchy in economic organizations. A more detailed account of its interrelating features is reserved for the two forthcoming chapters. Secondly, this chapter takes note of Cole's alternative reasoning and states his counter proposals. It is important to acknowledge his influence. It has been recognized that the classical notion of participatory democracy, developed significantly by Cole, forms the intellectual background of modern cooperatives.[1] So although the analyses in the following chapters go beyond Cole's work, a thorough account of his theory of the functional principle is a prerequisite for the discussions that follow.

Part One: Oligarchy Inevitable

In the preface to *Political Parties*, first published in 1911, Michels declares that democracy 'has encountered obstacles, not merely imposed from without, but spontaneously surgent from within' (1999: 6). Such hurdles will never be totally surpassed, as democracy contains an 'oligarchic nucleus'. For Michels, oligarchy in organizational life is inevitable, the growth of which imposes difficulties upon the realization of democracy. The need for groups to 'constitute cliques and sub-classes' is, he affirms, a sociological law; a law he refers to an 'iron'. The key word to highlight here is 'tendencies', it is oligarchic tendencies that for Michels amount to laws. They correspond to the laws of physics, and are inevitable, regardless of any effort to nullify them. In Michels' thesis, the iron law is an 'essential characteristic of all human aggregates'. The complexes of tendencies which prevent the fulfilment of democracy are difficult to unravel and formulate. Nevertheless, he maintains that they may be classified as being dependent upon a), the nature of the individual b), the nature of the political struggle and c), the nature of organization. It is upon these premises that he constructs his iron law. To survive and succeed large organizations need leadership. The very nature of organization is, however, such that those who hold subsidiary positions have no means by which to secure the accountability of leadership. 'Organisation is, in fact, the source from which the conservative currents flow over the plain of democracy, occasioning there disastrous floods and rendering the plain unrecognisable' (1999: 62). The tendency for power to pass from many

1. This is to the benefit of producer cooperatives. 'If co-operatives are the contemporary manifestation of the ideas underlying Guild Socialism and workers' control, they are all the better for that' (Young, M. & Rigge, M. 1983: 30).

hands into the few, and from those who use it infrequently to those who exercise it in the course of their work, is (virtually) unstoppable. Michels, therefore, believes we are confronted with this irresolvable dilemma: in order to have institutions like states, political parties, trade unions, religious bodies etc., the power to run them must be placed in the hands of the controlling minority (Michels, R. 1999: 6–7, 73–7; Parry, G. 1969: 22, 30–1).

Towards the end of *Political Parties*, he provides a useful summary of his thesis. All leadership systems are incompatible with the postulates of democracy. The tendency for leaders to consolidate their interests, the gratitude the represented feel towards their leaders and the overall passivity of the masses are all determining causes of the inevitable development of oligarchy. However, the principal cause is the 'technical indispensability of leadership'. The process begins as a result of the differentiation of functions within the organization. It is then completed by a range of qualities the leaders develop due to their estrangement from the rank and file. Initially, leaders are sincere and their functions gratuitous. But they very quickly become professional leaders, and after this latter stage of development they are rendered 'stable and irremovable'. Michels is adamant that the iron law is not restricted to political parties, it has a universal application. 'The formation of oligarchies within the various forms of democracy is the outcome of organic necessity, and consequently affects every organisation, be it socialist or even anarchist' (Michels, R. 1999: 364–6; Lipset, S. M. 1999: 15).

To test his hypothesis, Michels studied organizations within the socialist movement, especially the German Social Democratic Party (SPD). He found that the law of oligarchy was indeed one of its key properties (1999: 50). I have no wish to challenge Michels on this point; it is the relation between his theory and economic organizations that forms the focus of this book. Michels is characteristically sceptical towards the possibility of sustaining workplace democracy, as his brief remarks on syndicalism and producer cooperatives indicate. He stresses that although the notion of self-government is central to the syndicalist movement, it still acknowledges that organization is indispensable. For Michels, the antidote to organizational oligarchy cannot possibly emerge from a method which is premised upon a principle of representation:

> The syndicalists wish to stop where logically there is no stopping-place. All that the syndicalists have written upon political parties in general, and upon their big brother the Socialist Party in particular,

> applies to themselves as well, because it applies to all organisations as such without exception. (Michels, R. 1999: 318–19)

The syndicalists, he insists, have no immunity against the 'sociological laws of universal validity' (1999: 317–19, 321, 324). With regards to workers' cooperatives, Michels acknowledges that their organization of production offers the best hope for democratic collaboration. They consist of similar elements from the same trade and homogeneous manners of life. As all workers share a common professional competence, there is little difference in technical knowledge, and management may be carried out by all members. These circumstances are auspicious for the formation of a democratic organization. In spite of this though, Michels follows the argument that if every sphere of work is done by small democratic cooperatives in which all members have an equal say in management, there is every possibility that the economy would succumb to its cumbrousness. So producers' cooperatives must confront a dilemma. They either capitulate to the disputes and disunity that will inevitably stem from all members having the right to interfere with administration, or they submit to the will of a few and lose their cooperative nature. In order not to perish, Michels concludes, they are forced to sacrifice the former (Michels, R. 1999: 161–2).

NED is not syndicalism; it does though share with syndicalism a rejection of liberal capitalism, an endorsement of a principle of representation and an acknowledgement that organizations are indispensable to industrial self-management. Given what Michels has to say about workplace democracy, it seems certain he would have regarded NED as no exception to his universal law that oligarchy is a 'preordained form of all social aggregates'. Michels holds no hope for the survival of organizational democracy in any domain, be it political or economic. Oligarchy as an inherent element of all large organizations is the result of organizational and psychological factors, especially the former. As the introductory chapter indicates, he provides three different yet interrelated theories about the origins and development of oligarchy. There are two weak and one strong conception of oligarchy. They are a theory of transaction costs, a theory of membership lethargy (weak theories), and a theory of elite control (strong theory). The weak theories are critical of direct democracy, that is, that all members of an organization are able to participate equally in the collective decision-making process. The strong theory stresses that the interests of elites and those of the masses will inevitably develop fundamental different interests (Parry, G. 1969: 42–3; Kitschelt, H. 1990: 86–7).

This is the basis of Michels' thesis. There can be little doubt of its continuing influence as a rational for explaining oligarchic development. Since *Political Parties*, the process towards oligarchy of what begins as organizational democracy has been widely accepted as inevitable. Democratic organizations with no bosses or followers are assumed to be delicate, unstable affairs. Eventually a dominant and controlling leadership emerges, changing the organizations' defining characteristics. The tendency for power to concentrate at the summit of an organization is, unquestionably, an omnipresent phenomenon. As Rothschild and Whitt observe, this is the cornerstone of twentieth century social science (1986: 1). In contemporary society, Michels' work has broad applicability. 'Mainstream organisational and management theories typically ignore or dismiss the possibility of internal organisational democracy and, following…Michels, take for granted the presence of hierarchical, superior / subordinate relationship, and oligarchic control' (Rothschild, J. & Whitt, J. A. 1986: 23). Michels regards the socialist society of free individuals to be absurdly naive. His seemingly accurate predictions about the future behaviour of democratic organizations, and the fact that he defined and stipulated the tendencies for them, has ensured that *Political Parties* is widely acknowledged to be one of the most influential books in the canon of political sociology.

Part Two: G. D. H. Cole and Functional Democracy

Cole accepts Michels' logic only up to a certain point. He agrees that when it is impossible for all members of an association to deliberate together, problems of governance are likely to emerge. Large associations are compelled to assign a degree of power to certain members, and to establish a representative legislative assembly. In these more complex associations, the executive committee generally remains separate from the legislature, and is confined to implementing its decisions. The difficulty Cole acknowledges is that whenever people act together, they inevitably develop a sense of community. The flip side is that representative committees, as well as the rank and file, will generate this community essence. The presence of a degree of committee loyalty will affect how committee members perform, however well intended, their duty to the other members. It is here that the members' will is sometimes 'twisted' as it passes through the intermediary of the representatives. Cole calls the tendency for representatives to substitute their wills for those they are supposed to be representing 'perversion', a degree of which he admits is inevitable. It is liable to occur in all types of representative bodies. Although these dangers are less applicable with functional representation, they do not vanish completely (Cole, G. D. H. 1920a: 118–21, 123, 185–7).

A further point of congruity between their reasoning is on the issue of undifferentiated representation. Michels notes that political life is becoming more and more complex. 'As this complexity increases it becomes more and more absurd to attempt to "represent" a heterogeneous mass in all the innumerable problems which arise out of the increasing differentiation of our political and economic life' (1999: 76–7). Cole would have agreed with this; he may also have added that it is all the more reason to reject a mass political party-based system, for Michels accurately describes the consequences of non-functional representation. There is then a significant point of accord between the theories of Michels and Cole. Yet there are also fundamental differences. Cole argues that in functional democracy, individual wills are not obliterated. A representative cannot take the place of the represented. This is because the former does not represent the whole personalities of the latter. Representatives only represent a part of their constituents. For Cole, it is purposes held in common that can more realistically be represented. Functional representation accepts some distortion as inevitable, but not to the extent that organizational democracy is eradicated. Although the representative group cannot claim to represent its members as 'centres of consciousness', it can still approximately represent that part of them that they 'put into associated effort'. Hence, a 'real democracy is to be found, not in a single omnicompetent representative assembly, but in a system of co-ordinated functional representative bodies' (Cole, G. D. H. 1920a: 104–8, 162).

It is on the potential of organizations to introduce the representative principle while simultaneously preserving their internal democracies that Michels and Cole part company. As clarified above, Michels believes that the representative system is logically impossible (1999: 73). Cole has deep reservations about this. He acknowledges that in large communities democracy cannot really avoid representative government. But it can be democratic if it prevents the substitution of the representative's will for the wills of the represented (1920b: 31). Throughout his guild period Cole held that there was nothing inherently undemocratic about representation, although the following must be understood:

> The essentials of democratic representation, positively stated, are, first, that the represented shall have free choice of, constant contact with, and considerable control over, his representative. The second is that he should be called upon, not to choose someone to represent

> him as a man or as a citizen in all the aspects of citizenship, but only to choose someone to represent his point of view in relation to some particular purpose or group of purposes, in other words, some particular function. All true and democratic representation is therefore functional representation. (Cole, G. D. H. 1920b: 32–3)

On this reasoning, parliamentary democracy distorts the democratic principle in two ways. First, electors have very little, if any, control over their representatives. Secondly, an elector is asked to choose one person to represent him or her on all matters. But for Cole, as true representation is functional, there must be for every distinct group of functions a corresponding number of groups of representatives. Although citizens cannot be represented in general terms as individuals – for individuals, fundamentally speaking, cannot be 're'-presented – a representative can nevertheless represent a common viewpoint that a group of individuals hold in relation to a particular and specific social purpose. Consequently, individuals must have the same number of different functional votes to match the amount of separate matters that need associative action in which they are interested (which can change as society does). This democratic principle applies not only to individuals as citizens, but to any domain in which they cooperate to perform a social function or share a common social interest (Cole, G. D. H. 1920b: 30–4). This is the basic sticking point between Michels and Cole – one denies, and the other affirms, that organizational democracy can be sustained using the principle of functional representation.

In contrast to Michels, Cole contends that functional electorates are far from politically impotent, and are not powerless to avoid the substitution of wills (perversion). For Cole, it is only when perversion is *conscious*, *deliberate* and *continuous* that it indicates either the electorate or the method of representation is badly at fault. Rather than criticize people for being 'clannish', he suggests appropriate methods for dealing with 'clannishness': first, ensure that the powers and sphere of action are marked as clearly as possible; and secondly, secure the conditions whereby the constituency can become 'active and continuously resourceful'. Cole's claim that these conditions can be realized is substantiated during his discussion on the relationship between functional representatives and their corresponding body of electors after s/he has been chosen. He begins by noting the controversy around whether to elect representatives or delegates. The dilemma is whether elected officials should follow their own wills, or to the greatest possible extent follow direct instructions from their functional constituencies. With regards to delegates, there is not much difference between the two methods of representation. As unpredictable complications are commonplace, attempts to restrict the elected person by fixed instructions are liable to break down regardless of the representative form. Representation with no instructions or counsel, on the other hand, can lead to the substitution of one will for the many, even within a functionally demarcated association. Cole maintains, though, that the progression from undifferentiated to functional democracy provides the necessary corrective. 'It enables us to combine representation with constant counsel from the constituents, and thus makes it possible to abandon the theory of delegation without imperilling democratic control' (1920a: 109–10). In Cole's reasoning, the main problem of exercising democratic control over representatives in the modern state is that it is not possible to counsel or criticize them in any meaningful way. The difficulty is that electors are not collectively active throughout their representative's tenure of office. But as functional associations have a permanent being, functional democracy overcomes this obstacle. The group does not need to instruct their representatives definitely, because it can critique and advice them throughout their time in office. As a final safeguard, it has the use of the recall. Cole's contention is that in functional democracy elected officials will not be delegates, but representatives acting mainly upon criticism and advice from an instructive and active constituency. In contrast to Michels, he is optimistic about the likely successes the functional principle will engender. In particular, the electors have some knowledge about the job the representative has been chosen to do. The association's business in their business, and they can therefore act intelligently in relation to it (1920a: 110–14, 121–3).

So the basic discord between Michels and Cole is centred on matters of degree and permanence. They both recognize that the substitution of one will for many poses a dilemma to organizational governance. In the case of undifferentiated representation, there is a shared acknowledgement that this is virtually insurmountable. When the representation is functional, however, Cole infers that while this danger does not disappear, it is less applicable and need not be continuous. Provided methods are secured whereby the represented can constantly instruct, counsel, criticize and advise their representatives, the tendency to misrepresent wills can be averted. So for Cole, communications are more amenable and responsive to full-time organizations like the workplace. This is largely because rank and file members will be better equipped to direct policy, and to control and guide their leaders. As such, the workshop is the location where the most radical demands will be formulated and the greatest concessions secured.

If these pivotal structural changes in self-governance are not adopted, Cole accepts, officials will become increasing distant from rank and file members. The responsibilities for the internal conduct of industry must be entrusted to organized groups of producers (1972: 69–73). The ability of the guild cooperatives and the wider guild structures to uphold their internal democracies is therefore the issue that the following two chapters explore.

Part Three: Rationale

With Michels' pessimism and Cole's optimism established, I would like to conclude this chapter by briefly reiterating the rationale behind, and the structural layout of, the forthcoming chapters. Michels' discussion on the nature of the political struggle as it existed in his day has very little relevance to the analysis of NED's organizations. The differences are far too radical. NED's political economy operates within a re-politicized civil society, and it has no place for competing mass undifferentiated political parties. It is his arguments on the nature of the individual and the nature of organization, especially the latter, that can be meaningfully applied to NED. My refutation of Michels will, therefore, focus exclusively on these last two sets of tendencies; tendencies that for Michels are omnipresent. As we have seen, it is the combined outcome of his three interrelated theories of weak and strong oligarchy that lead him to pessimistically state that the iron law is, as its name suggests, universally pertinent. He consequently despairs at the forlorn fate of organizational democracy. In stark contrast, the following chapters outline and analyse Cole's sanguine proposals for the preservation of organizational democracy as they tacitly relate to these respective three theories. A great deal of both Michels' and Cole's work is critical of the same phenomena, social democracy. To some extent they are constructing similar arguments. But although Cole does briefly endorse Michels' critique of the mass undifferentiated political party system (1920a: 122), he is confident that the guilds are equipped to withstand the oligarchization process. It will be shown why his confidence is well founded. From here one of Michels' biggest errors is highlighted. The outcome from his primary analysis on political parties does not entitle him to reach far wider conclusions concerning the nature of organization in any political community. The aim is not so much to provide a critical evaluation of *Political Parties*, but rather to show why NED contains plausible democratic responses to the impediments to organizational democracy Michels stipulates. My conclusion that Michels was mistaken to suggest 'who says organisation, says oligarchy', constitutes a rejection of his jump from tendencies to laws. In this sense, an objection to his reasoning is expressed. My primary purpose, though, is defensive rather then aggressive. I am chiefly concerned with upholding NED against the charge that its organizations are incapable of sustaining democracy.

One final point, to substantiate my argument there is a need to move beyond Cole's texts and engage with both the theoretical and empirical literature on producer cooperatives in which the oligarchic question is directly addressed. The commentary on the Mondragon complex and the plywood cooperatives is especially useful in this regard. Further, in one of the most illuminating inquires of its kind, Rothschild and Whitt's *The Co-operative Workplace* (1986) identifies and analyses the internal conditions whose presence assists, or absence hinders, the progression of the most fundamental organizational feature of cooperatives: 'decision-making procedures based on participatory democracy'. As such, this text is also referred to frequently throughout the following two chapters. Significantly, in this literature the phenomenon of oligarchic tendencies is immediately encountered; Rothschild and Whitt acknowledge that it is the force of Michels' argument that presents the most severe theoretical challenge to workplace democracy (1986: 2–3, 13, 24). It is for this reason that a response to Michels is obligatory in a book that argues organizational democracy can, in the appropriate material setting, be upheld.

5

The Theories of Transaction Costs and Membership Lethargy

This chapter will demonstrate how the guilds in NED will counter the anti-democratic tendencies Michels describes in his weak theories of oligarchy: transaction costs and membership lethargy. Starting with the former, it begins by laying out his argument, and then clarifies the interrelated factors – the inevitable differentiation of function, the monopoly of expertise and the technical indispensability of leadership – which, he insists, apply to all large organizations. As the chapter proceeds, a counter-argument is developed. In order to show why the indispensability of leadership does not dictate that individual leaders are equally essential, Cole's proposals for choosing and controlling the guild committees are introduced and analysed. The works, district and national bodies are all considered. Although vital, as these procedures are only likely to partly halt the oligarchization process, the introduction of additional structural mechanisms like role rotation and balanced job sharing schemes are required. The analysis demonstrates that in the manner in which these innovative measures help prevent expert knowledge from impairing the guilds' internal democracies, they are a prerequisite for the preservation of guild democracy. This first part of the chapter is divided into three sections, a), 'The Entrenchment of Oligarchic Control', b), 'The Division of Function, the Monopoly of Expertise and the Indispensability of Leadership' and c), 'Expertise'. The second part of the chapter discusses Michels' theory of membership lethargy, and is introduced fully at the time.

Part One: The Entrenchment of Oligarchic Control

Due to the actual numbers involved, Michels suggests that it is mechanically and technically impossible to sustain direct forms of democracy. Where large numbers are involved, there is a need for a system of representation. As soon as cooperative actions reach the size that justifies the label organization, they are compelled to develop a division of labour and hierarchies in order to fulfil 'technical imperatives of efficiency':

> The technical specialisation that inevitably results from all extensive organisation renders necessary what is called expert leadership. Consequently the power of determination comes to be considered one of the specific attributes of leadership, and is gradually withdrawn from the masses to be concentrated in the hands of the leaders alone. Thus the leaders, who were at first no more than the executive organs of the collective will, soon emancipate themselves from the mass and become independent of its control. (Michels, R. 1999: 70)

Michels' point is that organizational growth will affect its internal government. As an organization expands, so its democracy declines. This is because the growth of leadership power is mirrored by the expansion of the organization. Every large organization has a differentiation of function. With the development of the organization, its administrative matters become increasingly enlarged, complicated and specialized. Tasks not only grow in numbers, their higher quality creates a more extensive differentiation of function. It therefore becomes impossible to observe them all at a single glance. Members cannot even supervise, let alone control the whole process of administration. They have little choice but to allow officials to fulfil tasks. Officials consequently become familiar with conducting business without consulting the masses. In the interests of efficiency, technical administration inevitably becomes the exclusive concern of the leaders, who gradually become more professional and more secure. The number of functions transferred from the electoral to the executive escalates, and a complex edifice quickly solidifies. With the resulting indelible division of labour, executive authority is correspondingly sub-divided. The outcome is a 'rigorously defined' hierarchical bureaucracy. This inevitable hierarchy, which is simply more cost-effective than participatory democracy, is constituted through technical conditions. The influence of the rank and file is simultaneously undermined. So as leaders become experts, they will command greater power. Their monopoly of expertise ensures that members are dependent upon their arbitration, and as such are controlled by them. As soon as professional leadership emerges, Michels contends, democratic control is reduced to a minimum (Michels, R. 1999: 64–6, 70–2; Hands, G. 1971: 164–6).

The rigid bureaucracy, along with the technical indispensability of leadership, ensures that power and control will inevitably concentrate at the top of the organization, weakening rank and file influence. Due to reasons of technical and administrative necessity, Michels insists that a solid leadership is required by a strong organization. It is this entrenchment of professional leadership that signals the end of democracy. Due to the increasing complexity of political life, it is ridiculous to claim that an undifferentiated heterogeneous mass can be adequately represented by elected leaders. Michels forcibly concludes that the oligarchic tendency is the inevitable outcome of the actual principle of organization. This is due to the impossibility of the representative system (Michels, R. 1999: 72–3, 76–7; Kitschelt, H. 1990: 86). When applied to NED, some of what Michels says about transaction costs can only be granted a secondary significance. The guilds are guaranteed representation in the communes. As they are not competing for the right to legislate in the body politic, they do not need to organize their vote, seek support or raise contributions in the same way that mass political parties do. Unlike a political party, a guild does not have an external struggle to contend with. So there is no reason to suspect that the guilds will be plagued by the tendencies to grow Michels identifies in organizations that openly compete for power. In addition, at the level of the guild cooperatives, it will be recalled from Chapter 2 that as soon as a cooperative grows beyond 500 members, it is required to divide into two cooperatives. This decentralizing strategy is enforced by the contract of association, and is upheld in the interests of democracy. Again, Michels' reasoning about organizational growth is not applicable here. But as politico-economic organizations that have been functionally demarcated, the national guilds and the guild cooperatives will need to fulfil technical imperatives of efficiency, which means they will contain a division of labour and a hierarchical structure. Further, they cannot operate without expertise and a technical indispensability of leadership. Although they are in a radically different political environment to the parliamentary system Michels correctly criticizes, they need to be resolute and on occasions resilient enough to continuously resist the oligarchic tendencies captured in the theory of transactional costs. An exploration of this issue forms the basis of the next two sections.

Part Two: The Division of Function, Monopoly of Expertise and the Indispensability of Leadership

In this section I shall address the problems to guild democracy posed by the division of function, the monopoly of expertise and the ensuing technical indispensability of leadership. It will be shown why the individuals who make up the leadership committees are not irreplaceable. The section concludes by acknowledging that although democratic committees are invaluable to the preservation of the guilds' internal democracy, by themselves they are not enough. It will be instructive to begin by outlining Cole's proposed methods for choosing and controlling the governing bodies.

He makes a preliminary statement about the key principle of guild democracy:

> the essence of the Guild idea is that it means government from below. At every stage, then, wherever a body of men has to work under the supervision of a leader or officer, it must have the choice of that officer. And, in the same way, every committee must be appointed directly by those whose work it is to preside. (Cole, G. D. H. 1972: 185)

So rather than authority stemming from the summit of the guild with delegated power descending through various grades of insubordinates, the impulse is for leadership to emerge from within and from below. Within a national guild, the district committee must represent the various localities, and the different classes of workers within its domain. Likewise, the national committee must do the same with the districts. The functions of these larger organizations must be kept to the absolute minimum, otherwise an excess of centralized power will generate a new bureaucracy causing the 'ossification of the Guild'. In his explanation of how the guilds will avoid centralization, Cole starts from the simplest unit and ascends gradually to the most complex. Within the works is the single shop, followed by the whole works, then the district and finally the whole guild (Cole, G. D. H. 1921a: 3–4; 1920b: 61–2; 1972: 184–5).

Using the example of an engineering guild, he begins by describing the methods for choosing the various committees. The works committees will be elected by the workers in each shop. As these decisions will be based around face-to-face relations, close personal contact between workers and committees will be easily maintained. It is when the process is repeated at the district and national levels that the democratic process of workers exercising a check on those they choose is liable to become stretched. Let us therefore view Cole's proposals a little closer.

> *'The District Committee will consist (1) of works representatives, elected by the Works Committee in each separate works, and (2) of craft representatives, elected by ballot of all members of each craft working within the district'.*

These district committees will coordinate production within the area, handle arrangements with other guilds in the same district and connect the individual works to the guild as a whole.

> *'The National Guild Executive will consist (1) of district representatives, elected by general ballot of each district, and (2) of craft representatives, elected by general national ballot of each craft'.*

Cole recognizes that workers cannot vote for their national representatives with the same degree of certainty as they can when they vote for one person to represent them on a local basis. He therefore proposes that every guild member have two votes: the first for his/her district and the second for her/his craft representative, the idea being that a counterbalance would emerge between district and craft interests on the executive itself.

> *'The National Delegate Meeting will be elected by general ballot of the members of each craft in each district'.*

The national executive is not the final governing body. This is a larger body, which will serve as a final court of appeal and initiate guild policy generally. This body, the national delegate meeting, represents the general will of the guild. As with the national executive, it must combine the interests of the crafts and the various districts. Cole proposes that not only should each district be represented by a group of delegates, but that each individual delegate should be a member of a craft (1972: 187–92). These are the varying methods Cole proposes, and NED adopts, for electing committees. The idea is that the procedure of electing representatives by a more restricted, yet more alert, electorate will enable the workers to control their leaders. In this sense, a paper democracy is transformed into a model of real self-government.

At this point it will be helpful to very briefly restate the key contrast between Cole's guilds and those of NED. The difference is that in the latter there is now a tightly monitored degree of competition between the quasi-autonomous cooperatives within each guild. It follows that one of the national elements in each guild must assume responsibility for monitoring competition within its domain. As the National Guild Executive is responsible for regulating exchange, this body is perhaps more suitable. With regards to democratic investment planning, it will be recalled that at the national and regional levels an external body with delegated authority, the Industrial Guilds Congress, is in charge of the planning and administration of investment. It is only at the local level that individual guilds are allocated funds for distribution to the cooperatives that submit successful appeals. The other revisions to NED's guilds are pointed out as we proceed.

It can now be shown why the individual leaders within the committees are not indispensable. Michels argues that as leaders become more secure and more professional, the influence of the rank and file will simultaneously decline. The leaders do not just become experts; they come to possess a monopoly of expertise. As a corollary, other members of the organization are rendered dependent upon their deliberations. Technical administration inevitably becomes the exclusive concern of the leaders, and in the process democratic control is reduced to a minimum. I am not disputing that, for technical and administrative reasons, a strong organization needs a solid leadership. But I am contending that the technical indispensability of leadership does not imply individual leaders will acquire the monopoly of expertise that would ensure their indispensability.

In every work there will be a variety of shops, each performing a unique function. 'Thus an engineering works may have its drawing office, pattern shop, foundry, toolroom, planing, milling, turning and boring, grinding, and fitting and erecting shops, its stores, and its various offices, receiving, shipping, financial, etc.' (1972: 187–8). For NED's guild cooperatives, instead of shops there are what may be more aptly termed departments. These include marketing, accounts and finance, personnel, research and development, quality and production; the latter being sub-divided into purchasing, industrial engineering, production planning and production plant.[1] Following Michels' logic, these different organs of the collective will create their own 'peculiar interests', which will bring each one in conflict with the collective interest (1999: 353). Members cannot observe at a single glance the whole process of administration. As such, a few salaried officials will become familiar with running the organization without consulting

1. This has been modelled on the Mondragon cooperatives (Whyte, W. F. & Whyte, K. K. 1991: 36).

rank and file members. Yet for Cole, while he recognizes that each shop (department) will have distinctive, as well as common interests, he stops short of saying they are in conflict. Goods need to be produced, so the different departments of a guild cooperative share a common purpose. In order to supervise the whole of the guild cooperative, the control board needs an overall awareness of operations in their entirety. The difference between the departments in a guild cooperative and a political party is that with the former, each member is full-time, permanent and salaried; these characteristic are not the exclusive domain of the leadership. This will have a positive influence upon their internal democratic structures; knowledge of productive processes is gained by everyone.[2] Turning and boring, milling or grinding may be individual skills that various individuals specialize in, but they all require a common grounding, all the workers would have served the same basic apprenticeship. Workers cannot work in the milling shop and remain ignorant to how the turning and boring shops function.

Further, each guild cooperative will also have a multifaceted clerical side. It will include financial, administrative and various other officers. The clerical departments will, as with their manual counterparts, have representatives on the control board. It is here that Albert and Hahnel's idea of 'balanced job complexes' can be reintroduced. Chapter 3 applied their proposal in relation to creative labour. It can now be re-established with regards to an egalitarian dissemination of productive knowledge. As the vast majority of workers will have the general (manual or clerical) knowledge required to become a competent member of the control board, they will not, if elected, be indispensable. The control board itself is indispensable, but as it does not command the kind of monopoly of expertise the leaders of political parties command, its individual members are not. Under these circumstances, they will need to be more receptive to the wishes of the rank and file. As far as the works within the guild cooperatives are concerned, the entrenchment of professional leadership will not signal the end of democracy.

Let us now see whether the officials on the district committees will be equally dispensable. The district committees – who will be constituted through representatives elected by the general assemblies and the various

2. It is significant that in the Mondragon cooperatives, knowledge and power are spread evenly. 'Separating the roles of the elected governing council from the informal management council, the input of the Social Council, and the oversight of the watchdog council encourages broad dissemination of knowledge and discussion, and avoids a concentration of knowledge and power in any one body' (Morrison, R. 1997: 75).

crafts of the component cooperatives – have an essentially different role from the cooperatives' control boards. While the latter are concerned mainly with the techniques of producing their goods, the district (as with the national) committees are to concentrate mainly on supply and demand; which, along with disseminating information widely and on an egalitarian bases, includes monitoring intra guild competition. There are two key issues that arise from this structural division of function. First, whether the opportunity to acquire the knowledge needed to fulfil these functions is beyond most workers and, secondly, whether it is inevitable that the district committees will attain a unified monopoly of expertise? Both relate strongly to the factor of indispensability.

With regards to the former, the district committees have two forms of representation, guild cooperative and craft. The idea is that they will be held in check by restricted electorates within the same guild. The control boards of the cooperatives will elect their district representatives from all departments of their cooperatives. The craft representatives will also represent the various clerical and manual trades. The finer technicalities of the positions cannot be learnt until the elected are in office. But on the provision that the general skills of representation are taught to all members of each guild, an adequate number of guild members will possess the basic essentials needed to join the district committees. Significantly, '[l]abourers and craftsmen have been found in the Building Guilds with considerable administrative ability' (Cole, G. D. H. 1921: 9). Restricting the scope of the individual district representatives to either cooperative departments or craft representatives ensures that the level of knowledge required in each is minimized. As a general command of either skill will be shared throughout each guild cooperative, the possibility that the elected will be endowed with the specialized and elitist knowledge imperative to indispensability is significantly impeded.

Neither will the district committees attain a unified monopoly of expertise. As there is a multitude of tasks to perform, there will be various departments within each district committee. 'On the Executive Committee not simply the various districts, but the various grades within those districts are represented, and the Executive itself is divided into departmental subcommittees which represent the point of view of the various grades' (Cole, G. D. H. 1919: 9). To ensure alliance between the various departments, information will regularly be exchanged; committee members will develop an overall knowledge of the internal affairs of the committee. This prevents any one department from generating the kind of monopoly of expertise that Michels insists is a corollary to the indispensability of leaders. When commentating on this kind of practice, Devine predicts that '[t]he general principle of openness of information, with each section's record open to scrutiny by any other, would provide a safeguard against the exploitation of one section by another' (1988: 228). Indeed, a basic intelligence would be gained by most sections within each department of the committee. It is unlikely that one department would be in a position to out-manoeuvre the others. By dividing the functions of the district committees, the chances that one section would be in a position to attain a monopoly of expertise, and hence render themselves irreplaceable, are reduced. So the fact that the district committees are indispensable does not mean they will be oligarchic. To reiterate, as a sufficient percentage of guild members will be able to seek election to the district committees, and as no one section of this committee will be in a position to attain a monopoly of expertise, a similar conclusion to that reached in respect of the works committee can be drawn. Although the district committees are indispensable, individual committee members are not.

Turning now to the national elements within the guilds, Cole acknowledges that in a large national body workers cannot vote for their national representatives with the same degree of clarity as they can with their craft or even district representatives. As such, it is worth taking note of the logic behind the voting procedures he proposes for the national elements. He is keen to avoid the delegate meeting being simply an 'enlarged replica of the executive committee'. Otherwise the larger body cannot adequately check the activities of the smaller body:

> 'The one will effectively balance the other only if different methods of election are adopted. I have therefore designed an Executive consisting half of representatives of all grades in each district and half of national representatives of the various crafts; but over against this body I have set a Delegate Meeting elected by each craft in each district severally.' (Cole, G. D. H. 1972: 200)

The executive represents the national craft and local all grades interests, which is balanced by the local craft interests represented by the delegate meeting. So even at the national level of the guilds, by installing two national bodies, each elected by different methods, Cole offers a system of checks and balances. The idea is that the dichotomy of the national craft and local all grades interests on the one hand, and the local craft interests on the other, helps prevent one body from ruling comprehensively. These proposals are a key aspect of the guilds' democratic armoury. It does seem possible, however, that their interests may frequently coincide. The danger being that the two national bodies would constitute interconnecting sections of what would effectively be the same body. Here the different methods of elections may not defend guild democracy as rigorously as intended.

Nevertheless, by drawing attention to their common, and then their distinct interests, it can be shown how this system can still approximate democracy. Cole asserts that both the national guild executive and the national delegate meeting will represent the general will of the guild. It is important that both bodies are also assigned distinct tasks. Cole mentions this briefly. The national delegate meeting, which is the larger body, will serve as a final appeal court and will determine the general lines of guild policy; to this I will add the task of enforcing the contract of association, which will involve working in close union with the guild bank. It is the national guild executive who will carry out exchange in the national market (1972: 190–1, 202–3); I have added to this the responsibility of regulating competition within its guild. Emphasis needs to be placed on the maintenance of this division of function as, following the district committees, the structural division between the two national bodies and the assignment of distinct functions to each will go some way towards restricting the chances any one section in either body has of consolidating a monopoly of expertise.

The democratic procedures visualized by Cole can, then, to some extent counter the decline into oligarchic control at the three main levels. But only to some extent, as a few solemn yet realistic reflections on the capability of workplace committees to fulfil their democratic role will indicate. Albert and Hahnel stress that although formally democratic committees are necessary, by themselves they cannot sustain workplace democracy. Lower-grade workers, even with voting rights, have less influence than managers who draw up budgets or construct products. The opportunity to develop skills in decision-making remains unequal. Workers performing mundane tasks are not encouraged to think deeply about their work, they become familiar with merely following orders. So even in democratic assemblies, the people whose jobs confer a richer knowledge of their firms operations will tend to dominate decision-making (1991: 18–19). It was shown in Chapter 3 that when work is boring and frustrating, it depresses skills and self-esteem; when it is interesting and challenging, they are enhanced. These qualities affect the degree to which participation in decision-making can be meaningful. In a similar vein, Rothschild and Whitt acknowledge that in large organizations the democratic and participatory ideals are impaired when the knowledge and skills required to fulfil essential tasks are unevenly distributed (1986: 104). The next section analyses the methods by which these particular obstacles to workplace democracies can be negated.

Part Three: Expertise

This section begins by explaining the reason why expertise can potentially undermine democracy in NED's guilds. It is immediately stated, however, why this problem is not impassable. The structural devices workplace democracies have at their disposal to maintain the democratic essence of their organizations are then highlighted and assessed. The section concludes by confirming that although their implementation involves certain trade-offs, the threat posed by the exclusive control of expert knowledge can be averted.

Cole states that the works experts will be chosen by the works committee – in NED this translates into the guild cooperative experts will be chosen by the control board – the district experts by the district committees, and the national experts by the national committees. Technical experts are not so much leaders but consultants who will mainly offer advice. As their selection does not affect the democratic issue, it is satisfactory that the committees elect them. A more immediate democratic method is not essential because they will not directly control any group of workers. He recognizes that the mass vote cannot always be used on technical matters that are only understood by a few experts, and that this is not necessarily elitist (1972: 195–8; 1920b: 50–4). This may appear a pragmatic approach to the dilemma of selecting technical experts. But there remains a potential threat to guild democracy. For Michels, as leaders become experts, their positions become more secure. Within a short period, a monopoly of expertise is established. This ensures that the rank and file become increasingly dependent upon their deliberations; the influence of the latter is significantly undermined. Michels' logic and the manner in which Cole distinguishes between the leadership jobs where election from below is appropriate (supervisory roles) and the positions where appointment is more suitable (technical experts) is not an identical comparison. Michels draws attention to the professionalization of the leaders themselves, and how in the process they develop their own expertise in the art of leading. Cole, though, wishes to keep the leadership bodies – the local, district and national committees – separate from the much smaller groups of experts whose role, as consultants, is mainly to advice. These two bodies are, however, obviously closely interconnected. In the case of amalgamation, collusion is the probable outcome, with experts effectively becoming part of the leadership group. Much of Michels' reasoning about the indispensability of expert leaders would then apply. Although his distinction between technical expertise and political leadership is at times blurred, it is likely that the internal democracy of the guilds would face a serious threat.

Echoing Michels' concerns, Rothschild and Whitt affirm that a major problem with expert knowledge is that it is prone to monopolization, which obviously stands in contrast to the egalitarian principle. The monopolization of knowledge, and the ensuing intensification of knowledge inequality, raises a serious dilemma for workplace democracies. It constitutes a key source of power that is instrumental to oligarchic control (1986: 104–8, 110). So due to their specialized knowledge, experts within the guilds are liable to exert, self-consciously or inadvertently, a disproportional influence on the committees' deliberations. Whether they are democratically elected or chosen by the various committees does not in itself alter this. This difficulty, however, is not insurmountable. The power of expert argument is, as Hands explains, 'double-edged'; the *depth* of expertise is often inversely proportional to its *breadth* (1971: 166). In large complex organizations like the guilds, the combination of depth and breadth in one small body would significantly increase the chances of that group becoming irremovable. One corrective strategy involves the establishment of procedures by which bodies of expert knowledge are disseminated to the greatest extent possible, thereby averting exclusive concentrations of expertise. This point is addressed by Devine. He suggests that although individuals cannot be experts in all matters, each person can excel at something. This negates the opportunity for the intelligentsia to monopolize expert power. Rather than simply impair the attainment of expert opinion, he recommends it should be generalized within the workplace. The tyranny of the expert is challenged by establishing a pluralism of expertise in every designated area; it is seldom the case that experts are in complete agreement on all issues. Consequently, '[t]he demystification of professional expertise requires openness of information and opinion. It also requires alternative expert opinion to be available to people and to self-governing groups' (Devine, P. 1988: 180–2).

So the question is how can NED's guilds *generalize* and *pluralize* expertise? Certain producer cooperatives have experience in pursuing this goal. Some of the worker cooperatives Rothschild and Whitt studied sought to replace specialized expertise with a more egalitarian distribution of knowledge. The formal and bureaucratic division of labour was, as a rule, minimized in these organizations. Rather than encourage experts to monopolize their knowledge as bureaucracies do, they attempted to reduce differentials in knowledge. Separations between intellectual and manual work, and between administrative and performance tasks, were deliberately reduced. Work roles were often more integrated, multifaceted and holistic. Expertise – which is considered an organizational, rather than an individual resource – was shared through the internal educational mechanisms of role rotation and task sharing. This resulted in a demystification of previously exclusive and elitist bodies of knowledge (1986: 60, 70). Once again, balanced job complexes can be referred to, now with regards to the generalization and pluralization of expert knowledge. It is these measures – role rotation, task sharing, balanced job complexes and the ensuring demystification and diffusion of knowledge – that generalize and pluralize expertise. They are intended to help counter the Michelian tendency of expertise to monopolize. As such, they are a precondition for equalising influence, and are essential for the equal empowerment the survival of workplace democracy depends upon. But as we shall now see, they also require certain compromises.

Perhaps the most immediate problem is that these programmes cannot always be worked out quickly. In one of the cooperatives Rothschild and Whitt studied, the alternative newspaper *Community News*,[3] task sharing was adopted. It attempted to achieve its tasks without an inflexible division of labour with its concomitant monopolization of expert knowledge. It largely succeeded, but the *News* quickly discovered that minimizing differentiation is time consuming:

> The *Community News* spent 1 hour and 40 minutes of regular meeting time deciding when and how the staff should do a complete role rotation, another 8 hours and 40 minutes at a special Sunday meeting called for that purpose, and not having finished, they spent an additional 5 hours and 20 minutes at the following regular staff meeting. Attendance at these meetings was 100 percent. This particular job rotation, then, absorbed 15 hours and 40 minutes of formal meeting time and countless hours of informal discussion. (Rothschild, J. & Whitt, J. A. 1986: 61)

This highlights a larger and more general problem with the preservation of organizational democracy, it takes time. As Rothschild and Whitt observe, two-way communication structures tend to be slow. To compensate,

3. This is a fictitious name.

meetings often need to be 'streamlined', and some tasks granted a higher preference than others. This creates problems, for example which particular meetings are indispensable, and which kinds of decisions may be delegated before the democratic and participatory ethics become strained? Job rotation and task sharing are, therefore, difficult to realize. Assignment planning involves large changes like regular retraining schedules. It can also be unsettling for those who find their specific jobs satisfying. This was the experience of some at the *News*. In extreme cases cooperators may object to the extent that they leave the cooperative. Nonetheless, occasional casualties are accepted at the *News* because the rotation system is widely recognized as instrumental to the practice of diffusing knowledge. Although patterns of influence cannot be equalized completely – verbal fluency, fair-mindedness and levels of energy and responsibility are likely to exert more influence in the group – the *News* did make serious inroads into undermining bureaucratic authority and expertise (Rothschild, J. & Whitt, J. A. 1986: 64–5, 70–1, 108–10).

The planning of role rotation and task sharing is a pragmatic exercise. At the *News*, although composition, editing and production tasks were commonly combined into job assignments, people were not asked to change work tasks every other day. The sharing of assignments is an equitable system, designed to ensure everyone attains experience and knowledge of all aspects of their production. The frequency of role changes can be informed by the particularities of each firm. Albert and Hahnel reiterate that it is not necessary for each individual to learn everything. All that matters is that every person is in a position in which they have the opportunity to devise plans, coordinate tasks and assess alternatives. Although some will take to this scheme more readily than others, it is the same with learning other basic skills such as literacy; and we do not, thankfully, suggest that the slower learners should not be taught to read and write. To ignorantly dismiss the ability of ordinary people to assimilate new skills and participate in managing their own affairs is to fall head-first into ideological distortion. As Albert and Hahnel put it, '[t]he myth that most people are incapable of intelligent participation no matter what training they get rationalises an economic structure that forces most people to fill debilitating roles so others can rule' (1991: 24–5; Rothschild, J. & Whitt, J. A. 1986: 108).

This is not the whole story; there are other advantages to balanced job complexes. Albert and Hahnel suggest that the creation of egalitarian work environments will restrict the time and energy elites waste upholding their positions. As the time spent defending status and coping with bureaucracies decreases, more energy can be directed into research and other creative activities. This will compensate for losses encountered by the most gifted scientists having to undertake their share of mundane tasks. Further, in response to the argument that without fixed hierarchies authority will deteriorate, they reply that appreciation of a team leader will not decline simply because s/he receives direction from other leaders on different teams. On the contrary, '[f]ar from diminishing the credibility of legitimate leadership, eliminating fixed hierarchies will undercut many impediments to efficient expression of leadership, for example, class hostilities' (1991: 24–5). Neither do they believe it will take excessive hours training work-forces to cope with a diverse schedule. They acknowledge that the more areas in which skills have to be developed the longer it will take, but the mutually enforcing benefits gained from the wider knowledge, together with a feeling of enrichment engendered by the practice of experiencing diverse responsibilities, will compensate for the extra training costs. Likewise, Rothschild and Whitt add that the time taken up by meetings is not a waste. Participation in decision-making tends to generate commitment to the outcome. When individuals have been active in a decision, they are less likely to resent its consequences. So for Rothschild, Whitt, Albert and Hahnel, the above educational mechanisms have the potential to enhance positive attributes in rank and file workers that would otherwise remain dormant (Albert, M. & Hahnel, R. 1991: 24–5, 35; Rothschild, J. & Whitt, J. A. 1986: 65).

Despite the use of a pragmatic approach and the value of democratic participation, the process of demystifying knowledge still contains a dilemma:

> Co-operatives employing relatively developed forms of technology must pay serious attention to sharing knowledge or risk eventual control by the experts. Sharing tasks, rotating jobs, creating apprenticeship systems and other means of demystifying knowledge enhance personal learning and perhaps member satisfaction, but time spent learning is time away from the production tasks of the organisation. (Rothschild, J. & Whitt, J. A. 1986: 111)

The guild cooperatives will perhaps need to trade some degree of efficiency and productivity, at least initially, in order to maintain their egalitarian existence.[4] But one critical point is clear. The contribution of role rotation, job

4. This is exactly what Rothschild and Whitt found in the cooperatives they studied. They conclude that 'schemes that broke down the conventional patterns of differentiation

sharing, balanced job complexes and the ensuing diffusion and demystification of knowledge towards the strengthening of organizational democracy cannot be dismissed as fanciful, inoperable, unrealistically utopian or such like. At the *News* for example, members were prepared to make the sacrifice in return for the non-monopolization of knowledge. Even though task sharing and rotation plans are time-consuming, the expenditure of effort makes sense when their value to democratic participation is taken into account. These devices would, therefore, be a necessary addition to NED's guild cooperatives. Although they will not replace the democratic election of guild officials, they are a valuable supplement. The strong tendency for expert knowledge to monopolize – a dynamic central to Michels' theory of transaction costs which, if left unchecked, is a powerful medium towards the entrenchment of oligarchic control – does not pose the same problems to the guilds as it does to mass political parties. The policies in the above programmes will ensure that organizational democracy can be approximated, even if it cannot be perfectly attained (Rothschild, J. & Whitt, J. A. 1986: 64, 109–11).

I would like to end this section on a point of clarification. Michels draws attention to the manner in which the differentiation of function produces oligarchic tendencies in an organization, a mass political party, which incorporates a multitude of diverse interests. Cole on the other hand grapples with how functions are best divided within a politico-economic organization that has initially been demarcated, a guild. The difference is considerable. Within a productive functional organization in which all members are full-time, not only is the range of contestable issues likely to be less extensive, it is also probable that the majority of members will be reasonably informed about the most immediate arguments for and against each one:

> Naturally the power of any individual worker-owner is diluted as the organisation enlarges, but it is still related to a fairly coherent and manageable range of activities and responsibilities in which they are heavily committed through their work, rather than to a disparate and distant set of activities in which they are only marginally involved. (Sayer, A. 1995: 161)

On this point Sayer is absolutely correct. It follows that the opportunity for the local (guild cooperatives), district and national committees to

---

did strengthen collective control, but they also entailed at least short-term losses in organisational efficiency' (1986: 112).

continuously deceive the various bodies of workers and the other auxiliary committees from which they were initially elected is, to some extent, undermined. It is true, however, that the more distant the governing body is, the harder it is to maintain democratic accountability. This applies only minimally to the committees in the guild cooperatives, to a larger extent at the regional level and to an even larger extent at the national level. But as the next chapter will argue, there are organizational structures that can prevent the polarization of the local and national levels. It will also be shown when representative democracy is embedded with a rich participatory context, the democratic ideal is more easily sustained. Taken together, these arguments will reinforce the conclusion of this section: the tendencies Michels identifies in his theory of transaction costs can be managed so that they will not drive the guilds towards rigid oligarchic control.

Part Four: Membership Lethargy

In Michels' thesis, the theory of transaction costs is just the first process. Organizational oligarchic tendencies are fortified by largely negative psychological imperatives: leaders develop an irresistible urge to dominate others while the masses have a need to be guided and require leaders to venerate. In one way or the other individuals have a universal identity: they share irreducible psychological characteristics. So as with the theory of transaction costs, Michels treats rank and file apathy as another universal category. This second part of the chapter begins by introducing the essentials of his theory. A short critical evaluation then follows by means of which I conclude that rank and file apathy will be overcome in functional democracy. In NED, the guild cooperatives will invoke sufficient participation. From here I infer that membership lethargy is not, in contrast to Michels' argument, due to the nature of the individual. There are two sections in what follows: a), 'Mass Apathy', and b), 'Participation in the Workplace'. The discussion in the latter is on the brief side as its contestable nature is, I believe, fairly minimal.

Mass Apathy

Michels stresses that rank and file members of an organization will generally not be endowed with either the intellectual or the emotional capacities to participate effectively. The majority are, he suggests, apathetic towards public concerns. To sustain membership influence members need to be active within the organization, maintaining a general knowledge of the major problems within it. The pull of work, however, limits the time and energy they can realistically invest in the group. It is only when political matters affect their private interests do they show any great interest in them. Most of the time people are only concerned with their own affairs, not the good of the collective. The majority of the members of modern democratic parties are indifferent to the management of the organization's activities; they are quite prepared to allow the few who regularly attend meetings to settle tactical and administrative questions. Consequently, the active minority dictate the laws to the apathetic and indifferent masses. So for Michels, along with the political indifference felt by the masses, their need for direction honours the leader, who in turn becomes powerful and indispensable (Michels, R. 1999: 85–8, 90–1; Parry, G. 1969: 44; Kitschelt, H. 1990: 86–7).

Michels goes on to claim that in political matters, there is a link between apathy and technical incompetence. To be effective political knowledge must be organized, and as the masses are too apathetic to do this they have a psychological need for guidance and are grateful for it. They are, he suggests, glad that the responsibility of decision-making is taken out of their hands. This only adds to the supremacy of the leaders, who become famous for defending the people, often at great personal cost. The collective feeling of gratitude helps guarantee the leaders' continual re-election, thus ensuring their perpetuation:

> The incompetence of the masses is almost universal throughout the domains of political life, and this constitutes the most solid foundation of the power of the leaders.... Since the rank and file are incapable of looking after their own interests, it is necessary that they should have experts to attend to their affairs. (1999: 111–12)

In addition, Michels argues that the masses feel a strong veneration towards their leaders, a deep respect that echoes a sentiment of hero worship in the former, and enhances the power of the latter. In this sense, the lethargy and incompetence of the masses only serves to consolidate the leaders' power. The specialized knowledge and the necessary amount of authority needed in the business of management means that a degree of despotism is largely unavoidable. So, the compliance, political incompetence and the submissive nature of the masses strengthen the conditions for the leading minority in the organization to increasingly distance themselves away from the apathetic masses (Michels, R. 1999: 92, 96–7, 110–14; Parry, G. 1969: 44).

Participation in the Workplace

In Michels' argument, the incompetence of the masses appears as an eternal category. This fairly short section will argue it is far more likely that this is a result of particular economic and technical conditions, rather than an inherent trait of every system. I will first indicate the practicality of, and benefits to, democratizing the workplace. It is then shown why the success of a cooperative is augmented by high levels of participation. Finally, in response to the claim that a self-governing culture may not by itself instigate a rise in participation, I conclude that balanced job complexes are indispensable to stimulating the interests and increasing the participation of a cooperative's entire membership.

With regards to workers there is little difference between a remote state elite or a remote private elite. 'Reducing what is done in the name of the state matters not one whit if the tasks are taken on by large-scale private corporate bureaucracies' (Hirst, P. 1990: 29). Cole also makes this point (n.d: 3–4). The solution is to design new structures that can make participation more meaningful. This is best achieved by making the workplace the centre of democratic participation. In the workplace individuals understand their surroundings, an environment without the vague glamour politicians fabricate to veil their own domain. Guild officers will be unable to follow the politician because the rank and file cannot so easily be deceived. Political demagogues are successful only because the electorate does not possess adequate checks upon them. Imagine that while electing their leaders the workers choose a poor representative/supervisor, what would be the likely outcome?

> At every turn, every hour of every day, the workers in the shop will be conscious of the incompetence of the man they have chosen. He will be dealing with matters that they themselves understand, and his interference will soon be resented by men who know his business better than he knows it himself. When the day of re-election comes round they will have had enough of him and his sort to make them choose a more capable man in his place. (Cole, G. D. H. 1972: 167)

It seems almost indubitable that the rank and file members in the guild cooperatives would be anything but lethargic. Any suggestion to the contrary – workers will be too apathetic to choose suitable supervisors and therefore lose an opportunity to create a genial work environment – would be almost disingenuous. Even Michels agrees that when a given political question affects the private concerns of the masses, their interests are likely to be aroused (1999: 85). The same can be said of their work. By injecting what are primarily economic bodies with a political content, they bring the democratic issue closer to the average worker's heart. In the workplace, where workers are under the daily instructions of their supervisors, workers would surely have much interest in how their supervisors are elected and/or appointed. It would seem that life in a genuine workplace democracy will have a great effect upon the workers' desire to participate.

The value of this cannot be overemphasized. Collective participation in decision-making is essential because it is actually a prerequisite for an efficient cooperative. Profit sharing has, by itself, not always been shown to be a reliable motivational driving-force. A case in point is Fitzroy's empirical research. In conventional capital-controlled firms, he infers, a slacking worker does so to the cost of absent shareholders; in all probability, other workers will be behaving in a similar fashion. But in profit-sharing firms, the same worker slacks to the detriment of her co-workers, who will be inclined to bring their collective weight upon her, especially if the group is cohesive. Yet it is not enough for cooperatives to only share their profits, there must in conjunction be high levels of participation. As Fitzroy explains, profit-sharing without participation in decision-making can weaken incentives. Individuals are likely to feel their personal contribution to profit is inconsequential, in which case their motivation will not be stirred. If profits stem only from managerial decisions, this will be treated as a random variable, and will invoke little inspiration. When profit-sharing exists alongside participation though, workers will expect a reward from their involvement with decision-making (1980: 191–2). Fitzroy investigated firms which had worker-participation, and others which shared their profits:

> To test the hypotheses, we divided our firms into two groups. One had a high degree of participation, the other low. In the group with high participation we found that profit-sharing had a positive and statistically significant effect on productivity, whereas in the group with the low degree of participation profit-sharing had no statistically significant effects. (Fitzroy, F. 1980: 192)

Fitzroy believes participation and profit-sharing can exist without any major changes in property rights; he does not call for a fully cooperative solution (like NED) to the problems in the existing political economy. Nevertheless, his research shows why it is crucial that cooperatives sanction a high degree of participation.

It has been claimed, however, that a culture of self-governance has not always engendered high levels of participation. For example with regards to the Yugoslavia system of self-management, Nove points out that the desire to participate was not universal. Many workers showed little interest in joining committees, or to learn the knowledge required of a co-manager. This was one of the main reasons why the power of management remained considerable. Workers can be assumed to be intelligent, but in their work capacity they are unlikely to be familiar with the demand patterns of their products, relative costs or the economic benefits of various innovations. Nove's point is that the Yugoslav experience indicates that participation in self-governing structures can be limited (1983: 137). Maybe; but caution must be shown when reference is made to the old Yugoslav experience. During his discussion of commodity fetishism, Howard claims:

> the adherence to a traditional hierarchical division of labour within the firm, the failure to extend democracy from the particular firm to the economy as a whole, and the suppression of political freedom in Yugoslavia require us to regard the Yugoslav case as an imperfect example of self-management. (2000: 82)

This system – in which Communist Party officials typically appointed directors to local firms, which as Howard stresses did very little for their accountability to the workforce (2000: 143) – is hardly conducive to rousing participation in the ranks. It is significant that the Mondragon, Plywood and Hoedads cooperatives have all at some stage enjoyed success in instigating an increase in levels of participation. There is no reason why NED cannot follow in their footsteps.

Nevertheless, Nove is probably right that the less workers know about their immediate working environment, the harder it will be to generate their interest to participate. Here the educational mechanisms like role rotation and balanced job complexes can be reintroduced. As they are intended to increase levels of participation, it is appropriate to re-emphasize their value in relation to stimulating the interests and energies of shop-floor workers. They ensure that knowledge of all aspects of production will be disseminated on a wider scale. No single work team will be acquainted with all of the variants. This is not the intention of balanced job complexes, but they do guarantee far more than a small minority will understand at least one of them. Workers can be expected to participate more when their interests are aroused, and with balanced job complexes everyone's workload will include a degree of interesting work. Under these productive conditions levels of participation can be expected to rise considerably; workers can then quickly grasp the lessons of self-government. It is hard to imagine them remaining apathetic and incompetent. The causes of voter apathy are, as radical democrats have always correctly argued, not to be found in human nature, but in the way society has conditioned the electorate (Parry, G. 1969: 152–3). Apathy may just as easily be a result of a lack of encouragement, rather than evidence of its impracticality.

Before we leave this chapter, I would like to offer one final remark. It is probable that by stimulating the rank and file members of a guild cooperative to participate in their guilds internal politics, the stimulus will be carried through elsewhere. As the workers in the guilds are also consumers and citizens, the desire to engage may well spread to these spheres. The idea is to encourage consumers to reflect upon their actions and to participate politically, not just in terms of personal desire satisfaction. In this sense, just as the democratic issue is brought closer to the workers' hearts, so it could be brought closer to the citizens' hearts. This kind of democratic impetus is certainly what Cole had in mind. 'What a man was in his daily labour, that would he be in his leisure and as a citizen' (1956: 246). This position is far from unique. Developmental and participatory democrats like Rousseau, Wollstonecraft, Mill, Macpherson and Pateman stress that participation breeds participation. 'Once people become active subjects, making things happen, in one aspect of their lives, they are less likely to remain passive objects, allowing things to happen to them, in other aspects' (Devine, P. 1988: 159). Chapter 3 reinforced this claim with empirical evidence. It would seem, then, that although Michels is not wrong about the nature of rank and file apathy in the representative democracy of modern Western politics, he is mistaken to universalize this outside a context in which mass undifferentiated political parties predominate.

Conclusion

The above arguments constitute NED's response to Michels' two weak theories of oligarchy. To very briefly recap, with appropriate procedures for electing guild officials, and with structural mechanisms for the demystification and pluralization of expert knowledge – realized mainly through task sharing and balanced job complexes, the tendencies Michels captures in his theory of transactional costs can be negated. It was then shown in relation to his theory of membership lethargy that the chief arena for democratization in NED will be the workplace. Together, these kinds of political participation will neutralize the tendency for particular leaders to become indispensable. So, rather than speak in terms of 'the nature of the individual', perhaps Michels should have restricted his assertions to 'the nature of the individual in liberal democracy'.

6

A Theory of Elite Control

Michels treats the theories of transaction costs and membership lethargy as weak forms of oligarchy, which constitute the preliminary elements of his theory. The strong theory stresses that an organization's leadership will evolve along internally cohesive lines; it will distance itself from the rank and file and assume its own unique set of interests. His argument is at its strongest when he is addressing the 'autocratic tendencies of leadership' and 'the exercise of power and its psychological reaction upon the leaders'. The main part of this chapter is divided into two sections; each one named in accordance with Michels' discussion. In both sections I outline the essential points and respond to them. My contention is that NED's guilds and guild cooperatives have, with the introduction of certain innovations, the potential to resist the factors that give rise to the strong notion of oligarchy. The chapter concludes with an additional section, 'The Social Councils', which demonstrates why these bodies provide the forum through which oligarchic tendencies will be negated.

Part One: Autocratic Tendencies of Leadership

This section addresses the two tenacious issues of leadership stability and the struggle between the leaders themselves. Addressing the former, Michels states that when officials remain in their positions for long periods, dangers to democracy arise. The longer they stay in office, the greater their influence over the masses. This serves to increase their independence. Leaders need a socialization period in office to become familiar with their work, which needs to be for a considerable time. Further, leaders will not give 100% if it is likely that dismissal can easily follow. The official needs a sense of security. Once leaders 'stick in their grooves', they tend to see themselves as 'God given leaders'. Short terms in office may be democratic, but for technical and psychological reasons, they are impractical. With the rapid succession in positions of command, the resulting confusion in regulations and orders will render control difficult. Although rotation in office corresponds to the democratic principle, it is compensated by these drawbacks. Due to the lengthy stay in office, the leaders are transformed into a 'closed caste'. On the rare occasion when the masses are evoked to the extent that the leaders' position is threatened, the latter present themselves as a 'compact phalanx'.[1] In which case, the governing bodies of organizations can act at their own discretion, in virtual independence from the represented. The general practice is that the governing bodies, and only the governing bodies, discuss the most important questions. These affairs are, Michels concludes, essentially oligarchic (Michels, R. 1999: 120–1, 123–5, 167–71).

This is the basis to Michels' leadership stability thesis. There are two preliminary discussions regarding his claim that a lengthy stay in office is both technically and psychologically practical. Michels is correct that newly elected officials will need a period of time for their new surroundings to become familiar. But as we have seen, a reasonable percentage of guild members will have a basic understanding of the general tasks in the guild cooperatives, district and national committees. Hence, this time period need not be excessive. This also bears affinity to the psychological worry of easy dismissal. It should be noted though the conditions Cole places on the democratic device of the recall.[2] Its usage should not, he insists, be unrestricted. Before a leader can be removed, s/he may appeal to his or her fellow managers. If there is sympathy the issue goes before a higher committee within the guild (1920b: 58–9). This measure is intended to guard against personal vendettas. On the provision that officials act fairly and efficiently, they will have no reason to feel insecure. Due to the bottom-up dynamic of guild democracy, it is far more likely that officials will experience anxieties of dismissal if they fail to represent the interests of those who elected them. That is, the psychological worry of easy dismissal is

1. Michels places great emphasis on this, mentioning it in two separate discussions (1999: 122–6, 167).

2. With his customary scepticism, Michels states that conservative tendencies within the organization will restrict the use of this right, and so reduce the supremacy of the sovereign mass to an illusion. Nevertheless, even he is forced to acknowledge that '[u]nquestionably this defence possesses a certain theoretical value, and the authoritarian inclinations of the leaders are in some degree attenuated by these possibilities' (1999: 167).

likely to rise concurrently with an increase in oligarchic decision-making. So this particular argument may be used in support of democracy, rather than against it.

Michels goes on to argue that partly as a consequence of their long stay in office, the leaders of an organization become increasingly detached from party rank and file. They will tend to fill in any emerging gaps in their ranks directly through their own volition, rather than by means of popular elections. When the rank and file are asked to select candidates, the central executive will often insist on the right of veto. Consequently, the leaders show a tendency to isolate. They form a closed institution, only allowing those who are in agreement to enter their ranks – a privilege that has an essentially oligarchical character (1999: 126–7). Cole is fully aware of this tendency. Commenting on the desire of the postal workers to form a national guild, he states their priority must be to bring the whole question of appointments and promotions under collective control. 'As long as promotion lies in the hands of the departmental officials who are thus able to administer rewards and punishments without regard to the opinions of the workers…it is useless to look for democracy' (1919: 4). Officials appointed by the bureaucracy will remain dependent upon it for further promotion. As such, they absorb the 'bureaucratic standpoint', while simultaneously losing the sense of co-working with the ranks from which they initially emerged. He therefore seeks not only real control over promotions, but also the inalienable right of workers to retain within their own ranks promoted officials. He repeats the claim when discussing the same issue in relation to the railway industry. 'The railwaymen have only to control the promotion of men from the ranks and to preserve control over those whom they have promoted. Having done that, they will have established, in its most essential features, a National Railway Guild' (1919a: 6).

Likewise, in NED's guild cooperatives the control boards will not retain the privilege to fill in gaps in the hierarchy through their own determination. One of the cornerstones of the guild constitution is that leadership positions are elected from below through popular elections; with the exception of the management members who are appointed by the control board – which itself is elected by the cooperative's sovereign body, the general assembly. Simply put, the control board does not hold the constitutional powers to reject new members elected by the general assembly. As such, even where committee members have a long stay in office, as they cannot choose their own recruits, they will not be transformed into a 'compact phalanx'. As Burnheim observes, '[o]nce the people already in power have no control over who their colleagues are going to be they will not be able to enforce secrecy' (1985: 167). This casts a doubt on Michels' claim that governing bodies of organizations can 'act entirely at their own discretion, maintaining a virtual independence of the collectivity they represent'. In a functionally demarcated politico-economic organization like a guild, the bottom-up nature of democracy will restrict the unmitigated use of discretion. In this sense, a 'virtual independence' is prevented.

Turning now to the second theme of this section, the struggle between the leaders themselves, Michels' argument is twofold. First, he suggests that every oligarchy harbours suspicion to anyone who attempts to join its ranks, seeing them as competitors ready to supplant them. The established leaders are naturally inclined to suppress or even deliberately sabotage the efforts of the new aspirants to leadership. To lose their command is to lose their importance, so they will not hesitate to use repressive methods to preserve their positions. The leaders may justify such behaviour by arguing that the organization is in conflict with powerful opponents and hence needs to maintain strong leadership. Attempts to challenge organizational policy or criticize leaders can be portrayed as treachery to the organization.[3] The result is that leaders will debilitate the rank and file and govern the party to suit their own interests. Secondly, Michels insists that usually one group of elites does not simply replace another. Rather, there is an ongoing process of intermixture, with the older sections absorbing and assimilating the new elements:

> Very rarely does the struggle between the old leaders and the new end in the complete defeat of the former. The result of the process is not so much a *circulation des elites* as a *reunion des elites*, an amalgam, that is to say, of the two elements. (Michels, R. 1999: 182)

On the occasions when they are seriously threatened by a new band of aspiring leaders, if they do not wish to stand down the old leaders may agree to enter a power-sharing pact with the newcomers. The submission of the old leaders, Michels suspects, is merely a ploy to undermine their younger rivals' influence. By conceding posts to their most conspicuous rivals, they impose obstacles in their way. As the new aspirants begin to share responsibilities with their old opponents, their activities become confounded. In this sense oligarchies can debilitate insubordinate yet influential opponents, and avoid an uprising against their own authority

3. Michels repeats these assertions (1999: 213–18).

(Michels, R. 1999: 172–3, 176–9, 180–3; Kitschelt, H. 1990: 87; Lipset, S. M. 1999: 17–18).

This is Michels' double-edged argument concerning the struggle among the leaders themselves. I will respond to each, beginning with his claim that leaders are able to legitimize the suppression of their internal competitors by pointing to powerful external opponents their organization is in conflict with. On the productive side of NED, external competition between the guilds will not occur. Guilds have little to gain by out-manoeuvring their counterparts. It would often be quite the opposite. Closely connected guilds have 'interlocking directorates', which involves a 'mutual exchange of seats on the governing bodies of the Guilds' (Cole, G. D. H. 1920b: 68). An ambience of fierce competition is not conducive to the maintenance of reciprocal relationships. In NED there is, however, a role for a regulated *intra* guild competition. Not all Marxist-inspired thinkers would be impressed by this. 'The modifying influence that one would expect to come from workers electing their own manager is more than offset by the regime of production for the market and its pitiless logic of profit maximization' (Ollman, B. 1998: 101). This is no doubt true in market forces economies, but in NED the competitive ethic is contained within each demarcated industrial sphere. A workplace's 'powerful external opponents' would be no more than their guild fellows in separate cooperatives. Cole believes that there will be a 'spirit of healthy emulation' between the different workshops of the same guild (1920: 14). It must also be remembered that in NED the financial returns for high output are monitored by guild committees who are themselves constituted through representatives from each cooperative. The guild contract of association will also strengthen mutual aid and prevent economic opacity within the guild.

Further, the regulating and redistributive functions of the regional and national guild committees, together with the bodies who administer the democratic investment fund, will ensure that although production for the market will continue, decision-making will not be solely determined by the 'pitiless logic of profit maximization'. Again, Mondragon's political structures of mutual aid illustrate this point well. Mondragon has a proud history of upholding cooperative values. For example the cooperative group Fagor, a large and successful cooperative group which consists of 13 cooperatives, pioneered the practice of risk sharing. If a cooperative is experiencing serious difficulties, it receives a subsidy from the currently successful cooperatives in the group so that it can return to efficient performance. In addition, during the 1970s a de-sizing in one cooperative resulted in 94 redundancies. Of these, 69 were relocated in another cooperative, and the remaining 25 were provided with adult education. 'The members of the Group directly financed this by agreeing to the subtraction of 1% of the gross income from their monthly pay checks to cover these costs' (Greenwood, D. J. 1991: 41, 74). This is hardly the cut-throat competition that capitalist society is said to thrive on. The same cooperative values will be upheld in NED's guild cooperative groups. Here the terms 'conflict' and 'enemies' does not seem warranted, at least not to the extent that the perceived threat of external 'rivals' can be invoked to justify the suppression of internal challenges. Whether reference is to inter- or intra-guild relations, the guild leaders cannot use the excuse of powerful external adversaries to defend repressive methods against emerging bands of potential new leaders.

Let us now see why Michels' second argument, that elites will not replace one another but amalgamate, will not affect organizational democracy in the way he suggests. Cole acknowledges that on the occasions when a *reunion des elites* does occur, it is indeed a major threat to organizational democracy. He describes how after the First World War the state recognized the power of the trade unions. But instead of granting the workers real control, he suggests it offered them a 'sham partnership' that disarmed them. It captured and then pressurized trade union officials into distancing themselves from the recalcitrant rank and file; the outcome was a hindrance to labour's fortunes (1916: 1). Along similar lines he warns that in recognizing the workers' demand for freedom, the public and private employers will reason:

> Let us grant a little, since we must; but let us make our grant in such a form as to tie the workers' hands from asking for more... They demand a share in management; let us place a few of them on boards of directors, provided that we remain in a safe majority. A handsome bribe will soon make them content. (Cole, G. D. H. 1914a)

Not surprisingly, he insists that leadership positions on the local, regional and national committees in the guilds must be filled from below. The existing leaders will not then be at liberty to concede posts to their most conspicuous rivals.[4] As explained above, the control boards in the guild cooperatives cannot appoint whomever they wish. Now the dynamic is

4. Cole had experience of this tactic. It was used by Beatrice Webb who set out to harness the energies of an aspiring group of serious-minded students, among whom was Cole. She attempted to 'undercut their critical potential by drafting them into the various

repeated in relation to the issue of relinquishing position. It is the guild cooperatives who determine the personnel on the higher representative bodies. The established leaders are obliged to enter into a power-sharing pact with the newcomers, a pact that is not of their own choosing. This will affect the dynamic within the committee. Freshly elected officials with the full support of the electorate are far less likely to be intimidated or manipulated by the experienced leaders than if their position had been consciously relinquished or directly appointed by the latter. Finally, when an amalgamation of leaders does occur it may be that the old leaders do hold on to their positions. Yet this will often be at the expense of compromising their policies. As Hands points out, this may help secure policy agreements. In this sense the dynamic may enhance democracy, rather than undermine it (1971: 162–3). So although the activities of the old and new bands of leaders interconnect, it does not seem that the former can undermine the challenge to their own authority, and subsequently that the latter will find their influence incapacitated.

To summarize, it is the combination of these facets that help prevent leadership groups from evolving along internally cohesive lines. In which case, the above tendencies underlined by Michels will not impair the internal democracy of NED's guilds.

Part Two: The Exercise of Power and its Psychological Reaction upon the Leaders

There are two main themes in this section of Michels' thesis. In the interests of convenience, I begin by briefly establishing their key features, before introducing the rationale of this section. First, Michels notes that at the beginning of their careers, leaders are genuinely convinced that the principles they advocate are laudable; their altruism is sincere. Over a period of time, however, the actual practice of leadership produces a profound change, a change that affects their moral character in a way that is destructive to democracy. Along with the organization's evolution, the leaders also evolve mentally, transforming their personalities. The consciousness of power creates a sense of personal greatness. 'He who has acquired power will almost always endeavour to consolidate it and to extend it, to multiply the ramparts which defend his position, and to withdraw himself from the control of the masses' (1999: 206). For Michels, the desire to dominate is an

sub-groups of her Control of Industry Committee' (Mathews, F. 1979: 161). Cole promptly resigned from the Fabian society and devoted himself to the guild socialist movement.

elementary universal psychological fact. Once people experience the exercise of power, it is difficult to persuade them to return to their old positions. Secondly, he argues that leaders of an organization tend to demand conformity from the rank and file, who should obey the orders given to them promptly and without critical reflection. 'To the leaders it is altogether inconceivable that the actions of the supreme authority can be subjected to criticism, for they are intimately convinced that they stand above criticism, that is to say above the party' (1999: 206, 217). These two factors – the psychical transformations caused by the experience of power and the refusal to acknowledge criticism – combine to ensure that the emerging party leadership will develop a particular self-interest at odds with those of the rank and file. They quickly become a power elite and cultivate attitudes that stem from their position within the privileged element. Michels' point is that due to an exclusive reserve on decision-making, organizational policies will reflect the interests of the leaders, not the masses. He once more rejects the idea of a representative leadership.

With regards to the psychological metamorphosis of the leaders, it seems probable that the experience of power will engender psychological changes in those who wield it. Although Michels states that exercising power produces an ineffaceable change in the holder's character, he is aware that other variables are also influential. For example, the 'factor of individuality', individuals will react in different ways to the same environment. Yet despite arguing that the personal element should be considered along with the environmental, he is unmoved:

> It is nevertheless true that in the course of party evolution, as the led becomes a subordinate leader, and from that a leader of the first rank, he himself undergoes a mental evolution, which often effects a complete transformation in his personality. (Michels, R. 1999: 209)

It is the move from opposition to power that transforms the leaders' mentalities. For Michels, this transformation in personality will only strengthen the oligarchic impulse (1999: 206, 209–10). In response, I would like to suggest that psychological changes are also a major characteristic of other power positions. A prison officer, a barrister or even a parent are all likely to be changed by their experiences of prison, the judicial system and the family. We are all to some degree changed by our experiences. It is not that power will have no effect on those who wield it. Rather, it is that there are a number of circumstances other than the factor of individuality that are likely to engender cognitive transformations. For example if the leadership group could be prevented from dissociating itself from the led, the influence on their mentality will be less dramatic. By averting the tendency for the leadership and led factions of an organization to polarize, the psychological changes in the leaders will be of a less oligarchic nature than when the two groups pull in opposite directions.

This section concentrates on how a democratic enterprise like a guild can achieve this goal. I will outline and assess the methods used by two larger cooperatives who, although not identical to the guilds, share enough of their essential features – in particular their federal basis – to warrant comparison. Hoedads, a forestry cooperative based in Oregon, has over 300 members, divided into teams of 15–20. Then there are the plywood cooperatives; in these 14 firms, the range is from 80–350 members (Greenberg, E. S. 1984: 175; Gunn, C. 1984: 145). As their size renders the decision-making process difficult, it is helpful to see how they deal with the problem of self-governance. Both Hoedads and the plywood cooperatives make use of consensus decision-making and larger representative bodies. Their complex and multilayered structures are designed to maximize group freedom while simultaneously securing the survival of the organization itself. I first introduce the various mechanisms these cooperatives adopt to counter the tendency of their respective representative bodies to evolve into a distant alien institution. It is shown that as they are largely successful it is a), possible to combine direct and representative democratic forms and b), how they compensate for each other's weaknesses. Attention is then drawn to a further essential facet of the plywood cooperatives – the leaders continuing to work part-time in the teams who initially elected them – which, as it plays a vital role in maintaining communication between the leading bodies and the work teams, is pivotal in preventing the polarization of the leader and led factions. From here it will be explained how the implementation of a similar scheme into NED's guilds will invigorate their democratic structures. It is then illustrated how, through the institutionalization of regular forums for criticism, the tendency for leaders to ignore or dismiss valid criticism can be directly challenged. Finally, attention will return to the issue of the leaders' psychological metamorphosis.

Hoedads implements both participatory and representative democratic forms. Each work team reaches decisions through consensus. In addition, every team chooses a representative who sits on regular meetings with the other representatives. Like the guilds, Hoedads has higher level committees to address the matters that need extensive research. It is here, the negotiation of solutions to complicated issues at the wider cooperative level, that the democratic process faces its greatest test. 'The committees walk a fine line between helping to provide leadership and informational input for long-term planning and for policy and operating decisions on the one hand, and impeding the democratic process of the co-op on the other' (Gunn, C. 1984: 151). The committees do not determine policies solely on their own deliberations, nor do they affect the decisions of the work teams. But as they influence decisions by expressing varying levels of interest for each issue and through the presentation of their analysis of relevant information, they do have considerable power. In light of this, the committee's role is restricted to giving advice, elections are frequent and work teams are recommended to rotate their representatives every 6 months. Additionally, in relation to the large geographical scale which consequently makes information flows problematic, Hoedads has its own internal publications within which each member can contribute. Finally, there are the general meetings, attended by the whole membership, in which plans concerning the long-term direction of the firm are discussed. Decisions taken are usually controversial policy issues, those that involve large sums of money and rules that make something compulsory. As the meetings can be drawn-out and tiresome affairs, they are held at weekend summer retreats where members can mix work and leisure. It is in this sense that Hoedads combines participatory and representative forms (Gunn, C. 1984: 145–6, 148–9, 151–2; Jackall, R. & Levin, H. M. 1984: 139).

A similar set-up occurs in the plywood cooperatives. The workplaces make the decisions which affect their own affairs, while those relating to wider policy formation are taken by the key democratic institution, a board of directors. The board is elected each year by the membership. Greenberg is keen to establish whether the board is responsive to its constituency, or whether it evolves into a remote institution of professional politicians whose policies are inconsistent with the wishes of the membership. His conclusion is that no closed group continuously dominates the board and enforces its opinions upon the rest of the membership. So in respect to policy decision-making, ultimate control rests with the general membership. There is more than one reason for this. First, there is the strong worker participation in elections. As well as their knowledge and frequent discussion of company policy, which typically increases over time, 31.5 had run for election, and 17.5 had at one time succeeded. Secondly, there are the disadvantages of being a board member. Although the psychic rewards of status and prestige are in themselves gratifying, members are not compensated for the extra hours they dedicate to cooperative business. Being a board member, Greenberg discovered, can be a burden rather than a comfort. Thirdly, there is the high turnover rate in the boards. When this became so severe it threatened stability, controls were introduced. As one worker explains, 'each year we elected all nine members on the board. Now we... elect only three and the people serve for three years' (quoted in Greenberg, E. S. 1984: 204, 203–5; 1986: 50–3; Jackall, R. & Levin, H. M. 1984: 139–40).

So, Hoedads and the plywood cooperatives make use of larger representative committees/board of directors. Both Gunn and Greenberg claim they not only demonstrate that direct and representative democratic forms can co-exist, they also mutually enhance and enrich each other's positive attributes. Due to the variables of size and time, a large politico-economic enterprise like a guild needs representative institutions. The guild cooperatives though can still be active in the decisions that determine the general direction of guild policy. As the Hoedads and plywood cooperatives have shown, the 'pervasive participatory democratic milieu' is the key premise upon which this claim can be substantiated. It would seem that the mixture of direct and representative methods helps prevent oligarchic tendencies from manifesting in large democratic organizations. Echoing Michels, Greenberg identifies the central problem:

> Almost all of these problematic tendencies are related, in one way or another, to the distance and lack of communication between a professional political class intensely engaged in governance and a largely uninformed, irrational, and apathetic mass population. (Greenberg, E. S. 1984: 212)

Yet in contrast to Michels' predictions, this kind of problematic distance did not exist in the Hoedads and plywood cooperatives. To reiterate, frequent elections, the open flows of information, general meetings, regular policy debates and the high turnover and rotation of board members all contributed towards creating a well-informed membership. Through these measures, communication between workers and supervisors is a two-way process, and is not seen by workers as hierarchical control (Gunn, C. 1984: 146–52; Greenberg, E. S. 1984: 211–13; 1986: 78–9).

Both Hoedads and the plywood cooperatives have, then, using different variations of the same methods, found ways of institutionalizing communication and preserving close contact between their respective representative bodies and the various work teams. This is a fine achievement. In representative democracies, as government and governed are separated, the task of politics is to create instruments by which citizens may exert some control over their leaders. A combination of democratic forms has enabled both Hoedads and the plywood cooperatives to successfully meet this challenge.

Representative democracy invariably stratifies, this is an omnipresent phenomenon. But as Greenberg explains, as representative institutions can be embedded within a vibrant participatory environment, they can fulfil their function without undermining self-governance.[5] This combination successfully ensured that the representatives remained accessible to the represented. He concludes that a professional political class does not dominate the board, and that the board is not plagued by the problems of rigidity and remoteness characteristic of representative institutions (1984: 203–5, 212; 1986: 64). Likewise, Gunn concludes that the outcome is a democratic organization which is able to cope with large physical distances. In this sense it can avoid the fragmentation that might otherwise stem from the diversity of projects at the local team level (166–7, 152). These are, to repeat, crucial findings. They indicate that the democratic fate of large-scale politico-economic organizations is, in the right circumstances and with the appropriate structural features, sanguine.[6] Along with the plywood cooperatives, Hoedads is 'readily reproducible as an organisational form' (Gunn, C. 1984: 167). NED's guilds will, accordingly, implement similar measures. Although the guilds district committees and national bodies are vested with authority, any measure which is likely to engender substantial change can only be passed through guild referendum. As a corollary, the

5. Gunn reaches the same conclusion (1984: 152).

6. This was indeed the case with the Mondragon superstructure. Decision-making in the cooperative group Ularco is complex, but it is genuinely democratic. A good example that illustrates this is the process by which a compensation policy was finalized. The guiding principles did not reflect exclusively the values of those leading the decision-making process. The decision-makers were aware they had to offer members a clear rational in terms they could understand, and a new pay formula was eventually accepted. The end result, though, did far more than display the power of management to enforce its own agenda. To gain widespread acceptance for its proposal, management were obliged to qualify the formula in order to accommodate members' expressed wishes (Whyte, W. F. & Whyte, K. K. 1991: 148). Likewise, Greenwood's et al. empirical research into Fagor, found that although there were problems with the operations of the workplace, the organizational structures of the Fagor cooperatives have been successfully democratized. They conclude that over time Fagor has not only become to an increasing extent a participatory and accountable system, with an equality of accessibility of all members to the structures of governance, it has remained an effective decision-making body. 'It appears that the higher organizational complexity and greater professionalization of management have not significantly impeded change initiatives arising from many different locations within the Group' (1991: 91). This, sustaining a democratic business in a collectively of over 6,000 members, is a highly impressive achievement (1991: 11, 21, 91).

higher guild committees cannot determine policies entirely by themselves; they are obligated to consult the general membership on issues that have a compulsory endorsement. In these circumstances, a genuine guild democracy is far from unattainable.

This claim will now be substantiated through an analysis of an additional feature which will play a decisive role in preserving close contact between the guild committees and the local cooperatives – the manner in which workers become informed and active in the process of general policy formulation. Greenberg observes a democratic tendency in both Hoedads and the plywood cooperatives, the overall availability of information. The minutes of meetings are always published. Copies are then placed in lunchrooms and posted on bulletin boards. This coincides with the cooperatives' policy that all documents are obtainable on request. 'The impressively widespread availability of information necessary to develop informed judgment and the high level of continuous discussion about this information and the policy decisions for which it is appropriate became quickly apparent in the interviews' (1986: 50). On the occasions when this literature was read, Greenberg was impressed by the high levels of discussions and the resulting policy decisions. He adds, however, that just a small percentage of workers regularly take note of the published minutes. This implies a greater flow of information has to be secured by additional methods. In the plywood cooperatives this is achieved by board members continuing to work in their regular jobs, where workers have the opportunity to probe deeper if they believe their questions have not been answered satisfactorily (1984: 200–1). As one rank and filer put it, 'when I worked with George . . . he was on the board a lot . . . and I used to always get all the information from him' (quoted in Greenberg, E. S. 1984: 201). A similar procedure will feature in NED's guilds. Due to their workloads, it will not be practical to make the members of the cooperative, district and national committees part-time. But it is possible to construct a system in which committee members return to their initial localities 1 day in every 2 weeks. The rotation scheme will be staggered. On any given day no more than 10% (corresponding to 1 day of the working fortnight) of a committee's membership will be on what may be termed their day release programme. As there will be more cooperative committees than district committees and, in turn, more district committees than national bodies, their numbers will alter accordingly. The circulation will take longer with the district than with the cooperative representatives, and longer still with those from the national bodies. A possible schedule would be that every local work-group has a cooperative committee member working with them once a week, a district committee member once a fortnight and a national executive/delegate meeting member once a month. These shift ratios are based on approximate speculation, the finer details can be left to circumstance. The general idea, though, is clear enough.

Perhaps the most immediate drawback is that easy worker access to the board members can be stressful to the latter. To serve on the board an individual needs not only dedication, but also an ability to cope with pressure. As one board member of the plywood collectives put it, 'I sure get hell once in a while... They all jump on me... We've had quite a few guys who couldn't take it and had to resign' (quoted in Greenberg, E. S. 1984: 205). This may seem rather harsh, but it certainly appears to hold the board members accountable; and accountability is supposedly one of the key principles of democracy. Indeed, it is likely that 'getting hell' would be more than 'once in a while' if the board member had become an oligarch. The contribution this arrangement makes to the form of organizational democracy can, then, hardly be exaggerated. 'It is... apparent that the board does not become a distant and separate institution because of the inescapable fact that board members continue to hold jobs in the mill during their tenure and are accessible to the shareholders' (Greenberg, E. S. 1984: 205). This arrangement is, therefore, a prerequisite for guild democracy.

I now wish to respond to Michels' claim that leaders will be unable to take a balanced view of criticism. Rothschild and Whitt stress that a structural condition which helps prevent an organization from yielding to oligarchy is 'mutual and self-criticism'. They point out that critical exchanges aid the egalitarian and participatory ethics of producer cooperatives. When criticism is applied systematically, it greatly reduces inequality of influence. When the levelling effects of critical forums are institutionalized, the understanding that one's actions can be exposed to group criticism can undermine excesses of individual power. Their empirical evidence indicates that the accumulation of unvented resentments and the expansion of unequal influence is more likely to occur in organizations that do not install an arena for regular critical appraisals; groups who do implement a procedure for critical reviews show a tendency to develop informal rules of fairness that determine what may pass as legitimate criticism. Social pressures are applied to those who disregard the collectively determined rules of fairness (Rothschild, J. & Whitt, J. A. 1986: 84–6).

When put into practice, these measures have been hugely successful. For instance Reinharz (1983) consulted a collective bakery. Though ideologically committed to democracy, it was experiencing internal communication problems. Her initial assessment was that interpersonal difficulties were generated more by the organization's unstructured procedures than by differences in personalities. As the bakery had no 'institutionalized sanction mechanisms', there were no formal means by which criticism could be channelled. So the goal was to design a structure which would enable members to deal with the inevitable conflicts that exist in every workplace democracy. Her innovation was the introduction of 'feelings meetings' (a term coined by the bakers) into the decision-making process. These monthly evening meetings took place in the comfort of the bakers' homes and lasted for 1.5–3.5 hours. She concludes:

> The collective evaluates our 2.5 year relationship as having prevented the disintegration or bureaucratisation of the setting. Our meetings did not eliminate the collective's problems but provided an area where disturbing feelings were transferred into useful learning and new supportive structures. (Reinharz, S. 1983: 209)

The collective acknowledged that the successful preservation of its democracy is through the establishment of these meetings (Reinharz, S. 1983: 205–7). In a similar fashion, Hoedads holds 'crew meetings' in which interpersonal problems are addressed. Although they are recognized as being the most difficult, they also tend to be the most rewarding. 'There is a feeling held in common … that, however tortuous and personally painful crew meetings are, they are one of the focal arenas for personal and organisational development. It is there, for instance, that prejudices and power relationships are confronted' (Gunn, C. 1984: 150).

The group sessions may appear daunting, but they do not need to correspond to the infamous 'encounter groups' characteristic of rehabilitation concept houses. Although behaviour can be challenged, criticism can be carried out with tact; it can be informal and gentle, rather than vitriolic and abrasive; or it may be aimed towards the group, avoiding individual confrontation. At the food cooperative Rothschild and Whitt studied, on the occasions when the ideas of particular individuals were criticized, care was taken to make it clear that only the proposal and not the person was being rejected. Criticisms were often levelled with acclaim. The idea was not to give the impression that a personal attack was being made. The measures are undertaken in a 'context of ambivalence'. The group must strike a balance between criticizing in order to reassert collective authority, while simultaneously taking care to avoid deeply offending a loyal member. But a balance can be struck; criticism/re-evaluation meetings are frequently and successfully used by contemporary producer cooperatives to help equalize influence and to quash self-centred leadership ambitions before they materialize. By ensuring the leaders are legitimately held subject to the criticism of the rank and file, these forums directly minimize inequality of influence.[7] The sessions are, Rothschild and Whitt conclude, 'a powerful mechanism to regulate group behaviour' (1986: 85–7, 91). NED's guilds cooperatives will, accordingly, institutionalize mutual and self-critical groups. Pragmatically, they can be held at the local work-team level on the same days their representatives are on their day release programmes. This procedure nullifies the tendency identified by Michels for leaders to demand conformity from a rank and file who are dutifully obliged to obey orders uncritically. Structured critical exchanges can, and have, enhanced the democratic ethics of workplace democracies. As Rothschild and Whitt confirm, a sanctioned process of mutual criticisms negates oligarchic tendencies (1986: 84, 87).

So, it is possible to innovate various structural mechanisms, in particular the institutionalization of both a leadership 'day release programme' and 'mutual and self-critical group sessions' which, when combined, alleviate the tendency for leadership and led factions to polarize. These two structural arrangements are worthy of singling out. The implementation of these measures will help the guild cooperatives to maintain close contact with the district and national representative bodies. I now wish to conclude this section by returning to the issue of the leaders' psychological metamorphoses. We have just seen that the holders of subsidiary posts will be empowered to keep those in higher positions of authority accountable. As such, the psychological changes in those who hold office in the higher echelons of the guilds will be qualitatively distinct from leadership groups in other organizations – such as a political party – whose exercise of power is, due to their estrangement from the led, less constrained. Any psychological changes caused by the exercise of a controllable power are likely to be of a far less oligarchical nature than when the power wielded is unbridled. So with the former, the consciousness of power will not fully invoke the vanity or 'undue belief in personal greatness' Michels believes will compel leaders to consolidate and extend their power. This, I conclude, is a key premise upon which NED's guilds will preserve the democratic ideal.

---

7. Rothschild and Whitt cite one study of producer cooperatives (Sandkull, 1982) in which collective self-criticism was one of the main methods by which the groups sustained social control (1986: 90).

Conclusion

So far in this chapter I have addressed Michels' strong notion of oligarchy, the theory of elite control. The merit of his argument in terms of the mass undifferentiated political party system has not been challenged. What has been questioned is its universality. In NED's guilds the potential dichotomization between the leadership and the led can be structurally prevented. The opportunity for the former to engender a particular self-interest, and/or acquire a range of specific idiosyncrasies, distinct from the latter is largely curtailed. Insofar as bodies of guild officials can be prevented from first evolving along internally cohesive lines, and secondly from forming a closed and impregnable institution, accountability is secured. The guilds will, I submit, be institutions of democratic excellence.

Part Three: The Social Councils

The Social Councils encourages communication in both directions, from the bottom upwards and from the top downwards, but its existence is also an acknowledgement that even in a genuinely democratic enterprise the interests of the rank and file may require special representation. (Oakeshott, R. 1990: 189)

I would now like to draw my argument on the negation of oligarchic tendencies to a close by clarifying that in NED's guild cooperatives, along with the wider guild structures, the bodies entrusted with this demanding task will be the Social Councils. This final part of the chapter breaks down into two sections. The first, 'Democratic Forums', draws from the success of the Social Councils in the Mondragon cooperatives. I will indicate that although they will need to be far more extensive in NED, they are ideally suited to assume a key democratic role. In the second section, 'Management Training', it is shown why the Social Councils are well positioned to instigate training schedules for inexperienced members of management; an educational role that, in the manner in which it assures management teams will be to the greatest possible extent fully committed to cooperative values, is essentially anti-oligarchic.

Democratic Forums

As we have seen, the plywood cooperatives do not suffer from the problem of a polarization between managerial/technical expertise and the bulk of the labour force; they remain accessible to each other. Greenberg does though offer a word of warning; this could be due in part to the relatively homogeneous skill range typical of the plywood industry. It is possible that cooperatives operating in industries with an increased division of labour and a wider skill range may encounter problems of symbolic participation and the emergence of a distant ruling faction (1986: 59). It is for this kind of reason that the non-oligarchic structures in NED's guild cooperatives must be reinforced by arrangements that sustain creative labour. Once again, balanced job complexes are essential. Rather than deskilling large sections of the workforce as capitalist enterprises frequently do,[8] the goal must be to continuously re-skill an already multi-skilled group of work teams. Secrecy in conventional firms is obtained by ensuring each worker only knows a small part of the whole. But in NED, rather than a minute division of labour, there are multi-skilled work teams; here secrecy is routinely avoided. Chapter 3 explained how balanced job complexes will realize this in relation to negating alienating labour. It can now be appreciated that, in the way they decrease the range of skill levels, they will be instrumental in preventing the oligarchization process. As the design of new work forms will be the responsibility of the Social Councils, it follows that they are the most appropriate body to organize the arrangements that will give rise to non-oligarchic tendencies. The Social Councils will set forth an egalitarian dissemination of productive and administrative knowledge through the construction of balanced job complexes. By demystifying, diffusing and pluralizing expertise, they will uphold measures that can prevent the monopolization of knowledge. They will also organize other anti-oligarchic strategies like the monitoring of promotions and appointments, the day release programmes of the officials in the higher guild bodies and the mutual and self-criticism groups.

There is good reason to assume they can do this efficiently. In the Mondragon complex the Social Councils have enjoyed success along similar lines. They were initially set up to improve integration within the cooperatives by improving internal communications. The control board and management are obligated to take its advice when making decisions on matters to do with health and safety, welfare and compensation. Although the Social Council is not supposed to be a counter-veiling power in respects to management, it is legitimate for it to challenge abuses caused by management. If, for example, it strongly disagrees with the control board, it can bring the issue before the general assembly. In which case, the entire

8. Braverman's *Labour and Monopoly Capitalism* (1974) is still one of the leading texts on the deskilling thesis.

membership makes the decision. So ultimate power to determine major policy issues rests with the total membership of the cooperative, and the Social Councils cannot actually impose decisions on others. But:

> in clarifying technical aspects of management proposals and building an educational process to make management more aware of and concerned with the views of workers, and in helping workers understand the rationale behind management's recommendations, the advisory organs [of which the Social Councils are central] played indispensable intermediary roles. (Whyte, W. F. & Whyte, K. K. 1991: 149)

It is clear that the Social Councils in the Mondragon complex have improved the quality of communication between workers and management. It is important to add that the Social Councils do not just transmit information from the workforce to management, and from there onto the control boards; they also ensure information flows clearly and quickly in the opposite direction. With regards to Mondragon's work group redesign projects, all parties in the cooperatives observed how contact between the workgroups and management committees vastly improved (Morrison, R. 1997: 77; Whyte, W. F. & Whyte, K. K. 1991: 39–41, 119, 235). In addition, Thomas and Logan's empirical inquiry into 80 cooperatives found that although there was dissatisfaction about work conditions and that the participatory organs did not operate perfectly, the lower ranks regarded the Social Council as a means of self-expression and a vehicle to disseminate information throughout the cooperative. They also discovered that the higher ranks appreciated the advantages of receiving larger quantities of information. Of equal significance, they also found that competent management was greatly respected (1982: 191).

It is evident that a lack of technical and economic information did not prove to be a problem in the Mondragon complex. The minutes from the Social Council meetings of some of the largest cooperatives do not just describe the issues discussed and the conclusions reached, but also the strengths and weaknesses of each proposal. Whyte and Whyte were impressed by the efforts of management to provide information as thoroughly as possible and their keenness to safeguard communication channels. This, though, created other difficulties. Cooperators were often faced with the difficulty of how to cope with an abundance of information. Whyte and Whyte even wondered whether members suffered from 'information overload', where they are inundated with more complex information that they can absorb. Part of the problem is that in the large cooperative and the cooperative groups, information is communicated in an abstract form. Members can then find it hard to identify the relation between their particular efforts and the wider processes within their cooperative (1991: 226–7). Yet in spite of this, one critical point is clear – far from being unavailable, the circulation of information was, in general, unobstructed in the Mondragon cooperatives.

So, the Mondragon system of general assembly, control board, management and Social Councils is in no way an arrangement for the entrenchment of management control. Yet it does provide the stability required for the smooth running of the cooperative. It therefore comes as no surprise to find it has been empirically verified that the Mondragon cooperatives prevent the control board and management from polarizing through the coordinating functions of the management and the Social Councils. 'The whole object of the endeavour is to maximize the legitimacy with which management is seen by the shop floor and management's freedom to work in its own way once policy has been decided' (Oakeshott, R. 1980a: 185). It is for these kinds of reasons that the Social Councils have taken a central role in the design of NED's guild cooperatives. There is though one key difference; their powers will be notably enhanced. To fulfil their functions, the Social Councils will have direct relations with both the higher guild authorities and the local consumer councils. On the occasions when negotiations with the latter are required, they will be the highest authority at the level of the cooperative. That is, if the control board of a cooperative is in favour of producing the items determined by the local consumer councils, but the Social Council has reservations, it is the Social Council that has the final say. In cases on impasse, the Social Council is the sovereign body in the guild cooperatives. This will make a small but important revision to the Mondragon cooperatives. In the Mondragon complex the Social Councils are advisory and deliberative bodies, as they are in NED. Yet in the latter they will also hold the constitutional power of veto. This means they will need to be far more substantial than they are in the Mondragon cooperatives. Other than this, the structures in Mondragon's Social Councils are well suited for adoption in NED's guild cooperatives. As Chapter 3 explained, the members of the Social Councils in the former are elected for 3-year periods, on the condition that a third vacate their positions every year. Workers elect their representatives from their sections, with whom they meet weekly; and each cooperative holds a meeting every 3 months of their entire Social Council. These arrangements have fulfilled their democratic functions effectively, and show great promise for the future. As such, they will be fully appropriated in NED.

Management Training

The Social Councils can also provide another vital function. They can act as a training ground for individuals recently appointed to management positions. This is indispensable to the guild cooperatives democratic armoury, and can be illustrated by reference to the following problems captured succinctly by Horvat. First, time wasted in unnecessary discussion. If participants are unaware of important information or have not prepared, or if the technical details of the issue are not made clear beforehand, then meetings will be excessively drawn-out considering irrelevant issues. This means that in preparing proposals management can exert a disproportional influence on determining the agenda. This feeds into the second set of problems, the potential to abuse democratic procedures to fulfil private interests. The democratic substance can be killed in a number of ways: a), councils can withhold certain details so that requests do not come with adequate information, committees cannot then discuss them, b), the request is placed at the end of an exhausting agenda, consideration is then postponed; or when through tiredness proponents leave, the remaining clique members are left to reach a favourable decision, c), clique members can ask meaningless questions to cause confusion, d), when decisions made by the democratic assembly are not implemented by the executive – to respond, it is necessary to study the relevant minutes and then criticize the guilty body publically, few have the time and energy to undertake such a task and e), the issue can be returned to the body at a later date, whereupon it is possible that some new faces will be present and deliver a different verdict. Thirdly, if decision-making bodies are numerous, and if they are weighted down by a long list of regulating bylaws, the possibilities for abusing self-management rise. They arise even further when rules are revised frequently. It is easy to get bogged down in the resulting piles of documents. Management, whose job is to attend every meeting, hold an advantage over the remainder of the cooperative. They are better informed and can more easily manipulate the decision-making process. In the fourth place, Horvat draws attention to the misconceptions about control. By definition, self-management denotes control of managerial projects. Direct participation is though mainly needed on strategic decisions, not on administrative, professional or routine matters. The problem is the difficulty of separating political and administrative tasks. As managers will usually be better informed about given issues than other members, they will be more powerful – a power that is open to abuse (Horvat, B. 1982: 252–60).

These are real problems, and Horvat acknowledges that worker management is not a panacea. This would have come as no surprise to Michels, who was acutely aware of these and similar problems; he would have simply added it is all the more reason to doubt the survival of workplace democracies. However, Horvat believes that the progression of a self-managed culture is the best remedy. This can only be realized over time, with appropriate education and through prolonged participation (1982: 260–1). I think Horvat is largely right; although I would add that for a self-managed culture to progress it will need to do more to directly challenge the problems he highlights. Perhaps most notably, it must guarantee that management teams will be fully committed to cooperative values. The Social Councils in NED's guild cooperatives will play a key role in this regard. They will assume the required educational role, they will also be the forum through which prolonged participation will be encouraged and channelled. But, significantly, they can help secure suitable management. Whyte and Whyte point out that in the Mondragon complex some of the chief executives who form the management body have experience as members of either the control board or the Social Council. This means they are familiar with their workers' social concerns. Time spent in these bodies serves as a quality management training programme (1991: 235). This appears to me to be crucial. As such, it will be essential to provide newly appointed management members the opportunity to work part-time in a temporary subordinate role in their cooperatives Social Council. At the very minimum, they must be asked to serve as a non-active member in a 'shadow' role for a short period of time; perhaps 3, 6 or 9 months, I leave it to circumstance.

In this way, newly appointed managers will gain firsthand knowledge of how the Social Councils operate, the problems they encounter and how management teams can best assist in overcoming them. It will also make the latter aware that the underhand tactics surreptitiously employed in abuses of power are well known to the Social Councils. However, although the prospect of management members reframing from abusing their power solely through a fear of being exposed can hold some democratic utility, it is not the ultimate aim. The Social Councils will certainly seek to maximize transparency in decision-making, but they must instil management members with the values compatible with the spirit of the cooperative. It is an inescapable aspect of productive efficiency that management must monitor the preliminary discussions in advisory commissions; otherwise debate in meetings could be too drawn out to reach a consensus. Transparency will partially guard against the temptation of management members to negate the democratic substance by manipulating the way in which the agenda is determined. But the likelihood is that as management teams will invariably be better informed about the technicalities of given issues, they will be in a position to influence substantially the decision-making process. For these reasons management members must be as fully dedicated to the democratic ideal as the rest of the cooperative membership. This is not an unrealistic expectation. As clarified above, in the Mondragon cooperatives managers continuously displayed a devotion to self-governance (Thomas, H. & Logan, C. 1982: 191; Whyte, W. F. & Whyte, K. K. 1991: 226). Whyte and Whyte found that in the largest cooperative they studied, the workers did far more than merely rubber-stamp management and control board proposals. Senior management, though, still expressed concern that the Social Councils lacked initiative in the organization of work, in particular their reluctance to play a significant role in work redesign programmes (1991: 228). As Chapter 3 explained, this was to change as the Social Councils came to adopt a more deliberative role. But it does suggest that even when the Social Councils were mainly advisory bodies, management teams were still keen to uphold cooperative principles.

This is illustrated well in an example cited by Morrison (1997). In the Mondragon complex, decision-making is aimed towards generating a consensus. If there are still evident divides after inclusive debate, rather than forcing the resolution, a proposal will be withdrawn for amendment; the intention is to unite the group. This cooperative tactic occurred during a discussion in a Cooperative Congress Meeting in 1987, attended by 350 elected representatives, in which a proposal to increase the wage ratio from 4.5 to 6.1 caused considerable disagreement. One side supported the proposal in terms of efficiency; they believed it would attract well-trained technicians and managers. The other side thought it likely that the cooperative value of solidarity would be threatened. Eventually, the proposal was approved marginally. Congress opted, however, to defer the proposal until after the rules of its application had been drafted and then approved. The aim was to respect both sides of the debate. This cooperation solution ensured that all parties still agreed to support the group's decision (1997: 71–3). In addition, Bradley and Gelb's (1981) research found that there was mutual respect between management and work teams even before the role of the Social Councils was extended in 1982. Discipline, they point out, is partly regulated by educational seminars in which cooperative values are reinforced. The idea is to substitute discipline with self-discipline. But some monitoring is still needed, and for this to function smoothly, trust must exist between managerial and non-managerial cooperateurs.

They surveyed in total 15 cooperatives. In terms of 'perceived difficulty of representation', from 1,004 respondents, 589 reported that they never felt inhibited from expressing their opinions. In terms of 'perceived division between management and workers', from 992 respondents, 583 reported a small division, and 200 reported no division at all. In terms of 'perceived degree of participation in important decisions', only 395 from 993 respondents reported no participation (although 272 added that it was not always very extensive). Cooperateurs were asked which groups take into account their interests. Worker–manager trust was again revealed to be high; both groups ranked each other as the highest. Bradley and Gelb conclude that these results are especially impressive given the discipline within the cooperatives (1981: 11, 14–16, 20, 26–7, 29–30, 38; 1983: 54–5). These examples covered by Morrison and Bradley and Gelb demonstrate just how committed management is to cooperative values, how management is generally held in high regard by work teams and how the delegated authority of management is legitimated through shared democratic values. The extra provisions upheld by the Social Councils in NED's guild cooperatives can only enhance these values further.

To conclude this section, the Social Councils in NED's guild cooperatives provide the forum through which both creative labour and non-oligarchic structures will be sustained. They will also provide a vital training service to inexperienced individuals in the management teams. In providing these functions, they will be instrumental in negating oligarchic tendencies.

Conclusion

Perhaps the most famous line in *Political Parties* is '*who says organisation, says oligarchy*'. This short sentence alone captures Michels' pessimism about the inevitability of oligarchy. I have contended that this logic, although warranted if confined to undifferentiated mass political parties operating within the state-civil society dichotomy, is an exaggeration when elevated to the status of a universal law. As NED adheres to the concerns of workers' control and the need for direct personal contact between the governors and the governed, it favours a system of decentralized self-governing structures. These last three chapters have shown first how NED's functional institutions incorporate decision-making methods that wherever possible are participatory, responsible, small and above all accountable, and secondly why they are robust enough to resist the descent into oligarchization. To conclude, '*who says NED, says democracy*'.

7

Conclusion

Modern industry is shaped in such a way that the human spirit has been crushed; this was demonstrated in the introductory chapter with regards to neo-liberalism's toleration of sweatshop labour. It is imperative that new models in which human values can be pursued are articulated. The defetishized society stands as one such example. We have seen that the society of fetishism and alienation has no autonomy. In *Capital 1* Marx refers to a thing as a mysterious 'social hieroglyphic' (1977: 437), a 'receptacle' under which the social relations of production are hidden. These things are accorded particular social attributes not only because they conceal, but as we saw in Chapter 1, in the sense that they provide a connecting link between people they also organize productive relations. As Marx puts it, to producers 'their own social action takes the form of the actions of objects, which rule the producers instead of being ruled by them' (1977: 438). The solution to commodity fetishism and alienated labour can, for Marx, only be found in a thorough socialization of the means of production. The link between commodity fetishism, alienated labour and communal ownership is neatly captured in the words of Brus:

> Only when there is a genuine co-management of the means of production... is there a genuine socialization of the means of production. The connection between this idea, the theory of commodity fetishism and the overcoming of alienation is clear. (Brus, W. 1973: 66)

I will only add to this that 'a genuine co-management of the means of production' cannot possibly be achieved through a centralization of economic power into the hands of a body politic analogous to the modern state. State socialism's historical record of granting workers the autonomy to co-manage the means of production is poor, and is well documented in the literature. Rather, a non-statist social control over the direction of the economy is a prerequisite for transcending the phenomena of commodity fetishism.

The two key interrelated characteristics of the defetishized society are first transparency in the social relations of production so that they are, along with the products of labour, no longer reifications; and secondly demystified commodities, so that they are no longer personified. It is the argument of this book that these are best realized through a left-libertarian political economy that enshrines both creative labour and democratic organizations. That is, it is not just the ideals of creative labour and democratic organizations *per se* that are important, the material system that will preserve their continuing existence is of equal significance. Developing the critiques of alienated labour and oligarchic tendencies, together with sketching the organizational contours of a left-libertarian political economy in which they will be embedded have, therefore, been the central tasks of this book. I have stressed further that for a democracy to be genuinely participatory a cooperative and egalitarian economy is the principal prerequisite. The design of this economy has been informed by the argument of the young Marx that the advancement from political to human emancipation demands a move beyond the state-civil society dualism; NED represents this society. This concluding chapter will summarize and verify my argument. There are two parts, 'The Political Economy of the Defetishized Society Reiterated', and 'New Economic Democracy: The Defetishized Society'; the rationale of both is provided as we proceed. Together they confirm the position defended in this book, that NED represents the defetishized society.

Part One: The Political Economy of the Defetishized Society Reiterated

As we have covered much analytical ground, it will be useful to begin by taking stock of the key contentions in Chapter 2, the plan-market synthesis, Chapter 3, alienated labour and dealienation, and Chapters 4 to 6, the negation of oligarchic tendencies. This section breaks down accordingly into three sections, 'The Plan-Market Combination in New Economic Democracy', 'Creative Labour in New Economic Democracy' and 'Democratic Organizations in New Economic Democracy'. I will then, in the following section, bring them together and from there show how NED's radical political economy moves beyond commodity fetishism. This present section will clarify that in NED horizontal links replace vertical subordination. A constructive attempt to interweave an original approach to democratic planning with an unconventional method of monitoring a subordinated market system moves the plan-market debate into a new direction; a progressive synthesis of plan and market is theorized in NED. From here I will confirm that through the universal institutionalization of creative labour and democratic organizational decision-making, socio-economic relations are as far as possible transparent in NED's re-politicized civil society. Opacity in decision-making and the concealment of the productive relations between people will, therefore, be routinely avoided. As a corollary, producers will know how their products are used by consumers, and consumers will be aware of the conditions through which they were produced. NED, I will conclude, transcends the contradictions inherent in the commodity form.

The Plan-Market Combination in New Economic Democracy

This section summarizes why NED represents a plausible third way. It will indicate how the original approaches to participatory planning and market design have been integrated by use of an unorthodox method. In terms of honouring the democratic ideal, this task has been mandatory. In market forces economies, there is the constant danger that financial pressures will impair the democratic life in the workplace as cooperative policies must fall in line with market success; in cases of impasse between upholding democratic structures and the imperatives of capital accumulation and perpetual growth, the priority of the latter is unavoidable. Yet in all probabilities replacing market forces with centralized planning would merely substitute economic coercive power with political coercive power. This would not bring the democratic accountability dealienation and defetishization requirement any nearer. As I will now explain, NED offers the necessary corrective.

Defetishization can only occur through a thoroughly democratized civil society. Democratic planning is the key prerequisite to the defetishized society; a market device is the secondary institution. Particular attention has been paid to the democratic approaches to price-fixing and investment planning. It is NED's pluralist mediation of state and civil society that makes optimal use of participatory planning and markets. Economic planning proceeds through open dialogue and negotiated coordination between the demarcated interests of all those affected. The role of NED's planning agencies is to integrate and coordinate; they are not a set of socially alienated institutions of coercion. In stark contrast to the centralized planning of command socialism, NED adheres to a self-regulated cooperation. Some decisions are, subject to democratic adjudication, more suited to administrative instruction. But others, especially at the microeconomic level, may be bargained directly between individual consumers and the guild cooperatives. It is the former that takes precedence in NED; curtailed markets are inserted into the system of pluralist planning. The organizational base to NED's defetishized political economy has been designed so that the market mechanism will only operate within the guidelines established by the participatory approach to planning. The theory of commodity fetishism limits how the commodity and market forms may be exploited in a democratically planned left-libertarian economy like NED.

Handing the responsibility of monitoring the market over to the guilds, in constant dialogue with the two consumer councils, will ensure that aggressive competition can be routinely avoided. The guild cooperatives will collect and share information, negotiate and harmonize plans. An egalitarian dissemination of information will encourage inter-workplace collaboration. As the guilds will monitor competition stringently in their own demarcated domains, they will uphold the communal structures which are a prerequisite for cooperation, reciprocity and mutual aid. This mitigates antagonistic competition, secrecy of decision-making and economic opacity. The guilds are federations of individual, although not atomized, cooperatives. At the regional level the assemblies are constituted through elected representative from the control boards and the Social Councils of the component cooperatives. This ensures all cooperatives are equally represented within the higher echelons of their guild. There are other good reasons for believing the cooperative ideal can be upheld. In NED labour-power in not a commodity, its value is determined through social planning. Although the more efficient cooperatives will extract higher profit margins, the basic incomes for all industries will, corresponding to a skills ratio, remain consistent. Following Mondragon, intra-cooperative salary differentials will be regulated by the 6:1 principle. NED's guild banking system has also been informed by the cooperative bank in the Mondragon complex. The personnel of the guild banks will consist of elected representatives from the associated cooperatives, and staff salaries will be in line with the average profits of the guild cooperatives. A mutually supportive relationship will be established further by the contract of association, which sets out the organizational guidelines and informs cooperative activity. In NED, it is not possible for individuals to accumulate vast fortunes or excessive personal power, but the satisfaction of the desire for autonomy and genuine self-management, along with the opportunity to pursue professional expertise and an ethical lifestyle, compensate for this. For these reasons NED cannot in any sense be affiliated with a market forces economy. As such, it will not degenerate into possessive individualism.

To recap, although NED combines planning and markets, the content of both are unique in substance. The functional bodies in a re-politicized civil society will first determine social plans, and secondly monitor the functionally demarcated market sector. This is an original approach to democratic planning accompanied by an equally original approach to articulating a market system. Through this inclusive determination of the product-mix, supply and demand will be coordinated with a high degree of transparency. To conclude, NED develops an unconventional mixed economy. In the process it moves the debate on political economy into a new direction. In the absence of the overlords of both capitalist and state socialist societies, NED stands as a genuine third way.

Creative Labour in New Economic Democracy

Gorz insists that consideration must be given to whether the content of work creates the kind of people we would like society to be comprised of. The question he poses is does a person's work enrich or impoverish their being (1988: 80). This book recognizes fully the prominence of this question. Work does not only create wealth, it is also self-creation. Marx argues that as workers do not control their working conditions, they cannot be autonomous beings. Rather, their lives are determined unintentionally by impersonal exchange relations. Creative power equates with people's self-conscious participation in the framing of their material conditions. As such, it is literally the power to determine their own affairs that the workers sell to the capitalists. Work in capitalist society is transformed into involuntary servitude; the exposition of sweatshop labour in the introductory chapter illustrates this point clearly. It is in these senses that the workers alienate the full remit of their creative powers. The society of alienation, so understood, has no freedom.

The key question is whether alienation is essentially a feature of capitalist property relations, or inherent to all mass societies? Responding to the argument that alienated labour is, due to the intractability of the inevitable division of labour, unavoidable in any advanced industrial society, I stressed why NED's use of the functional principle offers an alternative approach to dealienation. It was shown how placing organized consumption on an equal footing with organized production modifies Marx's emphasis on the latter. This led the debate on the possibility of transcending alienated labour onto a new path. A full democratization of both spheres can prevent social relations from falling into relations between things. The specific way in which NED socializes the means of production ensures that producers are sovereign over the labour process, yet consumers are sovereign over the items produced. Insuring producers are directly accountable to consumers, and not state planners, engenders transparency in producer–consumer relations. Dealienation in NED can only be implemented on a macro level, with all the guild cooperatives following a similar organizational design.[1] This will be secured through a regionalization of social planning investment bureaus. The democratic investment planning committees in the Industrial Guilds Congress, and then the corresponding committees in the guilds at the local level, will value highly as their criterion for awarding grants to the cooperatives that have sanctioned creative labour. Finally, although NED's work forms are susceptible to economic forces, the guild-consumer council regulated markets will not engender imperatives that are detrimental to the development of new work forms. The consumer councils will express consumer demand, and with regards to requests for high-quality products, the flexibility to respond to changes cannot always be met through the old style rigid assembly lines. On the contrary, they require the kind of multiskilled workers and adaptable manufacturing systems embodied in the guild cooperatives. In these senses, creative labour will be enshrined in the constitution of NED.

At the level of the guild cooperatives, production can be arranged so that labour will be restructured progressively and in a creative direction. When workers do not participate in the decision-making process, but merely receive orders, they experience a loss of autonomy – they are then in no position to define the objectives of the labour process in cooperation with their associates. A universal application of balanced job complexes negates this workplace autocracy; it is therefore a consummate way of institutionalizing dealienation. Every worker's job complex will contain an equal mixture of responsibilities; this will ensure a similar qualitative impact. In this way the mode of work cooperation will maximize the development of skills and faculties, and by providing everyone with the opportunity to enjoy stimulating and aesthetic tasks, it will ensure work is to the greatest possible extent an interesting and fulfilling experience for

1. Significantly, had the development of work redesign programmes in the Mondragon complex been left to individual cooperatives, it could well have faltered. But as it was initiated through the management of the cooperative group, it progressed impressively (Whyte, W. F. & Whyte, K. K. 1991: 236).

all workers. So in NED's guild cooperatives, workers will produce in order to satisfy the creative impulses inherent in their being. Finally, a cooperative and egalitarian mode of production will, in all likelihood, give rise to a corresponding mode of consumption. It will be recalled that the two consumer councils are the social forums through which discontent can be conveyed. Their function is to operate collaboratively with the guilds, and to provide consumers with the opportunity to participate meaningfully in the determination of what items should get produced, irrespective of the prerogatives of personal wealth. In this sense, the consumer councils will have a vital role to play in directing the economy. They will, therefore, be central to negating the lack of autonomy associated with alienated labour.

In left-libertarian schemes like NED people are not treated as simple utility maximizers, they are seen as doers and creators with the ability to cultivate an excellence in a particular area. Further, people are understood as possessing an inherent ability for self-determination, which means if their efforts are constantly directed by others they will experience a separation from their human essence. In an alienated existence human capacities cannot be developed. Transcending alienation demands the end of both worker subordination and the objective situation of powerlessness. This can only occur in a democratically regulated cooperative economy, and not when the wielders of private property appropriate the surplus. Workplace democracy is essential to a non-alienated society. On the Marxian understanding alienation refers to the objective situation of workers in capitalist societies who, in their production, enter into social relations over which they have no control. Here it is impossible to develop the capacities of creativity and autonomy. Workplace democratization, as it can enhance these capacities, forms the pathway to dealienation, and by implication defetishization. My claim that creative labour can be institutionalized universally is not a utopian flight of fantasy. The Mondragon and the plywood cooperatives indicate that alienation can be negated, in particular with regards to the product and productive decision-making. In order to implement dealienation more fully, it must be invigorated by a supportive radical political economy fully committed to participatory democracy. As Greenberg concludes, the analyst is obligated to provide an account of the macro system within which workplace democracies will function (1986: 170–1). This book has done precisely that. To conclude, the real question is not whether creative labour can be uniformly upheld in the appropriate political economy, it can; the issue is whether the advantages of doing so outweigh the disadvantages.

Democratic Organizations in New Economic Democracy

> *On the cooperatives we have no pity. When a manager is not performing well the cooperateurs soon get rid of him... In a year often 12 cases occur when managers are dismissed... managers have often to justify their policies before the Direction Council and the collective.*[2]

Organizational democracy has proved to be such an elusive goal that the analysis of the basic structure of any modern society which places a high value on democracy is incomplete without a detailed response to Michels' analysis. A thorough understanding of Michelian tendencies can arguably do the most to aid the continuation of a democracy. Michels is still the most assiduous theorist of oligarchy, and an awareness of the tendencies he highlighted, along with the knowledge of the means to counter them, will be key to whether NED's functional organizations can preserve their internal democracies. This section will draw out the implications of the preceding argument that NED accommodates a progressive political economy as it develops a plausible critique of oligarchy. It is then acknowledged that the negation of oligarchic tendencies remains a demanding task; and it will involve, at least initially, certain compromises. Nevertheless, organizational democracy can be sustained – the Mondragon cooperatives illustrate this point well. From here I reiterate why a society demarcated by the functional principle of representation, and not a state-centralism of any kind, is the correct premise upon which to construct a genuine democracy.

Chapters 5 and 6 argued that NED advances a critique of oligarchy. The realization of organizational democracy is not, however, unconditional. Although the oligarchic tendencies Michels identifies can be resisted, this will involve certain trade-offs. Demystifying and diffusing knowledge by role rotation, job sharing and balanced job complexes entails planning. The preservation of organizational democracy is time consuming. It is also true that when workers are learning they cannot be producing. It is probable that workplace democracies will, initially, have to sacrifice optimal levels of efficiency in production to prevent expert opinion from monopolizing. In addition, even though NED's curtailed markets are subordinated to democratically determined production, they will still affect the guilds' internal democracies. The likelihood is that the tension between maintaining the democratic ideal, that is genuine collective participation in decision-

---

2. A Mondragon cooperator commenting on the ease with which incompetent managers can be dismissed. Quoted in Morrison (1997: 74).

making, and ensuring economic survival will continuously resurface.[3] So in all models that have any role for a market, however minimum, guaranteeing management competence and sustaining collective participation in the formation and continuous re-evaluation of policy remains a tall order. It is also clear that in order to realize this, it is not enough to analyse only the internal structures of the guild cooperatives. As indispensable as this is, it is equally important to consider the socio-economic environment the cooperatives are embedded in. The economic activities of production and consumption are, in NED, expressed democratically in an interconnecting political fabric. NED's critique of oligarchy has been premised upon a rejection of the doctrine of state sovereignty. Theories of sovereignty invite elitism because they contain the argument that not just all individuals, but the whole of individuals, can be included in a single organization. Whereas in a functionally organized society individuals belong to a variety of associations, each of which may only claim that part of the individual which relates to its social function. In diametrical opposition to any theory that upholds the sovereign state, the functional theory asserts associations may only partially express individuals' wills; associations can never exhaust complete individuals. A functionally organized society is far less likely to submit to oligarchic rule than one characterized by state sovereignty because functional associations are, as this book has shown, more truly representative.

It is likely, however, that even functional organizations will periodically experience problems sustaining their internal democracies, as Cole himself recognizes (1920a: 185–7). But this is not to the extent that the entrenchment of oligarchic control is inevitable. A commitment to economic democracy and functional representation, operating within a system of decentralized political pluralism, does not pose the same threat to organizational democracy as Michels convincingly demonstrates undifferentiated representation does to the German SPD. On the latter point, I have not suggested Michels' claim that mass political parties and large-scale pressure groups operating within liberal capitalism will inevitably degenerate into self-perpetuating oligarchies, which will in turn undermine democracy in respect of the state, is incorrect. This book has made no attempt to dispute Michels on this issue. On the contrary, the central

3. This problem has also been noted in the Mondragon complex. Whyte and Whyte draw a distinction between the social values that inform work redesign programmes in the cooperatives and the dictates of the market that will naturally cause management to direct its attention to economic survival (1991: 125–6).

thrust of his argument is fully acknowledged. If society is to count as a real democracy, then Michels provides all the more reason to reject the existing order. But he formulates his theory of an iron law within the state-civil society dualism, a society that is already seriously flawed. NED is a decentralized society with no such divide. Democratic participation is extended to the civil and economic realms, yet restricted to the functional bodies any one individual may belong to. So although a system of plural voting is embodied in NED, in contrast to other contemporary models of socialism like Nove's feasible socialism (1983: 197–8), it has no place for mass political parties. In respects of internal democratic tenability, this does little to discredit it. An undifferentiated heterogeneous mass cannot be adequately represented in a single body like a political party. Undifferentiated representation is, I agree, fundamentally flawed.

From NED's radical democratic perspective, there are two basic weaknesses inherent in liberal democracies, the disregard for both the functional principle and economic democracy. Michels also recognizes the problem of undifferentiated representation, which for him implies that the dominion of the represented by their representatives is unavoidable (1999: 76–7). From here he despairs; believing only charismatic leaders can smash their organizations' conservatism and stimulate the interest of the masses, he went on to embrace Mussolini's fascism. The real solution cannot be further removed from the far right. Only through the organizational arrangements of a new left libertarianism, constituted through a system of functionally demarcated decentralized producer and consumer democracies, can oligarchic power be neutralized. I have contended that in a system which replaces political parties with functional bodies as the central democratic institutions, leadership accountability becomes attainable. NED successfully combines the ideals of libertarian socialism and democracy. In contrast, the oligarchical forms of the social and political organization characteristic of the two main collectivist approaches towards socialism, which have both strengthened state power, only seem to enhance Michels' position. In the socialist tradition there have been two dominant modes of organization, social democracy and what is popularly called Marxist-Leninism. It is incontestable that both state socialist approaches have hitherto only offered oligarchic forms of emancipation. It is, therefore, clear that Michels presents democratic socialists with what appears to be an insurmountable challenge. Although Marx is right to claim Hegel's account of the assembly of estates does not transcend the state-civil society dichotomy, solutions which are essentially oligarchic will fare little better. A non-oligarchic theory of the transition from (to use the language of the young Marx)[4] political to human emancipation has to be articulated. A variable that must take a similar priority with the mode of production and the mode of consumption is the mode of organization. All the time society is divided between state and civil society, and public democracy is limited to undifferentiated political parties operating within the centralized state, oligarchies will continue to dominate. But with the decentralization and functional democratization of the economic institutions within the civil sphere, the danger of the entrenchment of self-perpetuating oligarchies subsides, even if it does not vanish. NED invokes a radical discourse that can help fill the void left by the two state socialisms.

To conclude, Michels' assumption of a universal law is too bold. The law of oligarchy, even though strong, is not made of iron. So in a sense analogous to the end of the previous section, the issue is not whether oligarchic tendencies can be negated, in the appropriate circumstances they can. As with alienated labour, the real question is whether the compromises are a price worth paying for the realization of the participatory democratic ideal? For anyone wishing to bring commodity fetishism to an end, there is only one answer: an unambiguous yes.

Part Two: New Economic Democracy: The Defetishized Society

With the original method to combining planning and markets, in which both creative labour and democratic organizations will be institutionalized, now fully clarified, this passage will confirm why NED moves beyond commodity fetishism. There are three sections to this second part of the chapter. The first section, 'Defetishism and New Economic Democracy', explains precisely how NED steers a path beyond fetishized social relations and fetishized commodities. Section two, 'Defetishization: The Social Councils and the Consumer Councils', begins by reiterating why the Social Councils in NED's guild cooperatives and the wider guild structures, in particular the guild banks, are indispensable to the defetishized political economy. It then does exactly the same with the two consumer councils. This section is largely one of clarification, but as the Social Councils and the consumer councils are both imperative to defetishization, they are worthy of singling out. The third and final section, 'From Power-Over to Power-To', returns to the work of John Holloway outlined in the second section of Chapter 1. Here I show that as NED reconnects the social flow

4. See his essay *On the Jewish Question* (1843).

of doing, it successfully meets Holloway's stipulations for what defetishism entails. The section concludes by reiterating the argument that has been developed throughout this book, NED can realistically be thought of as the defetishized society.

Defetishism and New Economic Democracy

In capitalist societies the non-owners of the means of production, the workers, are forced to sell their labour power in return for a paid wage. Marx was quick to add that due to the separation they experience from their productive capabilities and from contributing meaningfully in the productive process, the society of commodity fetishism and alienated labour has no autonomy. The solution is a radical material transformation in which a collective control over the direction of the economy is institutionalized. I have argued that defetishization cannot possibly occur in a political economy constituted through oligarchic organizations. Not only would there be little opportunity for self-determination, there would also be little assurance that visibility in productive processes could be sustained. This is a crucial point. It was shown in Chapter 1 that the central aspect of commodity fetishism is, due to reifications in the productive relations between people and the personification of inanimate objects, the obscurity of productive relations. It is in this sense that commodity fetishism conceals the underlying social relations; it casts a shadow over the divide between idealized surface appearance and hidden reality. So, logically, defetishizing the commodity form presupposes reversing the concealment of the social relations through which items are produced, and inversing the tendency to accord commodities magical attributes falsely assumed to be emanating from their intrinsic content. Defetishization is a double-edged process. First, there must be transparency in socio-economic relations so that material relations between producers are no longer subordinated to the social relations between things; this is achieved, at both the planning and market levels, through the guilds-consumer councils approach to coordination. Secondly, the material conditions through which commodities are produced must also be made evident in order to invoke their demyification; this is achieved through a universal institutionalization of creative labour and democratic organizations. These two processes, which to some extent can be seen as corresponding roughly to the social and technical divisions of labour respectively, clearly interact, and make the task of the other less demanding. As I will now show, in NED's political economy social relations are as transparent as economic realities will allow.

Political economy addresses the relations people establish with each other during the productive process. Yet in commodity production, as people are connected through the transfer of things, the things through which definite relations are established assume a social role; in the manner in which they connect otherwise separate individual they acquire a functional existence. That is, they have a social character that expresses a productive relation. So the things not only denote the productive relations among people, they also hold them together (Rubin, I. I. 1972: 31). Significantly:

> These functions of forms have a social character because they are inherent, not in the things as such, but in things which are part of a definite social environment, namely things through which people enter into certain production relations with each other. These forms do not reflect the properties of things but the properties of the social environment. (Rubin, I. I. 1972: 39)

This is not the case in NED's radical political economy; the products of labour will not perform a similar social role of integrating productive relations. That is, in NED's 'definite social environment', the social function the products of creative labour perform will not stand in opposition to the underlying productive relations between people. As Chapter 3 argued, NED breeds workers who are reunited with the goods they produce, their productive activities, their workplace associates and fellow consumers, and, crucially, themselves. Producers are not initially divided as they are in commodity-producing societies.

The properties of NED's social environment are constructed so that economic agents will meet each other first in extra-market terms. Democratic participation in both the workplace and over investment planning will negate alienated labour and commodity fetishism. This is largely because there will be direct relations both within work-teams and between producers and consumers. In NED it is not through the state that citizens overcome commodity fetishism, it is through the democratic institutions of a re-politicized civil society, the guilds and consumer councils, organizations that citizens are far more intimately involved with. As clarified above, in market forces economies commodities are produced through private labours, it is only market exchange that brings together otherwise isolated producers. Social relations between people are hence indirect; they are formed through direct relations to things. Personal relations are transferred onto commodities. Social form is one step removed from productive content. By way of contrast, in NED there will not be a parallel contradiction between appearance and (non-hidden) reality. Producers come into direct *technical* contact with their cooperative workmates through their labour – determined by multi-skilled work teams and not through the isolation of wage-labour, they come into direct *technical and social* contact with their guild colleagues through their internal guild structures, and they come into direct *social* contact with consumers through their communications with the two consumer councils. In these three ways, the social character of NED's cooperative labour reveals itself before the act of exchange. This will help negate the tendency to fetishize as citizens will be integrated in both the productive and consumptive spheres; structures of dialogue and negotiation then integrate the two sets of interests. In NED, then, citizens are not initially divided as they are in commodity production. So through an inclusive and participatory approach to planning, the displacement of interpersonal relations to the social relations producers have to things is prevented. That is, social relations will not be interpreted by producers as comparative relations between things.

NED's functionally demarcated market system is set within this democratically planned economy. Through constant dialogue between their two councils and the guild cooperatives, consumers will not be ignorant about the productive conditions through which their goods were made. In NED the products of labour have been determined socially through the consumer councils and the guild regulated markets. Further, in terms of production, at the level of the guild cooperatives transparency is sustained as a consequence of balanced job complexes; the universal application of the latter ensures that all members of society share an awareness of the technical conditions of production. At the regional level, the higher guild committees are responsible for circulating knowledge between the semi-autonomous cooperatives in their jurisdiction; and at the national level, the national guild executive will fulfil this task. Disseminating information and hence avoiding the secrecy and opacity common to conventional capitalist enterprises can work well, as the cooperation between the network of textile cooperatives in Emilia Romagna, Bologna – supported by the 'Centro Informazione Tessile dell' – have demonstrated (Wainwright, H. 1994: 174). As a corollary of visible and consistent relations of production, the characteristics of labour (meaningful, skilful, stimulating, etc.,) can appear objectively in the items it produces. So the way in which NED's market system is organized ensures that the products of creative labour will not be distorted and misconceived when they are exchanged on the market. As they will not have social qualities distinct from productive forms bestowed upon them, such qualities will not then be mistakenly interpreted as occurring in them naturally. In other words, as commodities are not attributed with mystical and magical powers or with qualities only people can possess, the personification of things will be negated.

If wage-labour is the basic social relation in capitalist society, then cooperative labour is the basic social relation in NED. In the former, commodity fetishism regulates and then dominates the lives of economic agents. In the latter, the social relations of production are not reified; that is, their properties are not transferred onto the properties of things, whereupon they are misinterpreted as occurring in them naturally. So in this sense, NED's demarcated market system will not engender a divide between people's existence and their essence. Consequently, commodities will not become people's master, and workers will not become object-less beings. The products of labour will still be objectifications of inter-subjective relationships, as they are in any society, but workers will not be debased to the level of objects; the subjective aspect contained in the commodity will not induce reification as it will embody no significant abstraction from the material conditions through which it was produced. As the various kinds of workers producing creatively in democratic structures are not initially fragmented, the guild markets will not serve to integrate their labour in a duplicate illusory form. The social character of production can, through democracy in the guild cooperatives and through the illuminating role of the consumer councils, be presented in the sphere of production. It follows that the tendency to reify is transcended in NED. This is a key benefit of the guilds-consumer councils approach to coordination.

So, the transparency engendered by establishing horizontal relations between organized production and organized consumption, corresponding to the functional democratic ideal, negates the tendency to confuse social facts as natural. To repeat: in NED the essence of the products of creative labour is immediately apparent because they will be comprehended in terms of the actual relations that produced them. The outward appearance directly coincides with the essence of things. In this way social attributes are not mistakenly conferred to the commodity. Commodities will not, therefore, be manifested with autonomy and independent powers.

Defetishization: The Social Councils and the Consumer Councils

This section will reiterate why the Social Councils and the two consumer councils are essential to the defetishized society. Starting with the former, I re-emphasize that the various Social Councils in NED's mode of production are the primary means through which defetishization will manifest. As the final section of the last chapter concluded, the Social Councils in the guild cooperatives are the social forums in which oligarchic tendencies will be negated. It will be recalled from Chapter 3 that they will also serve the same purpose with regards to alienated labour. This section summarizes both analyses in the briefest of terms. In the process, the value of balanced job complexes is reconfirmed. The responsibility of organizing balanced job complexes in NED falls to the Social Councils in the guild cooperatives. As such, the section proposes that the Social Councils must form an integral component of the wider guild structures. Attention then turns to the two consumer councils. Here I stress why they are just as vital to NED's defetishized political economy. The section concludes by confirming how the key themes discussed in the previous section will be embodied in the democratic structures of the social and consumer councils.

With regards to creative labour, the Social Councils are deliberative bodies, and they provide an arena in which an evaluation of experiments in work redesign programmes will take place. In the Mondragon cooperatives, work-team redesign projects were found to have greatly enriched productive tasks. In one case, the Social Councils objected to a proposed plan because they included new machines that would not change the dehumanizing aspects of the insipid conveyor-belt production. This ensured the design team had to rethink their proposal in order to make it more acceptable to the Social Councils. Workers were able to appreciate the real significance of their work. This gave them a sense of how they were contributing to the whole product. Within the new work groups workers felt valued members. The Social Councils have also increased the quality of communication between workers and management. All parties in the cooperatives reported that contact between the work groups and management in work group redesign projects greatly improved (Whyte, W. F. & Whyte, K. K. 1991: 39–41, 119, 229, 235). So when the Social Councils have participated in work redesign programmes, they have been effective. It follows that they are the most appropriate body to organize the arrangements that will give rise to creative labour. I have argued that in NED's guild cooperatives the introduction of the educational mechanism of balanced job complexes will be central to work design projects; they will also serve a similar function in relation to maintaining non-oligarchic tendencies. Through the design of balanced job complexes the Social Councils can, through demystifying and pluralizing expertise, engender an egalitarian dissemination of productive and administrative knowledge. They will also organize other anti-oligarchic strategies summarized towards the end of the last chapter. It will now be clear why balanced job complexes are an essential ingredient of the defetishized society.

In sum, the Social Councils in the guild cooperatives represent the human, rather than the commercial, aspects of workers. It follows that they are the means through which both creative labour and democratic structures will be upheld. As the Social Councils play such an indispensable role in the defetishization process, it will be necessary to secure their representation in the higher echelons of the guild to which they are affiliated. They must be embodied in the democratic investment committees at every stage of planning. That is, at the national and regional levels on the Industrial Guilds Congress, and within the individual guilds at the local level. In addition, it may even be desirable for a senior member of the consumer councils to sit permanently on the regional board of the Social Councils; the logistics of which are open to review as the system unfolds. Finally, at the level of the cooperatives the Social Councils will have direct relations with both the higher guild authorities and the local consumer councils. With regards to their communication with the latter, they will be the joint-highest authority within the cooperatives. In this way the Social Councils will be in the ideal position to fulfil their defetishization function.

Turning now to the two consumer councils, I have repeatedly claimed throughout this book that they are indispensable to NED's defetishized political economy; they are fundamental to both the democratic planning and the market regulating processes. As their role is essential in these regards, it will be useful to briefly reiterate their value. First, they constitute the political structures through which dissatisfaction can be directed. They hold the power, on the mandate of consumers, to intercept in the sphere of production and prevent controversial products from going to market. This implies that producers will act in response to organized demand which has been established by open market research and through non-discriminatory channels of consultation, rather than simply respond to the blind dictates of the 'free market'. There may often be fierce debate within these social arenas. This should be encouraged, for in the process socio-economic relations will become increasingly visible, and the resulting transparency will be vital to the negation of the mystification and concealing aspects of commodity fetishism. Secondly, consumer choices can be irrational, and they can be poorly informed through a lack of adequate knowledge. I stressed in the third part of Chapter 2 that meaningful consumption choice is dependent upon suitable education and the availability of less-imperfect information. In NED the information producers' need in order to respond effectually to consumer demand will be in a large part supplied by the consumer councils. The extra-market material they will broadcast can advance rational economic behaviour. By circulating non-price information, the consumer councils can control the social forces responsible for guiding consumer choice. As such, in NED there will be horizontal non-market links between producers and consumers. Again, the transparency of genuine democratic structures will reveal the material relations through which goods are produced.

Finally, if a tightly monitored degree of competition is the best means by which to stimulate technological innovations, then consumer councils offer the necessary check on how producers attract consumer attention. Gimmicky advertising that artificially stimulates people's desires will be superfluous in NED. The consumer councils provide the social forums in which the product promotions of the guild cooperatives can be scrutinized. The former's seal of approval negates the need for aggressive advertising. So due to the illuminating and deliberating role of the consumer councils, exchange relations can be arranged so they will not veil the social relations of production. The importance of this cannot be over-emphasized. It was clarified above that in NED the qualities that commodities are compared with will not be disconnected from the productive relations of the workers who produced them. To this it can now be reconfirmed that commodities will be treated as the products of human activity not only by producers, but also by consumers. For all these reasons, the two consumer councils constitute a political mode of coordination. Significantly, in the terms in which ethical and political consumption is advocated by the consumer councils, NED endorses a rational social structure of consumption. Only this can ensure that the mode of consumption is free from the fetishized commodity form.

With these emancipatory functions of the Social Councils and the consumer councils highlighted, this section will now conclude by briefly returning to the themes in the previous section. I have argued that human relations will not be turned into relations between objects, and the products of labour will assume a form consistent with their essence. We have seen that the metamorphosis of material relations between producers into the social relations between things will be routinely avoided. NED reverses the mystifying metamorphosis, and in sense sets forth demystification through a 'de-naturalization'. Socially objective appearance is not collapsed into a natural objectivity. That is, the form, surface relations, expresses the content, the interior reality: guild cooperative labour producing democratically determined use values, and only in a secondly sense producing use-values for their exchange-value. It can now be appreciated why both the Social Councils and the consumer councils are – through their mediation of producer–consumer intercommunications, through their provision of transparency and illumination, through their joint control over the social forces that influence economic decision-making, and through their political empowerment of producers and consumers – imperative to this process.

From Power-Over to Power-To

I would like to draw this book to a close by returning to Holloway's work on defetishization outlined in the second part of Chapter 1. It will now be clear that doing in NED is not organized along antagonistic lines. There is no class conflict as productive assets are owned collectively, and controlled by the guild collectives. Of equal importance, there is no wage-labour; labour is cooperative and salaried. In contrast to capitalist societies in which capitalists and wage-labourers are initially independent from each other, NED establishes direct technical productive relations without invoking any corresponding separation. In NED social relations do not take the form of private transactions. Rather, in the absence of both an oppressive market and an oppressive leviathan there is a socially regulated economy; productive relations between people are democratically planned. Individual roles, and their interrelationships, are consciously defined. The totally of the social relations of production correspond to a non-statist uniformly connected system. It is true that the guild cooperatives are quasi-autonomous firms, but they cannot in any sense be compared with the typical capitalist enterprise. With regards to overcoming intense competition, the contract of association ensures technical expertise will be pooled and disseminated along egalitarian lines. Of equal significance, following the cooperative industrial research centre of the Mondragon complex, Ikerlan, each guild will have its own research cooperative which will share information equally. This is by no means all; through membership to the federation of homogeneous cooperatives, through the contract of association, through the consequences of democratic investment planning and through the other structures of mutual aid in their guild, the concerns of the cooperatives will not be limited to only their own interests. There is an array of constitutional measures that mitigate against the private usurpation of social wealth. So production is not directed by independent and purely self-interested commodity producers. In addition, through the two consumer councils society prescribes the quality and quantity of items produced. This implies that in their capacities as consumers, people have a determined place in the process of production. NED's political economy will not, I infer, be socially divisive.

NED, then, reconnects the social flow of doing. The doers, the guild cooperateurs, are united with the means of doing – a non-statist communal ownership of the means of production. In addition, both the doers and the means of doing are, in conjunction with the advice of the consumer councils, in unity with the done, the products of creative labour. As such, the done does not stand dominant over the doers. In these circumstances workers will control their creative activity. Although comfort commodities will be produced and sold impersonality on the market, social doing is not severed. This is because in NED commodities already have a sociality before they are produced. It is not only the commodity that is recognized socially through the act of exchange. As this book has demonstrated, there is a transparency of decision-making within and between the guild cooperatives, and between producers and consumers at the local, regional and national levels. To reiterate, in NED's functionally demarcated markets labour relations are not veiled; the productive relations between people do not appear as the relations between inanimate objects as done is not fractured from doing. Through the empowering and revealing ideals of creative labour and workplace democratic structures, it is not only the interaction of commodities that is exhibited, the subjectivity of producers is also brought into view. In light of this, my contention is that Holloway's defetishization thesis prefigures NED's radical political economy.

Would Holloway be sympathetic to NED? As NED is a blueprint of the new society, possibly not. For Holloway the movement must be the process, not a fixed end. The flow, he insists, should not be programmed as it does not have any precise aims. 'The drive towards self-determination is not instrumental: we do not start from an aim and deduce from that aim the path we must follow to reach that aim' (2002: 221). Rather, we are 'walking in the dark'. On the other hand, his criterion for judging organizations is to ask whether they bring social self-determination any closer. If a society constituted through self-determining organizations is the ultimate ideal then, as Chapters 3 to 6 indicate, NED in the solution par excellent. Further, Holloway observes that radical discourse often discusses democracy, but not so often the organization of labour (2002: 239). Direct democracy must challenge the power of capital; the organization of doing must be radically transformed. NED does this thoroughly; radical democracy co-exists with a subordinated system of capital-free demarcated markets. Further still, Holloway declares that the Paris Commune and workers' councils are experiments in anti-fetishism – the struggle for self-determination and a genuine collective flow of doing. In NED for Paris Commune read the commune system, and for workers' councils read guilds. So at the theoretical level, NED can be thought of as exactly the same – an experiment in anti-fetishism. Finally, in the absence of private ownership of the means of production, the subject in NED is able to re-appropriate the object. Objects are not, as will now be clear, reifications. The processes through which given bodies of producers, the subject, create their products of labour, the object, is revealed. To echo Holloway, this resembles an anti-power, a reunification of subject and object.

One last point, Holloway rightly claims the orientation must be 'towards the establishment of a network of links between producers (and consumers) independent of the state', and, only 'as part of a thrust not towards a state but towards a commune of communes or councils of councils...that social planning can be an expression of social self-determination' (2002: 241). If I were to provide a rationale for the articulation of NED in two lines, I could not have put it any better. The democratic structures of social planning that define NED's constitution achieve precisely that, they establish direct links between producers and consumers 'independent of the state'. For these reasons, the contention of this book is that NED embodies a defetishized political economy.

It is on this note that I wish to conclude. Alienation, fetishism and non-participation are key problems in modern life. NED's left-libertarian political economy resists these de-humanizing features of capitalist society, and in this sense it tries to put more meaning, more belonging and a sense of mastery in people's lives. In attempting to create a more humane society, the defetishized society requires people have the opportunity to seize control over their own destiny. They can only do this when the direction of the economy is subject to a genuine self-management. In NED this is realized by substituting private ownership of the means of production with social ownership, by replacing markets partly with conscious planning, by minimizing inequalities in income and wealth drastically, by distributing economic and political power more evenly and, crucially, by upholding political and economic democracy.[5] The task has been to articulate an alternative cooperative mode of production and, of equal importance, a corresponding mode of consumption. This is achieved by redefining the lines of demarcation between a cooperative economy and a pluralised state; that is, through a re-politicized

5. This working definition is informed by Nove's stipulations on what a socialist society will seek to implement (1983: 7–8).

civil society in which both the productive and the consumptive spheres are fully democratized. Democratizing the social relations of production in the unique way NED does, adhering to the functional principle of representation, institutionalizing continuous dialogue between organized producers and organized consumers, subordinating exchange-value to use-value, democratizing investment planning and establishing a fair criterion for surplus appropriation provides the most desirable socialization of productive assets. If workers are free to collectively determine their cooperative's policy, they will not be subject to forces beyond their control. It is in this sense that the autonomy defetishization requires can be approximated. This, though, is only half the story. When it is coupled with the opportunity, provided by the two consumer councils, to participate in the determination of what items may be produced regardless of personal bank balances, an equality of influence is also realized in NED's mode of consumption. Hence, citizens will not, in either their capacities as producers or consumers, be powerless beings unable to influence the direction of the economy. It is within this radical political economy that the defetishization process can unfold. As NED has the economic and political structures capable of penetrating beneath superficial appearances, and as it can avoid reification of the productive relations between people and the personification of things by generating both transparency in the social relations of production and demystified commodities, it can instigate non-fetishized social relations. This book has first stated the centrality of creative labour and democratic organizations to this task, and secondly it has articulated the left-libertarian material conditions through which they can be sustained. NED, I conclude, can plausibly be thought of as the defetishized society.

Bibliography

Albert, M. & Hahnel, R. (1991) *Looking Forward: Participatory Economics for the Twenty First Century,* Boston: South End Press.

Arneson, R. J. (1987) 'Meaningful Work and Market Socialism', *Ethics,* Vol. 97, No. 3. April.

Avineri, S. (1968) *The Social and Political Thought of Karl Marx,* Cambridge: University Press.

Batstone, E. (1969) 'Some Aspects of the Economic Performance of French Producer-Cooperatives'. Paper presented to the Walton Symposium on Labour-Management, Glasgow.

Beetham, D. (1977) 'From Marxist Revolutionary to Political Sociologist', *Political Studies,* Vol. 25.

— 'From Socialism to Fascism: The Relation Between Theory and Practice in the Work of Robert Michels', *Political Studies,* Vol. 25.

Bottomore, T. B. (1965) *Elites and Society,* London: Routledge.

Bradley, K. & Gelb, A. (1981) *Industrial Alternatives: Internal Organization and Efficiency in the Mondragon Cooperatives,* An Industrial Relations discussion Paper, London School of Economic.

— (1981a) *Obstacles to a Cooperative Economy: Lessons from Mondragon,* An Industrial Relations Discussion Paper, London School of Economic.

— (1983) *Cooperation at Work: The Mondragon Experience,* London: Heinemann.

Braverman, H. (1974) *Labour and Monopoly Capitalism,* Monthly Review Press: New York

Breitenbach, H. (1990) *Features of a Viable Socialism,* Hertfordshire: Wheatsheaf.

Breman, J. (2009) 'Myth of the Global Safety Net', *New Left Review*, 59, September–October.

Brus, W. (1973) *The Economics and Politics of Socialism: Collected Essays*, London: Routledge.

Burkitt, B. (1984) *Radical Political Economy: An Introduction to the Alternative Economies*, Brighton: Wheatsheaf.

Burnheim, J. (1985) *Is Democracy Possible?* Polity: Cambridge

Callinicos, A. (2003) *An Anti-Capitalist Manifesto*, Cambridge: Polity.

Carpenter, L. P. (1973) *G.D.H. Cole: An Intellectual Biography*, Cambridge: University Press.

Carver, T. (1982) *Marx's Social Theory*, Oxford: University Press.

Clayre, A. (1980) *The Political Economy of Co-Operation and Participation*, Oxford: University Press.

— (1980a) 'Some Aspects of the Mondragon Co-Operative Federation', in his *The Political Economy of Co-Operation and Participation*, Oxford: University Press.

Cohen, G. A. (1978) *Karl Marx's Theory of History: A Defence*, Oxford: Clarendon.

Cole, G. D. H. (1913) *The World of Labour*, London: G. Bell.

— (1914) 'Conflicting Social Obligations', *Proceedings of the Aristotelian Society*, Vol. XV.

— (1914a) 7th November. *The Daily Herald*, 'The Meaning of Industrial Freedom-V1'. Cole Collection. Nuffield College. Box A1/47/1-72.

— (1916) 22nd April. 'Lecture to National Guilds League', Cole Collection. Nuffield College. Box A1/46/1-8.

— (1919) 'Postal Workers and the Guild Policy', Cole Collection. Nuffield College. Box A1/48/1-5.

— (1919a) Unnamed pamphlet on the possible creation of a national railway guild. Cole Collection. Nuffield College. Box A1/48/1-5.

— (1920) 4th March. *Kingsway Hall*, Lecture. Cole Collection. Nuffield College. Box A1/49/1-8.

— (1920a) *The Social Theory*, London: Methuen & Co.

— (1920b) *Guild Socialism Restated*, London: Leonard Parsons.

— (1920c) *Co-operation and the Guilds*, Cole Collection. Nuffield College. Box A1/49/1-8.

— (1921) 28th October. *National Guilds League*, Lecture. Union Institute. Clerkenwell. Cole Collection. Nuffield College. Box A1/50/1-6.

— (1921a) December. *The Guild Movement in Great Britain*, Cole Collection. Nuffield College. Box A1/51/1-7.
— (1956) *A History of Socialist Thought: Volume III, Part I. The Second International 1889–1914*, London: Macmillan.
— (1957) *A History of Socialist Thought: Volume II. Marxism and Anarchism. 1850–1890*, London: Macmillan.
— (1958) Foreword in Pribicevic, B. (Ed.) 1959. *The Shop Stewards' Movement and Workers' Control 1910–1922*, Oxford: Blackwell.
— (1958a) *A History of Socialist Thought: Volume IV, Part I*, London: Macmillan.
— (1972 [1917]) *Self-Government in Industry*, London: Hutchinson Educational.
— n.d. 'Outline of a Pamphlet on the Control of Industry – During and After the War' Cole Collection. Nuffield College. Box A1/46/1-8.
Colletti, L. (1975) *Karl Marx: Early Writings*, London: Penguin.
Corina, J. (1972) Introduction to Cole, G. D. H. (Ed.) *Self-Government in Industry*, London: Hutchinson Educational.
Davis, M. (2004) 'Planet of Slums', *New Left Review*, 26, March–April.
Devine, P. (1988) *Democracy and Economic Planning: The Political Economy of a Self-Governing Society*, Cambridge: Polity Press.
Elden, J. (1981) 'Political Efficacy at work: The Correlation Between More Autonomous Forms of Workplace Organisation and a More Participatory Politics', *American Political Science Review*, 75: 43–58
Elich, G. (2010) 'Sweatshop Manufacturing: Engine of Poverty', *Global Research*, 16 May.
Elster, J. (1985) *Making Sense of Marx*, Cambridge: University Press.
— (1986) *An Introduction to Karl Marx*, Cambridge: University Press.
— (1986a) 'Self-Realisation in Work and Politics: The Marxist Conception of the Good Life', *Social Philosophy and Policy*, Vol. 3. Part 2.
Fine, B. (1991) 'Commodity Fetishism' in Bottomore, T. (Ed.) *A Dictionary of Marxist Thought*, Second Edition, Oxford: Blackwell.
Foley, D. (1991) 'Commodity' in Bottomore, T. (Ed.) *A Dictionary of Marxist Thought*, Second Edition, Oxford: Blackwell.
— (1991a) 'Labour Power' in Bottomore, T. (Ed.) *A Dictionary of Marxist Thought*, Second Edition, Oxford: Blackwell.
Fitzroy, F. R. (1978) *Alienation, Freedom and Economic Organisation*, London: Acton Society Trust.

— (1980) entry in 'Discussion of Practical Arrangements' in Clayre, A. (Ed.) *The Political Economy of Co-Operation and Participation*, Oxford: University Press.

— (1991a) 'Exchange' in Bottomore, T. (Ed.) *A Dictionary of Marxist Thought*, Second Edition, Oxford: Blackwell.

Fromm, E. (1992) *Marx's Concept of Man*, New York: Ungar.

Geras, N. (1971) 'Essence and Appearance: Aspects of Fetishism in Marx's "Capital"', *New Left Review*, No. 1. 65.

— (1991) 'Fetishism' in Bottomore, T. (Ed.) *A Dictionary of Marxist Thought*, Second Edition, Oxford: Blackwell.

Gorz, A. (1988) *Critique of Economic Reason*, London: Verso.

— (1999) *Reclaiming Work: Beyond the Wage-Based Society*, Cambridge: Polity.

Gouldner, A. W. (1980) *The Two Marxisms: Contradictions and Anomalies in the Development of Theory,* London: Macmillan.

Greenberg, E. S. (1984) 'Producer Cooperatives and Democratic Theory: The Case of the Plywood Firms', in Jackall, R. & Levin, H. M. (Eds.) *Worker Cooperatives in America,* London: University of California Press.

— (1986) *Workplace Democracy: The Political Effects of Participation*, New York: Cornell University Press.

Greenwood, D. J. & Santos, J. L. G. (1992) *Industrial Democracy as Process: Participatory Action Research in the Fagor Cooperative Group of Mondragon*, Stockholm: Arbetslivscentrum.

Gunn, C. (1984) 'Hoedads Co-op: Democracy and Cooperation at Work', in Jackall, R. & Levin, H. M. (Eds.) *Worker Cooperatives in America,* London: University of California Press.

Hands, G. (1971) Roberto Michels and the Study of Political Parties. *British Journal of Political Science,* Vol. 1.

Himmelweit, S. (1991) 'Surplus Value' in Bottomore, T. (Ed.) *A Dictionary of Marxist Thought*, Second Edition, Oxford: Blackwell.

Hirst, P. (1990) *Representative Democracy and its Limits*, Cambridge: Polity.

— (1994) *Associational Democracy*, Cambridge: Polity.

Holloway, J. (2002) *Change the World Without Taking Power*, London: Pluto.

Horvat, B. (1982) *The Political Economy of Socialism: A Marxist Social Theory*, Oxford: Martin Rabertion.

Howard, M. W. (2000) *Self-Management and the Crises of Socialism: The Rose in the Fist of the Present,* Oxford: Rowman & Littlefield.

Jackall, R. & Levin, H. M. (1984) *Worker Cooperatives in America*, London: University of California Press.

James, D. (2000) 'Justice and Java: Coffee in a Fair Trade Market', Global Exchange, Sept/Oct. www.globalexchange.org

Jay, P. (1980) 'The Workers' Co-Operative Economy' in Clayre, A. (Ed.) *The Political Economy of Co-Operation and Participation*, Oxford: University Press.

Kitschelt, H. (1990) 'The Medium is the Message: Democracy and Oligarchy in Belgian Ecology Parties', in Rudig, W. (Ed.) *Green Politics One*, Edinburgh: University Press.

Levine, A. (2002) *Engaging Political Philosophy: From Hobbes to Rawls*, Oxford: Blackwell.

Lipset, S. M. (1999) Introduction to Michels, R. (Ed.) *Political Parties: A Sociological Study of the Oligarchical Tendencies of Modern Democracy*, London: Transaction.

Lyon, S. (2006) 'Evaluating Fair Trade Consumption: Politics, Defetishization and Producer Participation', *International Journal of Consumer Studies*, 30. 5.

MaCain, R. (2001) http://william-king.www.drexel.edu

Magid, H. M. (1966) *English Political Pluralism*, New York: AMS Press.

Martell, L. (1992) 'New Ideas of Socialism', *Economy and Society* Vol. 21, No. 2, May.

Marx, K. (1974) *Capital: Volume III*, London: Lawrence & Wishart.

— (1975) in Colletti, L. (Ed.) *Karl Marx: Early Writings*, London: Penguin.

—(1976) *Capital: Volume 1*, London: Penguin.

— (1977) in McLellan, D. (Ed.) *Karl Marx: Selected Writings*, Oxford: University Press.

Mason, R. (1982) *Participation and Workplace Democracy*, Carbondale: Southern Illinois University Press

Mathews, F. (1979) 'The Ladder of Becoming: A. R. Orage, A. J. Penty and the Origins of Guild Socialism in England', in Martin, D. E. & Rubinstein, D. (Eds.) *Ideology and the Labour Movement*, London: Croom Helm.

McLellan, D. (1971) *Karl Marx: Early Texts*, Oxford: Blackwell.

— (1977) *Karl Marx: Selected Writings*, Oxford: University Press.

— (1986) *Marx*, Second Edition, London: Fontana.

— (1995) *The Thought of Karl Marx: An Introduction*, Third Edition, London: Papermac.

Meszaros, I. (1975) *Marx's Theory of Alienation*, Fourth Edition, London: Merlin.

Michels, R. (1999) *Political Parties: A Sociological Study of the Oligarchical Tendencies of Modern Democracy*, London: Transaction.

Mohun, S. (1991) 'Capital' in Bottomore, T. (Ed.) *A Dictionary of Marxist Thought*, Second Edition, Oxford: Blackwell.

— (1991a) 'Value' in Bottomore, T. (Ed.) *A Dictionary of Marxist Thought*, Second Edition, Oxford: Blackwell.

Morrison, R. (1997) *We Build the Road as We Travel: Mondragon, A Cooperative Social System*, USA: Warner.

National Guild League. (1915) 20th April. *Rules*, Cole Collection. Nuffield College. Box D3/1/1-8.

— (1917) 7/8th April. *Annual General Meeting. Agenda / Minutes*, Cole Collection. Nuffield College. Box D3/3/1, 2.

Nove, A. (1983) *The Economics of Feasible Socialism*, London: Allen & Unwin.

Oakeshott, R. (1980) 'A Co-operative Sector in a Mixed Economy: Piecemeal', in Clayre, A. (Ed.) *The Political Economy of Co-Operation and Participation*, Oxford: University Press.

— (1980a) entry in 'Discussion of Practical Arrangements', in Clayre, A. (Ed.) *The Political Economy of Co-Operation and Participation*, Oxford: University Press.

— (1990) *The Case for Workers' Co-ops*, Second Edition, Hampshire: Macmillan.

Ollman, B. (1971) *Alienation: Marx's Conception of Man in Capitalist Society*, Cambridge: University Press.

— (1976) *Alienation: Marx's Conception of Man in Capitalist Society*, Second Edition, Cambridge: University Press.

— (1998) 'Market Mystification in Capitalist and Market Socialist Societies', in his *Market Socialism: The Debate Among Socialists*, London: Routledge.

Parry, G. (1969) *Political Elites*, London: Allen and Unwin.

Pateman, C. (1970) *Participation and Democratic Theory*, University Press: Cambridge

Perlman, F. (1972) Introduction in Rubin, I. I. (Ed.) *Essays on Marx's Theory of Value*, Detroit: Black & Red.

Powell, B. & Karbek, D. B. (2004) 'Sweatshops and Third World Living Standards: Are the Jobs Worth the Sweat'? *Independent Institute Working Paper*, No. 53, 27 September.

Prychitko, D. L. (1991) *Marxism and Workers Self-Management: The Essential Tension,* Westport: Greenwood.

Reinharz, S. (1983) 'Consulting to the Alternative Work Setting: A Suggested Strategy for Community Psychology', *Journal of Community Psychology,* Vol. 11.

Ritzer, G. (1992) *Sociological Theory*, Third Edition, Singapore: McGraw-Hill.

Roemer, J. E. (1993) 'Can there be Socialism after Communism?', in Bardhan, P. K. & Roemer, J. E. (Eds.) *Market Socialism: The Current Debate,* Oxford: University Press.

— (1994) *A Future for Socialism,* London: Verso.

Rothschild-Whitt, J. (1976) 'Conditions Facilitating Participatory-Democratic Organisations', *Sociological Inquiry,* Vol. 46. (2).

Rothschild, J. & Whitt, J. A. (1986) *The Co-operative Workplace: Potentials and Dilemmas of Organisational Democracy and Participation,* Cambridge: University Press.

Rubin, I. I. (1972) *Essays on Marx's Theory of Value*, Detroit: Black & Red.

Russell, B. (1919) September. *The Guildsmen,* Guild Socialist Papers. Nuffield College.

Sandkull, B. (1982) 'Managing the Democratization process in Work Cooperatives', University of Linkoping, Sweden. Photocopy, cited in Rothschild, J. & Whitt, J. A. (1986).

Sawtell, R. (1980) 'Industrial Co-operatives in Britain: A Note on Enterprises Owned and Controlled by the People Working in Them and on Some Possible Developments for the 1980s', in Clayre, A. (Ed.) *The Political Economy of Co-Operation and Participation*, Oxford: University Press.

Sayer, A. (1995) *Radical Political Economy: A Critique*, Oxford: Blackwell.

Schecter, D. (1994) *Radical Theories: Paths Beyond Marxism and Social Democracy*, Manchester: University Press.

Schweickart, D. (1993) *Against Capitalism*, Cambridge: University Press.

— (1998) 'Market Socialism: A Defence', in Ollman, B. (Ed.) *Market Socialism: The Debate Among Socialists*, London: Routledge.

— (1998a) 'Criticism of Ticktin', in Ollman, B. (Ed.) *Market Socialism: The Debate Among Socialists*, London: Routledge.

— (1998b) 'Response to Ticktin', in Ollman, B. (Ed.) *Market Socialism: The Debate Among Socialists*, London: Routledge.

Serra, N., Spiegel, S. and Stiglitz, J. E. (2008) 'Introduction: From the Washington Consensus Towards a New Global Governance', *The Washington Consensus Reconsidered.* Oxford Scholarship Online: www.oxfordscholarship.com

Shaikh, A. (1991) 'The Falling Rate of Profit', in Bottomore, T. (Ed.) *A Dictionary of Marxist Thought*, Second Edition, Oxford: Blackwell.

Shelley, E. (1921) June. 'An Inquiry into the Working of the Building Guilds'. *Garden Cities and Town Planning,* Cole Collection. Nuffield College. Box A1/51/1-7.

Stiglitz, J. E. (2008) 'Is there a Post-Washington Consensus Consensus?' *The Washington Consensus Reconsidered,* Oxford Scholarship Online: www.oxfordscholarship.com

— (2008a) 'The Future of Global Governance', *The Washington Consensus Reconsidered,* Oxford Scholarship Online: www.oxfordscholarship.com

Thomas, H. & Logan, C. (1982) *Mondragon: An Economic Analysis*, London: George Allen & Unwin.

Vanek, J. (1970) *The General Theory of Labour-Managed Market Economics*, University Press: Cornell

Vernon, R. (1980) Introduction to Cole, G. D. H. (Ed.) *Guild Socialism Restated,* London: Transaction.

Wainwright, H. (1994) *Arguments for a New Left: Answering the Free-Market Right*, Oxford: Blackwell.

Weisskopf, T. E. (1993) 'A Democratic Enterprise-Based Market Socialism', in Bardhan, P. K. & Roemer, J. E. (Eds.) *Market Socialism: The Current Debate,* Oxford: University Press.

Whyte, W. F. & Whyte, K. K. (1991) *Making Mondragon: The Growth and Dynamics of the Worker Cooperative Complex,* Second Edition, Cornell: University Press.

Williamson, J. (1990) *Latin American Adjustment: How Much Has Happened*? Peterson Institute for International Economics: Washington

Wood, A. W. (2004) *Karl Marx*, Second Edition, London: Routledge.

Wyatt, C. (2008) *The Difference Principle Beyond Rawls*, New York: Continuum.

Young, M. & Rigge, M. (1983) *Revolution from Within*, London: Weidenfeld and Nicolson.

INDEX